FASHION AND BEAUTY IN THE TIME OF ASIA

NYU SERIES IN SOCIAL AND CULTURAL ANALYSIS
General Editor: Phillip Brian Harper

Fashion and Beauty in the Time of Asia

Edited by
S. Heijin Lee,
Christina H. Moon, *and*
Thuy Linh Nguyen Tu

NEW YORK UNIVERSITY PRESS
New York

NEW YORK UNIVERSITY PRESS
New York
www.nyupress.org

References to Internet websites (URLs) were accurate at the time of writing. Neither the author nor New York University Press is responsible for URLs that may have expired or changed since the manuscript was prepared.

Library of Congress Cataloging-in-Publication Data
Names: Lee, S. Heijin, editor. | Moon, Christina H., editor. | Tu, Thuy Linh Nguyen, editor.
Title: Fashion and beauty in the time of Asia / edited by S. Heijin Lee, Christina H. Moon, and Thuy Linh Nguyen Tu.
Description: New York : New York University Press, [2019] | Series: NYU series in social and cultural analysis | Includes bibliographical references and index.
Identifiers: LCCN 2018030567| ISBN 9781479892150 (cl : alk. paper) |
ISBN 9781479892846 (pb : alk. paper)
Subjects: LCSH: Feminine beauty (Aesthetics)—Asia. | Beauty culture—Asia. | Fashion—Asia. | Clothing trade—Asia.
Classification: LCC HQ1220.A78 F36 2019 | DDC 646.7/2095—dc23
LC record available at https://lccn.loc.gov/2018030567

New York University Press books are printed on acid-free paper, and their binding materials are chosen for strength and durability. We strive to use environmentally responsible suppliers and materials to the greatest extent possible in publishing our books.

Manufactured in the United States of America

10 9 8 7 6 5 4 3 2 1

Also available as an ebook

CONTENTS

FIGURES

Introduction

S. HEIJIN LEE, CHRISTINA H. MOON, THUY LINH NGUYEN TU

Last September, the Metropolitan Museum of Art, after an extended run, closed the exhibit "China: Through the Looking Glass," on the "impact of Chinese aesthetics on Western fashion." This was not the museum's first costume exhibit on Asia—Orientalism and fashion have been well-trod themes within the costume museum world—and we suspect will not be its last. But in this latest iteration, the museum has had a harder time figuring China as a ghostly specter haunting the European imagination of Yves Saint Laurent and other fashion cognoscenti. When the singer Rihanna stole the spotlight at the opening night gala wearing Gou Pei, one of the only Chinese designers shown that evening, critics and consumers worldwide, many from China, denounced the museum and the fashion establishment for its business-as-usual exclusions. The kerfuffle made clear that "China" can and does disrupt Western narratives about itself rather than quietly serving as their backdrop.

This most recent encounter between fashion and "the East" presents an occasion to think about how the geographies of fashion and beauty have shifted, particularly in the ways that Asia has emerged as a cultural and economic force in this story. The "China" exhibit became the Met's most popular exhibition in its 145-year history (nearly 800,000 people saw it), driven in large part by international visitors (who accounted for 40% of the audience), but, most strikingly, primarily Chinese (14% in total, the Met's largest single group of overseas visitors).[1] The record-setting success of the exhibit came as a surprise even to its curators. After all, fashion has long been understood as the domain of the West, with Paris, Milan, and London as it epicenter (New York and to a certain extent Tokyo were only recently admitted into this exclusive club). In most studies of fashion, it is resolutely a product of Western modernity, birthed from the social and political transformations that it supposedly

1

inaugurated—industrialization, democratic revolution—and reliant on an ethos of "the new" that is supposedly anathema to those from tradition-bound non-Western cultures.[2] What was it that led an exhibit on China and fashion to garner such interest?

Despite prevailing narratives, China has had a long relationship with fashion, certainly as makers of clothing, but more recently as one of the most lucrative markets for Western fashion designers. (*Vogue* editor Anna Wintour's recent tour of China gives some indication of its rising prominence.) This kind of attention to fashion is not limited to only China. Across Asia, luxury goods have found enthusiastic consumers in Shanghai, Mumbai, Seoul, and Saigon alike, prompting endless popular accounts of an ever-expanding world of happy shoppers. In fact, in mounting their China exhibit, the curators were accused by some critics of "a calculated move to capture some of that gold dust," since Asia has become the "buzz of many conversations, in every sector from Hollywood to finance, travel to e-commerce."[3]

This comment highlights the immense (and, to some, immensely threatening) shift in the political, cultural, and economic power of Asia, evidenced in part through the consumption of Western goods in the region. But that is only part of the story. A fuller picture would take into account Asia's own flourishing culture industries—film, media, music, fashion, and beauty—which have also grown tremendously, vying for (and in many instances commanding) the markets in their local contexts. Korean and Japanese beauty products, for instance, are higher grossing than any European product in Asia—products that have long been the industry standard for luxury cosmetics across the region.[4] China's own fashion industries have expanded so vastly that Chinese entrepreneurs have now bought old Italian factories to reproduce and "preserve" the so-called Italian couture tradition, using the same machines and often employing experienced and aging Italian workers, *only in China*. There are more than 200 design schools in China (as opposed to just 53 in the United States), turning out fashion designers who will work in the sample rooms of factories making clothes for global design brands. Moreover, Chinese-owned manufacturing firms have been at the vanguard of seemingly "Western" concerns regarding fashion and "sustainability" on a mass scale, experimenting with zero-waste factory processes that produce fabrics without the use of water, while raising labor standards and developing codes of social responsibility and conduct with American and European fashion brands.

As these brief examples reveal, "fashion and beauty" and "Asia" are intimately related, and have long been so. Think, for instance, about how the arrival of the Chinese manteaux in 1700s Paris set off a craze that launched a thousand couturiers.[5] Or more recently, how the clothing industries in the United States and Europe became transformed by outsourcing to Asia throughout the 1970s and onward. And even before there was a fashion industry in the West, there was broad enchantment with the styles, goods, and images from the non-West. At the turn of the last century, elite women (and those aspiring to be so) routinely "embraced the East," in Mari Yoshihara's terms—dressing in rich silks, decorating their homes with porcelains—to demonstrate their class status.[6] The production, consumption, and distribution of fashion and beauty, in other words, have never been located in defined and static geographies. Rather, they move in multiple directions, transforming and becoming transformed by their local contexts, and giving shape to globalization in the spaces that they engender and inhabit: in the nail salon and beauty counters; the museums and malls; the sidewalks and runways.

These circuits and geographies are only just emerging as important critical sites in scholarly discussions within the West. Scholars in the fields of ethnic studies and women and gender studies have for at least two decades been calling for a "transnational turn."[7] But such a turn has been incomplete, as the disciplinary boundaries, geographic foci, and theoretical questions have remained largely distinct among these fields. Building on the work that has come before, while also being attuned to the continuing gaps and absences, this collection hopes to contribute to ongoing efforts to think transnationally and interdisciplinarily by bringing together the fields of ethnic and gender studies with area studies and fashion and cultural studies.

With some important exceptions, the fields of area studies/Asian studies rarely treat fashion and beauty as central to the histories, economics, and politics of the region, generally focusing instead on cold war and colonial histories and politics and their transformations by more recent processes of development and modernization.[8] Fashion and beauty figure as marginal, if not entirely inconsequential. And yet in places like Korea, beauty—in the form of cosmetics products and cosmetic surgery—is one of its most profitable export industries, even economically outpacing its manufacturing and shipbuilding industries, the two industries upon which the Korean economy was first built. Beijing dominates the world's cotton prices, with China overtaking the United States as the largest dispenser of cotton subsidies and world's largest cotton importer.[9] At the same time, cultural studies and fashion studies still continuously reference a primarily Euro-American history and mostly within the realm of dress and costume history, again with notable exceptions.[10] In other words, the more recent acknowledgment that Asia has become an important new luxury market—even within ethnic studies, which tends to see Asia as a backdrop or context for migrating subjects—has not led to a more thorough engagement with its histories and politics (again, with some notable exceptions), except to reaffirm the trope of its frenzied luxury consumers, exploited workers, or maker of knockoffs or copies.

For the authors of this volume, however, these tropes are a thin veneer, giving shape to a social phenomenon but incapable of containing its many layers of meanings and contradictions. Training their eyes on sites as far-flung and varied and yet as intimate and intimately connected as Guangzhou and Los Angeles, Saigon and Seoul, New York and Toronto, the authors here map a set of transpacific connections made visible and, in some ways only possible, through fashion and beauty. Such a map reveals how global commodities have tied people together but have not fixed them into static positions. Rather, the transnational circuits and "cartographic imaginaries," to use contributor Nellie Chu's term, animated by fashion and beauty have allowed some to shift, however slightly, the seemingly immovable lines between producers and consumers; developed and developing; subjugated and free.

In order to make these connections clearer, we have chosen work that attends primarily to East Asia and Southeast Asia. We do so in order to show, first, how the forces of globalization have been remade by developments in East Asia, where, for instance, more millionaires now live than in Europe. How has the growth of Asia's elite class and the rise in Asia's luxury consumption altered its cultural and geopolitical landscape, and been shaped by changes in its economic development? Moreover, as the various industries in East Asia have expanded and have led to mass migrations of workers from rural to urban centers, what do the workers in these locations buy with their industrial wages? In China alone, 14 million migrant workers have made their way to cities like Shanghai to work as nannies, caretakers, housemaids, and cooks for the growing middle and upper middle classes. What do we make of the consumption practices of these 99 percenters, whose purchasing power has also increased and whose access to "cheaper" "imitation" goods, often made in Asia, can also signal new horizons of possibility?

Our focus on East Asia also allows us to see how these "tiger economies" have shaped the region as well. As several chapters reveal, Seoul's economic and cultural presence in Southeast Asia, for instance, has outpaced the influence of traditional global cultural centers like Paris and New York. What does it mean for newly industrializing nations in Southeast Asia to value and aspire to the cultural practices and economic positions of South Korea, Japan, and China? What does this shift enable and what does it demand? How does it reshape the long-standing divide between the modern and the traditional, the innovator and the imitator? What do these Southeast Asian regional dynamics—operating at times in place of "the West" and at times as its proxy—tell us about the shifting terrains of power under globalization?

Of course, similarly complex dynamics are also at work in South Asia, much of which falls outside of our focus. But rather than include this region in a cursory manner, we hope that this collection will provide a helpful comparative example to others working on South Asia. We also hope that our focus on the regional and transnational dimensions of East and Southeast Asia will not only fill a scholarly lacuna in the United States but will draw our attention to the social, cultural, and political forces that are reshaping these geographies (and our world) and the role of fashion and beauty as its conduit.

This collection, in other words, understands fashion and beauty less as objects and more as a set of narratives and practices that map forms of Asian modernity. Though fashion and beauty are often treated as distinct objects—with their own histories and fields—they are very much of a piece. They are both material and immaterial practices of self-presentation that are deeply informed by their social contexts, meaning they are embodied and individual expressions of community, nation, and region. As such, in this collection we understand fashion and beauty as indexes of the modern formations taking place in and through Asia.

We draw on concepts like "regional modernity"—the ways that trans- and inter-Asian connections have shaped processes of social, economic, and political development—to think through how notions of the beautiful and the fashionable have been produced outside of—but not unconnected to—dynamics in the West.[11] This includes, of course, the region's history of colonialism and imperialism and their lingering effects—histories that are fundamentally shaped by encounters with the West. Yet it also emphasizes the ways that this geography has produced its own visions of the beautiful, whether as practice, material culture, or aesthetics.

Such visions are of course gendered, given that labor relies so heavily on women's work and consumption hinges so centrally on an imagined female user. In Asia, as elsewhere, femininity has been integral to the modernizing project. As transnational feminist scholars have shown, many "modern" ways of being—such as the professionalization of housewifery, the organization of kinship networks into nuclear families, or even women's entrance into educational institutions—were coercive norms that subjected women to novel forms of control and discipline even as they perhaps subverted other forms of patriarchy.[12] Beauty and fashion work are one of the modern techniques through which women have managed such deep transformations, including changing sexual and maternal roles.[13] For example, South Korea's modernity created major shifts in the practice of Korean womanhood. As a result, Korean women went from identifying themselves first as mothers, then primarily as wives, and now in the current era of consumer culture, as sexy individuals. As such, body enhancement and modification are a means of enhancing human capital that does not depend on "the womanly virtues of traditional ethics" such as motherhood "but on measurable and quantifiable factors such as height, weight, and BMI index."[14] In order to aid this transition from "citizens" to "consumers," a plethora of self-help books, experts, and mass media have emerged in recent years to urge women to transform themselves into neoliberal entrepreneurs, prioritizing self-management through a disciplined body that can be achieved in part through plastic surgery, dieting, fashion, and adornment.

Because consumption has historically been gendered female, beauty and fashion continue to be framed as feminine genres even when beauty and fashion practices take up male bodies or subjects. Cosmetic surgery, for instance, is still largely thought of as a woman's domain because "official" statistics in the United Kingdom and United States exclude men's treatments such as cosmetic dentistry and hair transplants. Moreover, despite the fact that 80 percent of breast reduction surgeries are performed on men, the procedure continues to be associated with women.[15] The same is true in Asia where, despite the fact that South Korean men are the top per-capita consumers of skincare products among men globally, the cosmetics industry continues to be feminized.

In this collection, we explore the ways female labor is obscured and female pleasures have historically been marked as frivolous. And yet, we also show how both have become integral to the formation of the modern subject and to the social reproduction of the idea that commodities offer a step toward "the good life." Analyzing what and who modern subjects look like, what they wear, how they work, move, eat, and shop offers us a view into the forms of modernity taking shape in Asia—the aspirations it expresses and the sensibilities it endorses.[16] The chapters herein share the conviction that self-care, stylizing, and sartorial markers are the material and immaterial forms that embody and tell alternative histories and reshape traditional hierarchies. These are stories of emergence, aspiration, and imagination—in short, the lived experiences of modern life. Much of the work here seeks to capture the chaotic conditions of a modernity so thoroughly infused with the labors, desires, and imaginations that have come to define fashion and beauty. How do people narrate their own personal and national histories through these goods? Where do these narratives emerge, in what spaces and under what conditions? In answering these questions, centering Asia in the study of fashion and beauty sheds light on three critical thematics: time, creativity, and labor.

What Time Is Now?

In many ways fashion and beauty travel through imaginations, aspirations, and experiences of time as much as they do through a specific geography. With the opening up of Asian markets, Western fashion and beauty companies have worked to understand "Asian style" and "Asian taste" in order to satisfy the "Asian consumer." Such discourses posit a somehow knowable Asia, ready to be captured by market research, a new "frontier" for profit. In order to push back against such essentialized understandings that are deeply entrenched in and informed by Cold War understandings of the region, we do not use an empirical framework that attempts to provide a comprehensive picture of an entity or continent called "Asia."

A concept such as "Asian beauty" might suggest that such a monolith exists, ready to be capitalized upon both by corporate interests and Western fascinations. But as the "time of Asia" in the title of this collection suggests, fashion and beauty are the quotidian markers influenced by, experienced through, and produced in the temporalities induced by Asia's recent history. On the one hand, parts of Asia have experienced a compressed modernity that has given way to a sense of quickness, urgency, and speed. For example, along with the other "industrial tigers" Singapore, Taiwan, and Hong Kong, South Korea is known for its "miracle economy," which in just two generations went from agrarian poverty to modern powerhouse.

This rapid industrialization has been attributed to South Korea's *bbali bbali* culture, a kind of impatient sensibility that favors speed in day-to-day matters and abhors waiting. Literally translating to "fast fast," *bbali bbali* is an ethos and practice of hurrying, rushing, and getting it done as quickly as possible. At its best, the term has become synonymous with efficiency and is often described as evidence of South Korean exceptionalism—the result or reason, depending on how one looks at it, for South Koreans' rapid developmental "success." This need for speed, for instance, authorized the military regime to push young girls working in South Korea's textile factories during 1970s to hurry up and make more goods for the national economy—in the name of efficiency. At its worst, *bbali bbali* is the kind of hastiness that led to the *Sewol* ferry disaster in 2014. The desire for speed in this case—the boat was carrying more than twice its proper weight in cargo in order to get more to the destination faster—resulted in the deaths of more than 300 passengers and crew, most of whom were high school students. This narrative today continues to underwrite the cosmetics industry, which prides itself on putting out hundreds of new beauty products a year, compared to Euro-American firms' few dozens.

This sense of immediacy is heightened by new forms of media. South Korea is currently the most wired nation globally, with the highest number of DSL connections per head worldwide, and these levels of connectivity are reflected in South Korean marketing, music, and business campaigns. Korean entertainment companies, for example, leverage their stars' pop music on social media sites as their main platform for launching and sustaining their global popularity. Visuality, both in the sense of pop music's tendency toward spectacle and in the emphasis on pop stars' aesthetic appeal, has become a key factor in K-pop's global production and distribution. This aesthetic appeal is then used to sell beauty products, cosmetics, fashion lines, and myriad other products, services, and goods domestically and internationally, most prominently in other parts of Asia, where the number of households with televisions and computers has also grown exponentially. In a spectacular example of technological "leapfrogging," Asians who just a generation ago did not have telephones (or toilets) now own multiple smartphones, used to conduct business, connect with family, view latest trends, buy consumer goods, and produce their own media. As evidenced by Emily Raymundo's chapter on beauty blogs, this global digital realm is allowing some to remake fashion hierarchies and even to rewrite seemingly settled narratives about race.

On the other hand, despite this speed, Asia is always painted as temporally behind, playing catchup to the West both figuratively and literally. As the United States' hot wars in Asia evidence, the region has largely been constructed as in need of US intervention, whether to ward off communism or to establish, maintain, and catch up democratically (the Korean War, Vietnam War, American military bases and presence in Japan, South Korea, the Philippines, Guam, Thailand, Taiwan, Singapore, Australia are just a few examples). As such, Asian progress in history, economics, literature, media, and popular culture is typically measured in its approximations to the West. In contrast to the "Johnny-come-lately" stories told about Asia, this collection foregrounds the new alliances, affiliation, desires, and demands forged within East and Southeast Asia.

For instance, the formation of ASEAN nearly a decade ago helped to establish an economic bloc out of vastly divergent nations and histories. These alliances both made possible and were facilitated by the circulation of cultural goods—from K-pop to Japanese cosmetics—within the region, which culturally solidified relationships. As Thuy Linh Nguyen

Tu shows in this volume, such exchanges are central to reshaping local ambitions and desires, from which skincare to buy and who to marry, to which nations make the most "suitable" political allies and trade partners. In this context, Asian capital and Asian bodies have become models and ideals for both intimate/personal and state-led/political investments that can rival and displace long-standing Euro-American notions of beauty and power.

Imitation, Innovation, and Other Myths of Creativity

In a competitive global economy, where time is literally money, *bbali bbali* is a demand felt far beyond Asia. In the fashion industry, where technological innovation means that entire clothing lines can be produced in just six weeks, as in the case of "fast fashion," this kind of lightning speed is only possible through much coordination and collaboration. It requires moment-to-moment decision-making in all aspects of the production process, from the sourcing of textiles to clothing assembly, even to the timing of when a product finds its way onto the container of a ship. Consumers today have access to new varieties and designs of clothing that is, in fact, only made possible through the cumulative knowledge of a complicated, cooperative, anonymous, creative, and market-driven production process. The fashion and beauty products that have emerged out of Asia within the last two decades are the result of large ecologies of shared resources and knowledge, interconnected across the region. It requires a lot of creativity to keep all of this going.

Creativity is an ephemeral quality, but one that has very tangible effects. In fact, according to influential thinkers like Richard Florida, creativity drives most things; it makes cities great and nations grow, it saves economies stagnating under deindustrialization and gives meaning to workers laboring without purpose.[17] Everyone can tap into their creativity, boosterists say, as all passion projects can become economically productive enterprises. While Florida's thesis has been challenged by many scholars who have asked what happens to the vast majority of people without the cultural, educational, and other forms of capital necessary to participate in the creative economy, in the fashion industry, these critiques have not stuck. There, creativity still reigns supreme and exists only among the privileged few. Coveted positions at prominent fashion houses are still passed between a handful of mostly white male designers, who supposedly have earned these titles by dint of their innovative imagination, not because of their education or social networks and locations.

In this context, to be deemed creative is to have access to social and economic capital. Like most other coveted resources, this one too is limited. Creativity should be readily available since presumably all humans have imaginations, yet it is constructed as scarce, endemic to few people and nations. Consider, for instance, the narratives that accompanied contemporary Chinese artists' entrance into the global art market in the 1990s. Stories of thousands of art students mindlessly copying master works or duplicating pop pieces for the international market sought to frame the innovations in contemporary Chinese art as no more than an extension of age-old Western aesthetics. More recently, K-pop's global popularity has met with the ubiquitous criticism that its artists and their music are manufactured, implying that K-pop artists and producers lack not only talent but creativity and originality and, as such, are merely weak imitators of Western pop.[18] In these accounts, artists from the non-West are rarely seen as innovators and instead are characterized as followers of forms and genres usually originating in the West.

This practice is common in fashion, where sartorial products from the non-West are still referred to as "clothes," "costume," "dress," rather than "fashion," defined in part as "the new." Despite centuries of tailoring expertise, decades of manufacturing experience, and many lifetimes of aesthetic practice, clothing manufacturers in Asia are still accused of mimicking styles from Paris and Milan. More recently they have been excoriated for outright copying them. These accusations have launched a thousand investigations, cost (and raised) billions of dollars, and involved legal institutions across several continents. In all of these copyfights, there is no mention of the ways Western designers have, since the emergence of the European couture system, "borrowed" or been "inspired" by the non-Western styles and materials. In settings like the Metropolitan Museum's "China" exhibit, this practice is seen as little more than cultural exchange. In fact, Western designers are often portrayed less as "borrowing" than as "improving" on non-Western styles (for more on this, see Minh-Ha Pham's contribution to this volume).

At this point in time, is it possible that we still need to argue for Asians' capacity to create? Maybe, but for us such an argument cannot hinge on a claim to any definitive origin or ownership. Creativity in fashion and beauty is not the product of an individual genius. It is a collective affair. Every dress we put on, every style we pick up, and every lipstick we own is sourced, made, marketed, and sold through the work of thousands of hands and minds. Each brings one thing to the process—a stitch perfectly executed, a mistake that becomes a new style, and a host of other innovations that are mostly imperceptible. It is little wonder, then, that Chinese manufacturers making the most maligned, "cheap," "copy" style see themselves, as Nellie Chu's chapter reveals, as designers with a broad imagination of the world.

In wholesale markets across East and Southeast Asia, from Shanghai, Guangzhou, Seoul, and Bangkok, there are blouses, or shoes, that might vaguely resemble all of the logos and designs of Chanel, Louis Vuitton, Michael Kors, and Tory Burch—companies that all produce in Asia—yet designed into one hybrid object. These are often created in urban villages throughout Asia known for their "shanzhai cultures," or "imitation cultures." It is easier to write off these amalgamations as mere "copies" than to understand them as the accumulation of a myriad design decisions and relationships in different arrangements of labor and technology (for example, digital printing, hand-stitched embroidery, machine sequinning, and so on), all created out of collective and local knowledges spanning multiple cities in Asia—just as it is easier for us to see fast fashion as only cheap and imitative. As Nellie Chu, Christina Moon, and Minh-Ha Pham's chapters in this collection reveal, what Asia shows us, perhaps more than any place in the world, is that the skills and ideas required for all these kinds of production are in fact creative. That they do not rely on a model of the individual author/genius and instead require forms of collectivity might challenge us to rethink how we define creativity.

Just as Asian producers are perceived as copycats, Asian consumers of fashion and beauty are likewise described as lacking in creativity and imagination. While these consumers are no doubt coveted for their economic value, their cultural value remains circumscribed. We have all heard about the growing middle class in China, India, and Vietnam, and routinely see media depictions of Chinese consumers waiting in line to get into the Beijing Chanel boutique or into famed Parisian stores like

Galleria Lafayette. These women, with money to burn and an insatiable appetite to boot, are the newly arrived belles of the ball. But despite their wealth, marketers working in so-called emerging markets have continually remarked that these new consumers have yet to learn good taste. As one editor at Elle Vietnam said about the elite class gobbling up luxury goods in Saigon's shiny malls: "These women, they don't really know how to have good style. They'll wear Chanel head to toe, they have no idea how to do high-low. And let's forget about 'effortless chic'—that's not a concept they get at all in Asia."

We have heard this narrative about many consumers: Chinese, South Korean, Indian, Middle Eastern, and even Russian women, whose sudden rise to billionaire status has not come with good taste. There is an implicit telos to these accounts of global fashion. Consumers in recently developed economies are always framed as latecomers to fashion— much as they are latecomers to freedom and democracy. "They don't have a feel for the game," as Bourdieu would put it. Instead, these nations of consumers purportedly have to play catch up, have to learn the ways of a sport they didn't invent and can only hope to master. This is not just a perception by outsiders. As Ann Marie Leshkowich's chapter reveals, the issue of what Vietnamese women should wear has long been a concern of local elite and state interests. The approval of Western "experts"—their stamp of good taste and good style—has and continues to be of great cultural and economic significance.

In this way, narratives of shoppers in Saigon or Singapore are accounts not just of class but also of civilization. "Asian taste" becomes a way to map Asian-ness less in a geographic sense than in a temporal sense—as late, as behind, as progressing in a trajectory that unfolds from the West to the rest. Denise Cruz, along with Minh-Ha Pham and Christina Moon, show us in this volume how the language of creativity and imagination have become proxy for race and nation. They make clear how it helps to hold up the dividing lines between who designs and creates and who simply sews and manufactures; between who is a style leader and who is a style follower; and, ultimately, who deserves the economic and cultural capital that creativity can convey. It also helps to hold up the lines between the civilized and uncivilized, traditional and modern, past and future, even as those ideas are being challenged by a world under transformation. How else can we understand this continued insistence on seeing Asia and Asians as always falling short or lacking in taste other than as an anxious scramble to maintain an order already beginning to fade? How else could Asia be at once a great hope and a great failure; the savior of fashion and its weakest pupil; the hapless imitator and the unruly consumer?

Laboring for Pleasure, and the Hard Work of Buying

Continuously circumscribed as coming late to the table, and lacking creativity and imagination, Asia in fashion and beauty is also routinely framed solely within the realm of labor. There is perhaps no more iconic image of this than the figure of a garment worker, head down, toiling away and feeding cloth into her sewing machine. The story of fashion is the story of global labor—growing and extracting cotton, spinning thread, cutting cloth, and sewing of garments, all these forms of production have long been global. From the 1970s onward, and particularly beginning in the 1990s, however, this global story has taken place in Asia.[19]

Whether on the assembly floors of production or as temporary technical designers in corporate design offices on Seventh Avenue, fashion's cultural workers have increasingly emerged from Asia. The Asian, female "docile" body was ushered into fashion production both by transnational corporations eager for cheap labor and from Asian states eager to put her "surplus labor" to work.[20] Throughout the 1990s and 2000s, this female worker, typically found in emerging Export Processing Zones of South China, Southeast Asia, and South Asia, was just old enough to make money for her family before she would have to return to her village to marry.[21] But as much as she desired a wage, she also desired her autonomy and the glamour and cosmopolitan life of the burgeoning cities, formed in part by migrations of women like her. She would likely leave behind her birth-land registration, making her ineligible for healthcare and other social benefits of citizenship. She would live inside a worker's dormitory, where both state and private enterprises would supervise and survey her life at work and at home. The little money she earned she would send home.

Increasingly, this figure of the suffering garment worker has been brought to the public's attention with films like *The True Cost* (2015), or books like Elizabeth Cline's *Overdressed* and Lucy Siegle's *To Die For.*[22]

As Miliann Kang's chapter addresses, recent news coverage of the manicurist toiling in toxic working conditions has become another representation of Asian beauty labor. Though these representations bring much needed awareness to the plight of exploited workers, they also depict workers as victims who can only be saved by the heroes of capitalist consumption—privileged women of the West who either *design* fashions under more "sustainable" and environmentally favorable conditions or *consume* and shop more "ethically." New ad campaigns among fashion companies now promote "truthful and honest labor" that reference "nature" and authentic "ethnic" expressions of practice and making (from hand-sewing, mending, knitting, and weaving). This "transparency," captured in image and film, is used in their marketing, evidencing clean factories, smiling faces and worker empowerment, and certificates of corporate responsibility and social responsibility (from institutions like the International Labor Organization).

Critics of the fashion industry and "ethically minded" fashion companies suggest that mass production in places like Asia are the root of evil in global capitalism, where "Made in China" stands for cheaply made, copied, and despised things. The victims are Western consumers unaware of these exploitative conditions and of their own exposure to China's use of toxic products. The heroes are also Western consumers, the most agentive actors against these exploitative practices, the bearers of good conscience qua good consumption. Denise Cruz's analysis of VINTA, a Filipino Canadian business specializing in couture ternos (traditional Filipina dresses), offers an alternative site, where the hallmarks of what we now deem "ethical practice" have been going on for years, unnoticed by most Western observers. VINTA's diasporic attempt at slow and ethical fashion goes against the easy consumption of Filipina labor and illuminates the unease and unevenness with which such endeavors are met.

In all of these popular depictions, we learn little about who actually works and what the work of fashion and beauty is. What does life look like and how is it experienced on and off the assembly line? How can we see fashion and beauty as part of the motivations and dreams for migrating, the enactment of the modest choices one has in this life?²³ A movie, new fashions, a pair of shoes, a tube of lipstick, a new hairstyle or skin cream—how may these represent, as Jessamyn Hatcher puts it in her chapter, "little freedoms"?

And yet, how might these "modest wish fulfillments" also be under-stood as important political spaces and sites for culture and its aesthet-ics in an understanding of lived experience? In South Korea, cosmetic surgery is a form of "body work" that encapsulates both work performed on the body through surgeries, and the work that the altered body is readied to perform (or perform better) in a national market economy. While some "body work" is performed in a doctor's office or on a surgi-cal table, Emily Raymundo shows us that such labors are also performed in the privacy of one's bedroom through the consumption of YouTube video tutorials that instruct consumers on the proper forms of makeup application. These chapters bring new light to how we think about who the "worker" is in fashion and beauty and the very nature of her work.

In this volume, the work of fashion and beauty takes on less clear pa-rameters, finding itself in places like nail salons in New York, K-pop vid-eos in the city of Seoul, and the spas and air-conditioned shopping malls of Saigon, where the distinctions between work life and home life and lei-sured life begin to blur. In fact, in many examples throughout this book, the labor of fashion and beauty occurs continuously, beyond the space of the workplace, and among many agents. Throughout are examples of the innumerable ways that paid work depends on the realm of unpaid labor, including the care and socialization of children, their grooming, cultivation, and presentation, as demonstrations of a family or household to a community, as investments for better futures. One is reminded of Terence Turner's "The Social Skin," wherein he describes Kayapo women who submit their children to standing still for hours on end, while paint-ing intricate and idiosyncratic geometrical designs on their bodies. They adorn children with accessories and cosmetics to reflect on the relation-ship between the painter and the child, and the child's relationship to the household, village, and community.[24]

More recent accounts of such maternal preening take on neoliberal dimensions in South Korea, where mothers act as self-entrepreneurs who model, mold, and shape their children toward market demands. As teens and adults, this grooming becomes reciprocal, with both parties shaping and shopping. Take, for instance, Etude House's 2013 "Mother and Me Healing Day" promoted by its global Facebook page. The page suggests a GOBACK Intensive Mask Sheet for mother and a Cherry Lip Gel Patch for daughter "to have a healing day with your mom." Such marketing not only presumes beauty work as women's work but as labor to be shared between mothers and daughters and thus passed off as imperatives masked as pleasure and bonding. Moreover, while the page suggests an intensive wrinkle-reducing mask for mom that will help her "GOBACK" to a presumably more youthful and thus more preferable appearance, it suggests a lip patch for "soft, luscious, kissable lips" for daughter, highlighting how differently aged bodies "need" different products in accordance with their sexual viability. In these ways, the surface of the body is a space of modernizing labor in and of itself, a site where buying and selling, loving and coercing, freedom and power all coalesce.

Collectively, the chapters in this volume highlight the ways that fashion or beauty can serve as the means for realizing all kinds of aspirations and possibilities, as a modest reward or investment, an opportunity or mobilization, an economic niche or cosmopolitan cultural formation. Fashion and beauty, whether commodity, practice, or imagination, evidence the mottled and heterogeneous experiences of modern life, and of the inter-Asian connections that have made new paths possible. As ethnographers, visual analysts, historians, and firsthand witnesses collaborating alongside nail salon workers, make up vloggers and designers, fast-fashion entrepreneurs, entertainment and beauty workers and others, contributors to this volume document fashion and beauty in its innumerable material and immaterial forms—a photo of a pose, an image on the bottle of skin cream, a $20 dress bought from the neighborhood shop, a plastic surgery GIF, the color of a nail polish. These objects are actually documentations of daily life, capturing fleeting moments and encounters that shape a world lived far beyond things. As such, they demand that we approach them as more than objects collected and archived behind glass, but instead as narratives and practices of those who make, wear, use, and imagine fashion and beauty. Only in doing so can we begin to see more clearly the alternative histories that we have come to think of as the time of Asia.

NOTES

1 Vanessa Friedman, "Exhibition on China and Fashion Proves Golden for Met," *New York Times*, Fashion and Style, August 29, 2015.

2 See, for instance, Giles Lipovetsky's *Empire of Fashion: Dressing Modern Democracy* (Princeton, NJ: Princeton University Press, 2002).

3 Friedman, "Exhibition on China and Fashion Proves Golden for Met."

4 Limei Hoang, "What's Driving the Goldrush for Korean Beauty Brands?" The Business of Fashion, July 24, 2016. https://www.businessoffashion.com/.

5 Joan DeJean, *The Essence of Style: How the French Invented High Fashion, Fine Food, Chic Cafes, Style, Sophistication, and Glamour* (New York: Free Press, 2006).

6 Mari Yoshihara, *Embracing the East: White Women and American Orientalism* (New York: Oxford University Press, 2003).

7 See, for instance, Inderpal Grewal and Caren Kaplan, *Scattered Hegemonies: Postmodernity and Transnational Feminist Practices* (Minneapolis: University of Minnesota Press, 1994).

8 Laura Miller, *Beauty Up: Exploring Contemporary Japanese Body Aesthetics* (Berkeley: University of California Press, 2006); Dorinne Kondo, *About Face: Performing Race in Fashion and Theater* (Cambridge: Cambridge University Press, 1997); Dorothy Ko, *Cinderella's Sisters: A Revisionist History of Footbinding* (Berkeley: University of California Press, 2005); Sean Metzger, *Chinese Looks: Fashion, Performance, Race* (Bloomington: Indiana University Press, 2014); Wen Hua, *Buying Beauty: Cosmetic Surgery in China* (Hong Kong: Hong Kong University Press, 2013); Ayu Saraswati, *Seeing Beauty, Sensing Race in Transnational Indonesia* (Honolulu: University of Hawaii Press, 2013).

9 Andrew Brooks, *Clothing Poverty: The Hidden World of Fast Fashion and Second-Hand Clothes* (London: Zed Books, 2015).

10 Sandra Niessen, Ann Marie Leshkowich, and Carla Jones, *Re-Orienting Fashion: The Globalization of Asian Dress* (New York: Berg, 2003); Maxine Leeds, *Ain't I a Beauty Queen? Black Women, Beauty, and the Politics of Race* (New York: Oxford University Press, 2002); Ginetta Candelario, *Black Behind the Ears: Dominican Racial Identity from Museums to Beauty Shops* (Durham, NC: Duke University Press, 2007); Rebecca Chiyoko King-O'Riain, *Pure Beauty: Judging Race in Japanese-American Beauty Pageants* (Minneapolis: University of Minnesota Press, 2006); Thuy Linh Nguyen Tu, *The Beautiful Generation: Asian Americans and the Fashion Industry* (Durham, NC: Duke University Press, 2010); Alexander Edmonds, *Pretty Modern: Beauty, Sex, and Plastic Surgery in Brazil* (Durham, NC: Duke University Press, 2010); Minh-Ha T. Pham, *Asians Wear Clothes on the Internet* (Durham, NC: Duke University Press, 2015); Tanisha Ford, *Liberated Threads* (Greensboro, NC: University of North Carolina Press, 2015); Martin Manalansan, *Global Divas: Filipino Gay Men in the Diaspora* (Durham, NC: Duke University Press, 2003); Nhi Lieu, *The American Dream in Vietnamese* (Minneapolis: University of Minnesota Press, 2011); Theo Gonzalves, *The Day the Dancers Stayed: Performing in the Filipino/American Diaspora* (Philadelphia, PA: Temple University Press, 2009); Vanita Reddy, *Fashioning Diaspora: Beauty, Femininity, and South Asian American Culture* (Philadelphia, PA: Temple University Press, 2016).

11 K. Sivaramakrishnan and Arun Agrawal, eds., *Regional Modernities: The Cultural Politics of Development in India* (Palo Alto, CA: Stanford University Press, 2003).

12 See, for instance, Seungsook Moon's *Militarized Modernity and Gendered Citizenship in South Korea* (Durham, NC: Duke University Press, 2005).

13 See Edmonds, *Pretty Modern*, for an excellent account of beauty's contradictory roles in Brazilian modernity.

14 Cho Joo-Hyun, "Neoliberal Governmentality at Work: Post IMF Korean Society and the Construction of Neoliberal Women," *Korea Journal* 49, no. 3 (Fall 2009): 17.

15 Toby Miller, "A Metrosexual Eye on Queer Guy," *GLQ: A Journal of Lesbian and Gay Studies* 11, no. 1 (2005): 112–17. See Ruth Holliday and Joanna Elving Hwang, "Gender, Globalization and Aesthetic Surgery in South Korea," *Body & Society* 18, no. 2 (2012): 58–81 for an account of how such mainstream trends are reflected in cosmetic surgery literature such that even in academic scholarship, cosmetic surgery continues to be analyzed as a phenomenon targeting mostly women despite the evidence that men also engage in such practices.

16 Here we are of course building on the work of the fantastic collection, Alys Eve Weinbaum, Lynn M. Thomas, Pritia Ramamurthy, Uta G. Poiger, and Madelyn Yuye Dong, *The Modern Girl Around the World: Consumption, Modernity, and Globalization* (Durham, NC: Duke University Press, 2008).

17 Richard Florida, *The Rise of the Creative Class: And How It's Transforming Work, Leisure, Community, and Everyday Life* (New York: Basic Books, 2002).

18 See, for example, Lucy Williamson, "The Dark Side of South Korean Pop Music," *BBC News*, June 15, 2011, http://www.bbc.com/.

19 See Edna Bonacich, Lucie Cheng, Norma Chinchilla, Nora Hamilton, and Paul Ong, *Global Production: The Apparel Industry in the Pacific Rim* (Philadelphia, PA: Temple University Press, 1994).

20 See the work of Chin Kwan Lee in *Gender and the South China Miracle: Two Worlds of Factory Women* (Berkeley: University of California Press, 1998) who explains how the breakdown of the communist workers unit that lead to massive rural to urban migratory flows also culminated in the introduction of the hukou registration status of Chinese citizens, a social control system which stratified Chinese society into an urban class with social welfare and full citizenship and a class of peasants, tied to the land for agricultural surplus for industrialization.

21 Aihwa Ong, *Spirits of Resistance and Capitalist Discipline: Factory Women in Malaysia*, second ed. (New York: SUNY Press, 1987); Chin Kwan Lee, *Gender and the South China Miracle: Two Worlds of Factory Women* (Berkeley: University of California Press, 1998); Leslie Chang, *Factory Girls: From Village to City in a Changing China* (New York: Spiegel & Grau, 2008).

22 *The True Cost*, Dir. Andrew Morgan, BullFrog Films, 2015; Elizabeth Cline, *Overdressed: The Shockingly High Cost of Cheap Fashion* (New York: Portfolio/Penguin, 2013); Lucy Siegle, *To Die For: Is Fashion Wearing Out the World?* (London: Fourth Estate, 2011).

23 Here we are reminded of the work of cultural and social historians Michael Denning, *The Cultural Front: The Laboring of American Culture in the Twentieth*

Century (New York: Verso, 2011), Nan Enstad, *Ladies of Labor, Girls of Adventure: Working Women, Popular Culture, and Labor Politics at the Turn of the Twentieth Century* (New York: Columbia University Press, 1999), and Alys Eve Weinbaum, Lynn M. Thomas, and Priti Ramamurthy and The Modern Girl around the World Research Group, *The Modern Girl Around the World: Consumption, Modernity, and Globalization* (Durham, NC: Duke University Press, 2008).

24 Terence S. Turner, "The Social Skin," in *Not Work Alone: A Cross-Cultural View of Activities Superfluous to Survival*, edited by Jeremy Cherfas and Roger Lewin (London: Temple Smith, 1980), pp. 112–140.

1

White Like Koreans

The Skin of the New Vietnam

THUY LINH NGUYEN TU

My first visit to Vietnam was in December 2000, a trip to escape the New York winter but, in retrospect, well-timed in many other ways. Just a decade had passed since the country had instituted its economic reforms and it had been only a month since President Clinton's visit, the first by a US president since the war. During my six-week stay, I lived in Saigon but traveled throughout the country. Americans—and I was surely one despite being born in Vietnam—were still an uncommon sight, especially outside of the city. Where we traveled, my partner and I inspired all sorts of responses, from a friendly wave and "hello," to stares and pointing. Vietnam was just beginning to rebuild. The Imperial Hotel's recent multimillion-dollar renovation was a sign of things to come. The Furama Resort had just opened in Danang, the first luxury hotel built on the beach where the United States had installed the army base made memorable to Americans by the hit television show, *China Beach*. Once, while sitting on its white sand, a woman selling guava, cut up and served with salt and spicy red pepper, approached our group. We bought several to share and as she was departing she turned to my cousin and asked if her friend—me—was American? She said she could tell because my skin was so white—a comment I would come to hear endlessly.

When I returned to Vietnam in the summer of 2012, much had changed. Saigon was packed with new and renovated hotels, restaurants, and shops. The 68-floor Bixteco Tower stood at its center, casting a long shadow over the central district. American, European, Australian, Japanese, Korean, and Thai tourists all slurped pho in beautifully appointed settings. On a return visit to Danang, the Furama looked like it had seen better days, overtaken by dozens of lavish resorts lining the beach, including the dazzling new Grand Hyatt. Strangers still found me comment-worthy, but not because of my absolute foreignness. "You speak Vietnamese very well for a Japanese person," a street-side coffee vendor in Hoi An told me. Once, at a Karaoke lounge, I was even mistaken for a local. My skin too had become rather unremarkable. Its much-praised lightness seemed to have disappeared in the intervening years.

A decade had passed between these two trips and the years had no doubt left their mark on my body. But my skin had not darkened significantly, nor had my features changed noticeably. How had I gone from "American" and remarkably "white" to "Japanese" or "Vietnamese" with rather unremarkable skin? These comments hinted at a shift in the signification of color, race, and nation. They compelled me to consider, following the insights of many historians and anthropologists of the body, how narratives about the body—here, the skin—are also ways of making sense of the world—in this instance, of a city undergoing rapid economic and cultural transformation.

In Vietnam, one particularly revealing place to observe these changes was at the upscale malls and boutiques—or shrines to skin, as I came to think of them—that had sprung up in the wake of postwar economic reforms. Like fast food restaurants and foreign cars, malls blew into Vietnam on the same winds of trade liberalization that delivered most other luxury items. But unlike most malls in the United States and elsewhere, whose main floor windows are filled with the latest fashion, here, cosmetics dominate the scene. Ads for beauty supplies, from low-cost shampoos to high-status lipsticks, also flood magazines, newspapers, and television—outpacing, in my estimation, advertisements for any other kind of consumer good. Not surprisingly, sales of prestige cosmetics, including brands like Shiseido and Lancôme, have far outpaced those of luxury clothing. In comparison to the cost of a new Prada purse, cosmetics are a relatively affordable luxury item. They attract a wider swath of consumers in part because they offer even those with modest income an opportunity to participate in the global luxury market.

If cosmetics reigned at these glittering spaces of consumption—by 2000, Vietnam had become the fastest growing market for cosmetics, outpacing even China in the Asia/Pacific region—it was skincare that really ruled. These products take up about 75 percent of the market. They are displayed in pristine glass boxes, proffered by women (and occasionally men) neatly dressed and perfectly polished—the very representations of what they sell. Indeed, these local Vietnamese look no different from the globally circulated advertisements that surround them. Their hair black and shiny, their faces heart shaped with wide eyes, their skin clear and, in their favorite word, "bright" (sáng).

These women, like the places they inhabit, seem to be shining with the new. And at the cosmetics counters, they sold more than just affordable luxuries. They promised, in their goods and persons, access to something more elusive and perhaps even more urgent: entrance to the modernity enveloping Saigon. As in other places in the non-West—Brazil, for instance, in Barbara Weinstein's fantastic history of São Paulo—this unfolding modernity has a color.[1] It is, simply put, white. But you might be surprised by what that whiteness looks like in Vietnam, what it means. Thinking back to my first visit to Vietnam, two decades ago now, it seems plausible that my light skin might signal my Americanness, that whiteness could be monopolistically tied to that geography. But by 2012, such associations were being unraveled by a dazzling Asian futurity, forged in the much-touted success of South Korea, Japan, China and their "tiger economies." To their Southeast Asian neighbors in Vietnam, these nations modeled a bright future, one figured most commonly by the Korean star, whose lightness glimmered. How do we read *this* whiteness, embodied on Asian skin and signaling both aesthetic and economic possibilities for newly developing countries in the region?

Answering this question required me to think about "skin talk," or local discourses and debates about skin, within the context of Vietnam's ongoing modernization, as well as the emergence of South Korea as a cultural and economic power in the region. Moreover, it demanded that I consider whiteness in both a more cosmopolitan way—that is, not dominated solely by a US racial framework—and in a more provincial way—that is, as it is represented and read, imagined, and realized in a local and regional context. Reading Vietnamese women's considerations of and practices of skincare in this way, I began to see their efforts and imaginations of beauty as classed and gendered projects of development. As Vietnamese men literally rebuilt their cities with a muscular entrepreneurialism, elite Vietnamese women developed their own bodies to reflect both their nation's aspirations and their own hopes for the "new Vietnam." Their desire for lightness reflected these ambitions.

Yet light skin signaled something quite different in Saigon. Light skin in the United States has long been constructed as delicate and fragile—as a sign of Western femininity, of white women's need for protection and care. Moreover, the fragility of whiteness has been further reinforced in recent years by populist narratives that have positioned white people (men in particular) as constantly under threat, from lost jobs to terrorist attacks. But, as I hope to show, Vietnamese women embrace lightness not as an emblem of feminine vulnerability or of threatened masculinity. Quite to the contrary, the Korean brand of lightness they desire conveys power and dominance, a mark of South Korea's cultural and economic position in the region—and a sign of the possibilities for their own positions, even in the face of these nations' incompatible histories.

Hierarchies of Lightness

Among the images that dominate visual representations of postwar Saigon, perhaps the most iconic is that of hordes of men and women riding mopeds, masks covering their faces. The heat, dust, and chaos are palpable. In some ways, this image narrates a kind of generic third-world urban disorder—this could be Dhaka or Delhi—but what locates it firmly within a Vietnamese context is the body of the women, covered head to toe and presumably sweating in the scorching sun. The commentary that usually accompanies this image is one about Vietnamese women's obsession with lightness, their covered bodies a testament to the lengths they will go to maintain a fair complexion. And, like other spectacular examples of covered bodies—women in burqas, for instance—this one elicits a lot of feelings. There is pity for these women, who apparently suffer under both the dominance of Euro-American beauty standards and local forms of patriarchy. There is perhaps even anger on their behalf, a desire to free them from their own sweltering veil.

Saigon bursts at the seams with mopeds. These motorized scooters, which outnumber all other forms of transportation, became even more prominent post-reform, when new models entered the market and when families began to accumulate enough capital to purchase them.[2] They are a symbol of the increased mobility, both spatial and economic, that many Vietnamese enjoyed in the wake of Đổi Mới, the economic reforms instituted in 1986 that sought to turn the nation into a "socialist-oriented market economy." Mopeds expose their riders to the elements—to rain, sun, dirt, and heat. Commuters from the city's peripheries routinely pack additional clothes, as their travel gear inevitably becomes soiled and sweaty by the time they arrive at work. Women cover up in this context to shield against all the elements, but the reading of their fastidiousness as a preoccupation with whiteness has become widely accepted, and not just by outside observers.

"These women are so worried about getting dark," Ma, an editor at Elle Vietnam told me, "they don't care what they look like, as long as they can hide from the sun and stay light." Ma was, as usual, impeccably dressed during our lunch meeting, wearing a white blazer over a black mini-dress that exposed her long, bare legs. I asked her if she ever worried about "getting dark" herself. Ma replied, "of course I want to have good skin, but I also want to wear fashionable clothes and not have to cover myself like người nhà quê."

Người nhà quê, a country bumpkin, or someone who lacks sophistication and cosmopolitanism, is a common derogatory term that hinges on a long-standing discourse in Vietnam about the spatial, cultural, and moral distinctions between the city and the country.[3] Ma's invocation of it struck me because it suggested that if Vietnamese women shared a desire for lightness, they understood that desire differently. For Ma, the fashion editor who wore her sophistication on her sleeves, this ambition to "stay white" was actually a sign of backwardness and was antithetical to what it meant to be fashionable. The image of the fully covered Vietnamese woman, so commonly understood to be representative of a widespread longing for the norms of modern femininity, was here being read as actually hostile to it. For Ma and her circle, the woman sitting astride her moped appears to inhabit the same city, but she actually lives in a different time.

Women like Ma rarely ride mopeds, preferring cars or cabs. These vehicles offer wealthy women not just a new way to travel but also a new relationship to their body. For enclosed in these cars, these women can be both exposed and protected. When they alight from the cab and enter the mall, there is no dirt or sweat on their clothes and no sign of the sun that has barely kissed their skin. In Saigon, cars sit at the top of the vehicular hierarchy. In the (ever-changing) rules of traffic, non-motorized vehicles (bicycles and cyclos) must yield the right of way to mopeds; mopeds must in turn give the right of way to four-wheeled vehicles. In a similar vein, this figure of fashionable femininity, whose wealth reshapes her body's relationship to the environment, reveals how the pursuit of whiteness is also hierarchically structured. In the eyes of Ma and her ilk, working-class attempts to "hide from the sun and stay white" are like the moped that these women ride: a symbol of aspiration that reveals its own distance from real power.

Our conversation raised as a question a phenomenon that I had previously understood as social fact. Scholars and social critics have written extensively about color and beauty and the privileging of whiteness in normative notions of attractiveness and desirability.[4] These norms, they say, have been exacerbated in recent years by cosmeceutical companies, which have sold billions of dollars of skin-whitening creams to young, urban, educated women in the global south by linking lightness with modernity, social mobility, and youth. Commentaries about cosmetics consumption in Asia and Africa center on this dilemma—on the ways women are asked to mimic Western norms of beauty, particularly light skin, and respond by widely consuming these dangerous products, which often contain high levels of the potentially carcinogenic chemical hydroquinone.[5]

The desire for whiteness in Asia and Africa is thus understood in part as one of the (for critics, tragic) by-products of modernization. As more images of Western beauty circulate, and more goods that can help women to approximate that image become accessible, modernization begins to look on women's bodies very much like Westernization. Whiteness in one formulation becomes a kind of currency, carried like a debt to colonialism, but also expended to demand payment for colonialism.[6] In places like South Africa, activists have successfully rallied to regulate or ban the use of these creams. But efforts to curb its consumption have more often taken a softer touch, through editorials and other public commentaries urging women to simply accept the color of their own skin.

The image of the covered woman in Vietnam seems to offer even more evidence for this type of argument, as does the ubiquitous presence of whitening creams at the city's cosmetics counters and in marketing outlets. Yet while these products occupy a fair share of the market, they hardly dominate.[7] And while shoppers do look for them, the Vietnamese women I encountered at Saigon's shiny malls do not use the term white (trắng) to describe their ideal complexion. They use instead the word sáng, or bright. Sáng refers not to a color, but to a quality, a luminousness that radiates from the skin. "Clean," "clear," and, increasingly, "healthy," are words women use to describe the ideal condition. Moreover, sáng is also commonly used to refer to brightness of another kind: intelligence. When someone is gifted with "mặt sáng" (bright face), they are bright-eyed, smart, but not necessarily light-skinned. Brightness is in this sense a broadly desirable quality not limited to notions of beauty.

Perhaps in response, much of the industry has changed its nomenclature from "whitening" to "brightening." While many products may have "white" in their name, they inevitably promise to "lighten" or "brighten skin." In some ways, "brightening" is only a euphemistic rendering of "whitening," but the shift in terminology is significant for Vietnamese consumers. Whitening products like those with high levels of hydroquinone are not commonly sold in malls and boutiques, but at market stalls, low-end shops, and door-to-door. These latter are the domain of the less affluent. My informants claimed that these products were popular among poorer and more rural populations, whose anxieties about their color led them to consume "harsh," "cheap," and even "dangerous" goods. Once again, they presented the pursuit of whiteness, which I had understood to be a widespread preoccupation, as a primarily working-class practice. This was not the aspiration of a modern, cosmopolitan woman. For these women, "bright" was the preferred terminology, and the preferred condition—shining outward, radiant in its status.

All this suggested to me that whiteness could be both an ideal to pursue and a relic to move beyond. Class marked that dividing line. Far from a homogenous and homogenizing force, the arrival of global beauty into Saigon only made more apparent the class distinctions heightened by Vietnam's new "socialist-oriented market economy." For those in pursuit of "brightness," where could they turn to find this new ideal?

In Place of Whiteness

It may surprise some to learn that, according to Kimberly Hoang, Vietnamese women hardly chase whiteness, since many already see their skin as naturally white. In the words of one bar hostess she interviewed: "[A]ctually the true skin color of women in Asia is white. When a baby is born in Japan, Korea, or Vietnam, what color is their skin? It is fair and white, right? Dark skin is from going out in the sun a lot. We are just trying to bring out our natural beauty."[8] In my own interviews, women often tell me they cover up to "stay light."[9] In other words, whiteness is something they already possess, not something they have to attain by using creams or other methods, though it is a state that is constantly under threat from age, environment, and other factors.

And, in fact, various groups in this region have at different points understood themselves to be white. Excavations of early Chinese texts show that Chinese writers saw themselves as light in distinction to their neighbors and were until the sixteenth century understood as white, even by Catholic missionaries and European traders.[10] This Chinese whiteness was achieved primarily through acts of conquest. We see this in the ways that the term *kunlun*, meaning dark and originally referring to indigenous Chinese populations, became associated exclusively with non-native peoples. Over the course of the Tang era, Chinese conquerors incorporated Malays, Javanese, Thais, Kmers, and various aboriginal groups from Champa (present-day eastern coastal Vietnam), who they routinely enslaved, into the elusive and ever-expanding category of *kunlun*. The darkness of these "black-bodied" neighbors, confirmed in later periods by sailors and merchants engaged in Southeast Asian trade, helped to affirm in the Chinese a sense of their whiteness. When Chinese travelers encountered neighbors who defied this dichotomy—who were fair or light—they reasoned that these anomalous persons were the product of intermarriage with Chinese.[11]

A similar process enabled shifting claims to whiteness in Indonesia, which has at various times been considered a characteristic of the Dutch, Japanese, and of Indonesians themselves.[12] At the height of Dutch colonialism (1900–1942), Europeans requisitioned whiteness as their sole property, transforming it from a quality that many—especially the Chinese—possessed, to one with racial prerequisite. During the relatively shorter period of Japanese colonialism (1942–1945), Japanese reclaimed whiteness as an Asian quality, a move that enabled them to reposition Asians—Japanese first, followed by Indonesians, Chinese, Arabs, and Indians—as culturally and politically above "non-Asian nationalities," including Europeans and Eurasians. This hierarchy, and claim on whiteness, was later transformed again by the emergence of Indonesian nationalism.[13]

As these brief examples suggest, within the region, whiteness as a status has accrued to varying groups of people who have been able to enact or demonstrate their capacity for sovereign power. Whiteness, as the Indonesian case makes particularly clear, is a dominant political position that can be embodied by a range of nations and people.[14] In contemporary Vietnam, if women attach any body to an idealized brightness, it is usually not a Euro-American "white" body. Nearly all the women I interviewed in Vietnam instead cited Korean and, to a lesser extent, Japanese celebrities as having a "look" they liked, the qualities they found beautiful, or most often the skin they revered or envied.

Korean stars adorn the covers of magazines; appear on television commercials; show up on billboards; and otherwise permeate Vietnamese visual culture.[15] At the Calla Spa where I conducted my research, women often brought in photos of Korean actresses to breathlessly narrate their beauty. In the treatment rooms, women updated one another about the latest Korean soaps. Tales of friends, families, and neighbors who had gone to Seoul, usually to undergo some form of plastic surgery, circulated among various networks, turning each into a micro-celebrity followed about by a flurry of excitement and speculation.

But it was not just Korean culture that made a mark on Vietnam. From face creams to fast food, from retail to real estate, Korean capital has flooded the new Saigon. In recent years, South Korea has become the biggest source of foreign direct investment (FDI) in Vietnam; between 1988–2009 its total registered capital amounted to USD26.9 billion, a figure that does not include various other informal or third-party deal-making.[16] Because the capital fueling the development of Saigon (and Vietnam) has come in large part from Korea, its imprints appear not just on movie stars' bodies but on the city's streets, buildings, and skyline. To many, Koreanness looks, feels, and in many ways is modernity.

We might call this a regional or pan-Asian modernity, which looks not to the West but to ascendant Asian nations for inspiration and aspiration.[17] As a model, Korea offers the possibility of a strong economy and a (perhaps even stronger) culture industry; both have dominated

Vietnam. This is what makes it so desirable, and indeed what makes it possible for Koreanness to appear so modern, so white.

In contemporary Vietnam, Koreans become imbued with this quality precisely because they have displayed their capacity to dominate. Scholars like Heijin Lee in this volume have written about how South Korea has invested in and deployed its cultural products for economic and political ends, indeed as a form of statecraft. The spell that Korean popular culture has cast on Vietnam was certainly a product of these efforts. This display of its strength, masked by the rhetoric of the "free market," has now structured Vietnam in a position of indebtedness economically (in the form of billions in loans) and culturally to its neighbor. Both serve as evidence of South Korea's power in the region—and its capacity for whiteness.

To be sure, Vietnamese interest in lightness predates the recent Korean invasion. As in many parts of the world, skin color here has also been used to mark many distinctions, including class and region. US military and cultural presence in Vietnam during the last few decades has only helped to reinforce the prioritizing of lightness. But "colorism" as a system of domination remains unevenly enforced in the country; wealth, education, and other privileges are not (or not yet) distributed solely along color lines.

Moreover, the widespread charges of Korean cultural influence suggest that the desire for light skin in this historical moment cannot be understood solely as a product of the global dominance of Euro-American standards, or the legacies of colonialism. While these standards and legacies are certainly still present, they also rub up against an emerging model of whiteness, one that does not rely on the historic links between white femininity and vulnerability or fragility. Lightness has in this region historically suggested a position of dominance—even, or especially, in the absence of white bodies. In aspiring to this Korean whiteness, women are reaching for a position of strength, one demanded both by the discourses of development—which equates strong economies with strong nations—and by the geopolitics of this region, in which nations jockey for regional dominance.

"I always tell women, you want your skin to be strong (manh)," Nga and other aestheticians at Calla repeatedly told me. Nga explained that though women sometimes came in seeking treatments to lighten their skin, she always advised the importance of strong skin, as a protection against the sun, dirt, and other toxins in the environment. "Lightening your skin can make it weak (yếu)," she went on, making clear that light skin was only desirable if it was also strong. Rejecting a vulnerable femininity, Nga advised women to reach instead for a brightness embodied by Koreanness, imagined as economically and culturally powerful, an appropriate model and path for their own brilliant futures.

Suitable Skin

Perhaps it is not surprising then that when surveyed about their beauty consumption, Vietnamese women often say they see Korean products as "especially suitable and well matched with Asian women's skin tones and facial features."[18] In my interviews, they described Korean cosmetics as "good for Vietnamese skin" and "good for this climate." One woman, a manager at an upscale hotel in the city, told me she found these products "appropriate for women like her," who work with an international clientele. She explained that it was important for women in her position to put forth "the best face of Vietnam." For her, Korean cosmetics were integral to this.

The Korean cosmetics industry has worked hard to insinuate itself in this way. They have publicized, most effectively and stealthily through the Korean cultural exports of K-pop and K-drama, the secrets to Korean women's flawless, porcelain skin and the miracle of Korean products. In advertisements, media accounts, and message boards, there is much waxing poetic over Korean skin: light, bright, glowing, and luminous are the words commonly used. The founders of Glow Recipe, a website that sells Korean products, characterized its distinctive qualities in this way: "radiance, luminosity . . . it's not about a shade of skin, but about an overall glow."[19] In other words, it is the kind of brightness Ma and her cohort embrace: a lightness that emanates outward, rather than a whiteness that requires constant coverage.

If a Korean glow is the most desired state, Korean products are the most in demand. Presented as the result of vast Korean scientific know-how, Korean brands boast rapid innovation; these companies claim to launch around 20–30 products per month while Western firms launch that many per year. In other words, Korean cosmetics are always at the industry's cutting edge.[20] As one magazine editor helpfully noted: South Korea is about "12 years ahead of the United States in terms of (beauty) technology," "outpacing all other countries in beauty innovation." In the skincare world, it has become "the new France."[21]

As such, it is perhaps not surprising that for the last decade, Korean cosmetics brands have taken the lion's share of the Vietnamese market, at about 35 percent. Its closest competitors hail from Europe (23%), followed by Japan (17%) and Thailand (13%), and finally the United States (10%). Products from the region, then, take up a majority of the market (65%), a surprisingly high percentage given the size and storied history of the Euro-American cosmetics conglomerates.[22]

Yet, despite talk of and genuine admiration for Korean scientific innovation, this is not what draws Vietnamese to Korean brands. While many praise Korean developments in science and technology, especially their cutting-edge cosmetic surgery industry, these views do not translate into a perception of quality. A consumer study of Korean cosmetics brands conducted at the Ho Chi Minh City International School of Business revealed that women in their survey almost uniformly *disagreed* with the statement: "Korean cosmetics are effective in solving skin problems (acne treatment, whitening, or anti-aging)." The study concluded, in fact, that quality, or effectiveness, was the characteristic women *least* identified with Korean brands.[23]

What drew them to these products then was not a sense of their quality, or at least not solely. Rather, as explained by the hotel manager I described above, they understood them to be "suitable" or "appropriate"—*hợp*. Suitability (*hợp*) is an important principle in Vietnamese culture, especially in residents' approach to health. Medicine is commonly thought to be effective only if it is suitable or compatible with the patient, and the criterion for suitability depends on a range of physical as well as social factors. Rather than take only what is prescribed for a particular condition, most Vietnamese will shop around for drugs that they perceive to be more generally well-matched to their family, based on family members' past experience, or on observations of a neighbor who might share their social situation if not their medical condition.[24]

When I asked cosmetics retailers what made Korean cosmetics suitable for Vietnamese skin, they suggested the geography. They pointed to Jeju Island, with its volcanic ashes, potent green tea, biodiversity, and mineral waters, from which is derived products that are so powerful they need only be misted on the face. (The popular brand, The Face Shop, sells one such item called simply "Jeju Marine Pure Water Facial Mist"). The Korean government has touted Jeju as one of the most botanically rich and least contaminated places on Earth—a skincare goldmine—but the salesperson did not stress these qualities to me. She told me instead that its value for Vietnamese women lies in Jeju's climate, which is much like Vietnam—a very surprising assertion, given that Saigon routinely ranks in the top ten most polluted cities in the world. "It's the same humidity, altitude, everything," she explained, "It's very good for Vietnamese skin."

In her estimation, cosmetics are very much like medicine; they cannot treat a specific condition without working on the whole person. Thus, a product is considered suitable not just because it effectively addresses a particular physical need, but because it signals a much broader sense of compatibility. Korean products are presented as suitable to "Vietnamese skin," to "Asian women's facial features," or to "this climate" as a whole. Vietnamese women's perception that Korean products were most suitable drove their consumer choices, it would appear, far more than did quality or price. It was their sense of or perhaps desires to produce compatibility between Koreanness and Vietnameseness that has shaped their preference for products that originate in (and represent) Korea.

What does it mean to see Koreanness as compatible with Vietnameseness? For pro-development boosterists, it enables the growing number of Korean-Vietnamese business partnerships to continue to remake Saigon in Seoul's skyscrapered image. It allows them to produce a narrative of harmony, despite a very recent history of conflict. During the Vietnam War, violence committed by Korean soldiers was, according to many Vietnamese, even more vicious than that by American soldiers. These acts of brutality have not disappeared from Vietnamese cultural memory, or from global politics. South Korea is today seen by the United States as sovereign, or at least human, in part because of its willingness to ally with Americans against the North Vietnamese, in radical distinction to its counterpart, North Korea, which is still figured as politically illegitimate and even savage.[25]

In its efforts to follow in the neighboring "tiger's" steps, the Vietnamese government has actively sought the help of Viet Kieu (overseas

Vietnamese) through a variety of legislation. For instance, in 2008 it passed the amendment to the Law on Vietnamese Nationality and allowed Viet Kieus to restore their Vietnamese nationality. This amendment followed on the heels of the passage of Resolution 36/NQTW in 2004, which mandated that government agencies make their policies more transparent and offer more support to Viet Kieus.[26] These legislations sought to encourage overseas Vietnamese to see themselves as a part of the nation, and to invest in it economically and otherwise. They helped to carve out a path to development that prioritized Vietnameseness, even as it remained open to other forms of foreign investment.

Writing about China's own efforts to produce and preserve Chineseness in its practice of modernization, Aihwa Ong has named these types of efforts "modernity without deracination." In the Chinese context, the reconciliation of "race" with "modernity" works through the institution of practices and policies that seek to retain "Chinese values" and identity while also remaining receptive to transnational capital—that, in other words, produces a strategic dichotomy between Chinese and non-Chinese foreigners.[27] By contrast, Vietnam's own "modernity without deracination" flattens out the differences between Vietnam and other Asian nations. It requires an imagination of affiliation or compatibility with places like Korea.

This remaking of South Korea from imperial aggressor to cultural ideal required the work of women. It demanded of an elite group of consumers the capacity to see in their very own bodies a reflection of Korea's new place in their world. For these women, the attribution of whiteness to Koreanness is less the observation of physical realities than the aspiration for a new social reality, one in which Vietnam *could* be like Korea. This aspiration was, of course, not universally shared. For those Vietnamese without access to the market's largess, Jeju Island is remembered not as the land of sparkling waters, but as the place where South Korea enacted violent communist suppression, helped along by US counterinsurgency forces. This particular history of course does not enter into narratives of cosmetic compatibility. Thus, while Koreanness has come to saturate Vietnamese economic and cultural development, only for some is it a beacon of modernity to be emulated.

The arguments about whiteness I outlined above—where it originates, how to attain it—reflect these differing, class-based perspectives.

The desires for whiteness, and prohibitions against its pursuit, are a reflection of different imaginations about Vietnam's place in the region. For the urban elite who zip around in their air-conditioned cars, Vietnam's ascendance is fast and assured, next up in the region's string of successes. Vietnamese businessmen who boast of having more money than Americans and Viet Kieus who return with wads of cash and entrepreneurial ambitions are emblems of this new Vietnamese economic power.[28] These men represent a virile new Vietnam, and the deals they make have literally transformed their country's skyline.

For the most part, women have had little hand in these dealings, except as the social lubricant allowing men to transact. But in many ways, the fresh-faced and fashionable women shopping at Vincom Mall are their necessary modern counterparts. Through discourses of skin and skincare, elite Vietnamese women could imagine their own place in this changing world. Cosmetics retailers often told me they were there to "teach women, to educate them," about skincare, beauty, fashion, about good style and good manners—in short, about modernity. They saw their work as more than just selling, and indeed, women came to the cosmetics counters often to ask for advice, try a sample, chat—far more often than they came to buy. Through these interactions, women began to see how care of the skin could translate to care of the self, and of the nation. After all, both required development. For those not involved in million-dollar real estate deals, skin was the landscape of a different kind of hope.

To realize these hopes, women needed to embrace consumption, but even more crucially, they needed to enact a labor-intensive regime of care. "Korean women start being proactive from a very young age and treat their skin and complexion like the ultimate investment," writes one so-called expert, in a typical characterization of Korean skincare. "It is not just financial investment but a time investment. So although you might be following a strict cleansing and moisturizing regime every night before going to bed, you are still not even coming close to some important steps that Korean women use to help them achieve that spotless, beautiful skin."[29] Accounts like these make apparent the laborious nature of skincare, even as they narrate it as a ritual of pleasure—a kind of pampering. Their self-discipline *qua* self-pampering nonetheless positions Korean women as models of diligence and conscientiousness, whose hard work has freed their skin of blemishes and moved their nations forward.

I have often heard women in Vietnam (and in the United States) speak with awe and admiration about Koreans' skincare regimen, widely understood as the most exacting. For most women, this goes far beyond their current efforts. It is a horizon to reach, rather than a position to take. I imagined this ethical imperative—toward better skin, body, and life—would be met with even more creams and cleansers, but for many of the women I spoke to, it required more than good consumption. Cosmetics products alone could not produce this desired glow, which required women to embrace a model of progress and futurity that depended on deep discipline and a get-ahead-or-fall-behind ethos. For these women, preserving their skin under the shield of clothing was the mere tip of the iceberg; to do no more would leave them no better off than the women riding outdated mopeds.

Elite women labored instead to produce skin that was "sáng, sạch, dep" (bright, clean, beautiful)—a mantra I heard often at the Calla Spa. If this sounds familiar, it is because it so closely mirrors the slogan urban planners and developers put forth to convince farmers and other holdouts about the need for urban redevelopment. If they vacated their land for new malls, developers promised, the city would become "xanh, sạch, dep" (green, clean, and beautiful), a place for everyone to enjoy, even as some (most) must be displaced to make it possible.[30]

In this context, I came to understand the debates about skin color in Vietnam as classed and gendered practices of development—a means by which women intervened in the transformations buzzing around them. I came to see skin as the arena in which women could debate and imagine what modernity should look like in Vietnam. The vision pushed by Ma and her cohort can be thought of as a regional, pan-Asian modernity, one that requires an imagination of compatibility (hợp) with the region's ascendant economies. If the disciplined care required to make Vietnam "look" like Korea seems a lot like the brand of neoliberal self-discipline the United States has been exporting for many years, this is because it is not so different. But the directive now seems to be emerging from elsewhere. The fascination with Korean skin hints at this shift. The face of the future looks different. And if it still appears white, it is surely whiteness of a different color.[31]

Conclusion

Returning to my initial questions, I want to offer some speculations about what all of this might mean for our understanding of skin color as an index of race and nation. When I tell friends that I am doing research on the global cosmetics industry, they always ask if I am writing about skin whitening. They have heard it is a big industry in Asia and Africa, where women crave lightness. I often respond that, yes, in general it is better to be lighter than darker in Asia, just as it is in general better to be lighter than darker in the United States. The industry is big and remains so because a shift in the location and meaning of whiteness has not led to the destigmatization of darkness, here, there, or anywhere.[32] As so-called white nationalists (white supremacists) gain political standing in the United States and Europe, often violently, parsing the complexities of lightness does little to counter their power.

But the story I want to tell here is less about the overthrow of racial ideology than about transformations that are still ongoing and a future that is yet unknown. Whiteness, brightness, and lightness are, as I have suggested, not just different colors but different ways of being in the world. Some take us back to a history and present of racial domination, while others move us toward new possibilities. If Korea is "the new France"—the presumed birthplace of beauty—and Korean skin is the new beautiful, can it really be said that whiteness is a standard to which all nonwhite people aspire, at their own peril?[33] Can the complex articulations of race, gender, class, and nation indicated by Vietnamese claims to whiteness offer us a way out of Euro-American styled supremacy, even as they might force us to reckon with new forms of domination?

If we take seriously how people talk about and understand their bodies, we might see how they invest and divest in racial schemas, and more importantly, how these ideas shift in regional and local contexts. In my effort to provincialize whiteness, I hope to have shown how these ideas are forged through the regional dynamics that encourage (or discourage) people to see themselves in and to forge new relationships of affinity. I hope to have made clear as well how these debates about whiteness, which are framed by colonial histories, have also enabled Vietnamese women to debate and articulate their vision of the modern. It is possible to look ostentatiously white and American, as I had on my first trip to

Vietnam, and soon after to appear unremarkably light and not American at all. It is also possible to be white like Chinese, Japanese, and now Koreans. To grasp these changes is to see a world in the making.

NOTES

1 Barbara Weinstein, *The Color of Modernity: São Paulo and the Making of Race and Nation in Brazil* (Durham, NC: Duke University Press, 2015).

2 Allison Truitt, "On the Back of a Motorbike: Middle-Class Mobility in Ho Chi Minh City, Vietnam," *American Ethnologist* 35, no. 1 (February 2008): 3–19.

3 See, for instance, Eric Harm's account of this distinction in *Saigon's Edge: On the Margins of Ho Chi Minh City* (Minneapolis: University of Minnesota Press, 2011).

4 See, for instance, some recent works: Michael Edward Stanfield, *Of Beasts and Beauty: Gender, Race, and Identity in Colombia* (Austin: University of Texas Press, 2014); Blain Roberts, *Pageants, Parlors, and Pretty Women: Race and Beauty in the Twentieth-Century South* (Chapel Hill: University of North Carolina Press, 2014); Kimberly Jade Norwood, ed., *Color Matters: Skin Tone Bias and the Myth of a Postracial America* (New Brunswick, NJ: Rutgers University Press, 2013); Alexander Edmonds, *Pretty Modern: Beauty, Sex, and Plastic Surgery in Brazil* (Durham, NC: Duke University Press, 2010); Deborah L. Rhode, *The Beauty Bias: The Injustice of Appearance in Life and Law* (New York: Oxford University Press, 2010); Evelyn Nakano Glenn, ed., *Shades of Difference: Why Skin Color Matters* (Stanford, CA: Stanford University Press, 2009); Ginetta E. B. Candelario, *Black behind the Ears: Dominican Racial Identity from Museums to Beauty Shops* (Durham, NC: Duke University Press, 2007); Rebecca King-Oriain, *Pure Beauty: Judging Race in Japanese American Beauty Pageants* (Minneapolis: University of Minnesota Press, 2006).

5 See Evelyn Nakano Glenn, ed., *Shades of Difference: Why Skin Color Matters* (Stanford, CA: Stanford University Press, 2009), especially contributions by Nakano Glenn and Lynn M. Thomas, and Candelario, *Black behind the Ears*, which refutes whiteness as a homogenous ideal among Dominican women.

6 Patricia Goon and Allison Craven, "Whose Debt?: Globalisation and Whitefacing in Asia," *Intersections: Gender, History and Culture in the Asian Context* 9 (August 2003), http://intersections.anu.edu.

7 Despite broad consensus about their appeal, these products are not the most popular in the Vietnamese market (they lag behind cleaning and moisturizing). This may not be true in other locations on the continent, particularly outside of Southeast Asia. In South Asia, for instance, lightening creams like Fair and Lovely have long been a cosmetic staple, though it is not clear to me what share of the market it occupies. See Ong Thi Phuong Anh, "Determinants of Brand Equity in Vietnam Cosmetics Industry: Case Study of Korean Cosmetics," Thesis in Partial Fulfillment of the Requirements of the Degree of Bachelor of Arts in Business Administration, Vietnam National University, Ho Chi Minh City, 2013. See also

Nguyen Hu Mai and Serene Sirikhoon, "Cosmetics Market in Vietnam," master's thesis in International Marketing, Mälardalen University, 2008.

8 Kimberly K. Hoang, "Competing Technologies of Embodiment: Pan-Asian Modernity and Third World Dependency in Vietnam's Contemporary Sex Industry," *Gender & Society* 28, no. 4 (2014): 522.

9 In one indication of this, women's street fashion in Saigon is quite different in the evenings, when women uncover themselves after the sun sets.

10 Rotem Konner and Walter Demmel, "Introduction," *Race and Racism in Modern East Asia* (New York: Brill, 2012).

11 Don J. Wyatt, "A Certain Whiteness of Being: Chinese Perception of Self by the Beginning of European Contact," in *Race and Racism in Modern East Asia*, and Don J. Wyatt, *The Blacks of Modern China* (Philadelphia: University of Pennsylvania Press, 2012).

12 L. Ayu Saraswati, *Seeing Beauty, Sensing Race in Transnational Indonesia* (Honolulu: University of Hawaii Press, 2013).

13 Saraswati, *Seeing Beauty*.

14 Dredge Kang has made a similar argument in his dissertation, "White Asians Wanted," in which he shows how preferential desires for what he calls "white Asian" partners (i.e., Northeast Asians, Sino-Thais, and Chinese diasporans in Southeast Asia) in Thailand, signals not a desire for Euro-Americanness but for economic development and cosmopolitan modernity. White Asians, in his formulation, hail from developed nations like Japan and Korea and can claim this status because of their relative economic and cultural power. Dredge Kang, "White Asians Wanted: Queer Racialization in Thailand," Thesis in Partial Fulfillment of the PhD in Anthropology, Emory University, 2015.

15 While Saigon still showcases a fair share of American film and music, and the arrival of Brad Pitt and Angelina Jolie in Saigon for the adoption of their son had become something of an urban legend—tour guides still argue about which restaurants they frequented—these were not the central sites of reference.

16 Vo Tri Than and Nguyen Anh Duong, "Revisiting Exports and Foreign Direct Investments in Vietnam," *Asian Economic Policy Review* 6 (2011): 112–131.

17 See, for instance, Arun Agrawal, ed., *Regional Modernities: The Cultural Politics of Development in India* (Stanford, CA: Stanford University Press, 2003).

18 Ong Thi Phuong Anh, "Determinants of Brand Equity in Vietnam Cosmetics Industry: Case Study of Korean Cosmetics," Thesis in Partial Fulfillment of the Requirements of the Degree of Bachelor of Arts in Business Administration, Vietnam National University, Ho Chi Minh City, 2013. See also Nguyen Hu Mai and Serene Sirikhoon, "Cosmetics Market in Vietnam," Master's Thesis in International Marketing, Mälardalen University, 2008.

19 Cited in Sheryl Wischhover, "The Politics of Skin Whitening," *Refinery 29*, March 13, 2015, http://www.refinery29.com/.

20 Alicia Yoon, "Korean Beauty and the Search for Innovation," *Peach and Lily*, September 1, 2015, https://www.peachandlily.com/.

21 Kenya Hunt, "The New Skincare Superpower," *Marie Claire*, May 2011, 244.

22 Nguyen and Sirikhoon, "Cosmetics Market in Vietnam."

23 Ong Thi Phuong Anh, "Determinants of Brand Equity in Vietnam Cosmetics Industry."

24 David Craig, *Familiar Medicine: Everyday Health Knowledge and Practice in Vietnam* (Honolulu: University of Hawaii Press, 2002).

25 Eleana J. Kim, *Adopted Territory: Transnational Korean Adoptees and the Politics of Belonging* (Durham, NC: Duke University Press, 2010).

26 Andrew T. Pham, "The Returning Diaspora: Analyzing Overseas Vietnamese (Viet Kieu) Contributions toward Vietnam's Economic Growth," DEPOCEN Working Paper Series, http://www.depocenwp.org.

27 Aihwa Ong, *Flexible Citizenship: The Cultural Logics of Transnationality* (Durham, NC: Duke University Press, 1999).

28 Kimberly Hoang, *Dealing in Desire: Asian Ascendancy, Western Decline, and the Hidden Currencies of Global Sex Work* (Oakland: University of California Press, 2015).

29 Annabelle Atkinson, "The Super Easy Korean Skincare Routine (For Glowing Skin)," *She's in the Glow*, September 29, 2014, http://shesintheglow.com/.

30 Erik Harms, "Beauty as Control in the New Saigon: Eviction, New Urban Zones, and Atomized Dissent in a Southeast Asian City," *American Ethnologist* 9, no. 4 (November 2012): 735–750.

31 Matthew Frye Jacobson, *Whiteness of a Different Color: European Immigrants and the Alchemy of Race* (Cambridge, MA: Harvard University Press, 1999).

32 In fact, one of the main complaints US consumers have about Korean makeup (rather than skincare) is that there is a very limited color palette, ranging from pale to slightly less pale.

33 This takes us away, at least, from Homi Bhabha's classic formulation about colonial mimicry, in which the colonized are always "not quite, not white."

2

China: Through the Looking Glass

Race, Property, and the Possessive Investment in White Feelings

MINH-HA T. PHAM

Much of the media coverage of the Costume Institute's 2015 exhibition *China: Through the Looking Glass* shared a common structure. Reviewers, both professional and amateur, often begin by admitting they were "nervous"[1] about the show's potential for Orientalism (several reviewers mention that the title "reeks"[2] of Orientalism) and end by reassuring readers that the exhibition was actually fine after all (i.e., not Orientalist/ not racist). A review published on the popular fashion news site Racked captures the general sense of relief when it describes the show as "surprisingly respectful."[3]

A certain amount of wariness about fashion's representations of Asianness is justified given its checkered history of Orientalism. From Paul Poiret's collection in 1911 to Marc Jacobs's collection for Louis Vuitton in 2010 (and all the others in between, including more than a few by Yves Saint Laurent) to the long tradition of Orientalist costuming across high and pop culture—from Katy Perry's stage performances to Karl Lagerfeld's yellowface film,[4] the West's sartorial interpretations of Asian people, places, and things has been mostly limited to caricature. Still, I want to suggest that the question about whether *Looking Glass* is an Orientalist exhibition or not is the wrong one to ask—not least because that question has already been answered by the exhibition organizers. In curator Andrew Bolton's words, the style of the exhibition garments "belongs to the broader tradition and practice of Orientalism."[5] But, he clarifies, Orientalism is not necessarily a bad thing. The *Looking Glass* exhibition, Bolton explains, "attempts to propose a less politicized and more positivist examination of Orientalism"[6]—an approach to Orientalism that one of the exhibition labels terms "romantic Orientalism."[7] So, to be absolutely clear: The organizers don't deny the exhibition's Orientalism. They acknowledge it with the qualification that it is Orientalist in a feel-good way. "Far from being dismissive or disrespectful of its peoples and customs, Western designers have invariably looked to China with honorable intentions."[8] More information about the exhibition's brand of feel-good Orientalism appears on the museum's website and on the introductory wall text leading into the exhibition:

> [The exhibition] explores the impact of Chinese aesthetics on western fashion and how China has fueled the fashionable imagination for centuries [. . .] From the earliest period of European contact with China in the sixteenth century, the West has been enchanted with enigmatic objects and imagery from the East, providing inspiration for fashion designers from Paul Poiret to Yves Saint Laurent, whose fashions are infused at every turn with romance, nostalgia, and make-believe.[9]

If the exhibition's concept is neither original nor a matter of debate, it is also, for me, the least interesting thing about it. A much more relevant and, I think, useful discussion focuses not on the *what* of an exhibition organized around Orientalism but the *when* and *why* of it. This chapter considers the exhibition's Orientalism as a matter of context, not content. That is to say, my concern is not so much with the exhibition's Orientalism but with the conditions in which an Orientalist fashion exhibition—installed in a space that months before was renamed the Anna Wintour Costume Center after the imposing *Vogue* chief editor and the most powerful arbiter of Western fashion in recent memory—would be marketable and popular. (With 815,992 visitors over an extended four-month run, *Looking Glass* broke the Costume Institute's previous attendance record.)[10] By highlighting its contextual aspects, I want to shift the focus away from the usual concerns about Orientalism as a representational problem toward a discussion of its use and value as a curatorial/commercial strategy. In a sense, I want to take up the museum's point that Orientalism is not just about using racialized Asian aesthetics but the ways these aesthetics are being used, appreciated, and valued (in Bolton's words, as the "fuel" or raw material for Western creative production). Analyzing the exhibition in context rather than in isolation will also, I hope, show that the tendency to view fashion's Orientalism as a cultural misstep rather than an economic choice obscures the very conditions—historical, social, and material, in the case of *Looking Glass*—from which it emerges.

Any contextual discussion about this show has to begin with the fact that when this exhibition exploring Western fashion's relationship to China opened, that relationship was already undergoing significant changes in at least two ways. The first involves the growing importance of the Chinese luxury consumer to US and European brands. In 2015, the year of the exhibition's run, Chinese consumers accounted for 35 percent of all luxury sales, US consumers claimed 15 percent, and western European consumers were responsible for another 12 percent. Japanese, other Asians, and others not already mentioned shared the remaining 38 percent. As a whole, Asian consumers constituted more than half (60 percent) of the global luxury market.[11] US and European luxury fashion brands like Prada, Salvatore Ferragamo, Jimmy Choo, and Coach responded to China's growing market power by launching their IPOs (initial public offerings of common stock) in the Hong Kong Stock Exchange close to their new target market. Others, such as Christian Louboutin, Salvatore Ferragamo, Prada, and Rupert Sanderson, are courting the biggest and fastest growing luxury market in the world with exclusive collections purportedly tailor-made for Asian tastes, bodies, and lifestyles (many of which are only available in Asia).

The second change reflects China's dominance in the global e-commerce market. In 2013, China became the largest online retail market in the world when it "racked up $314 billion in online sales, easily surpassing the US, which tallied $255 billion."[12] By 2015, that gap had widened considerably. Chinese online sales reached nearly $600 billion while the United States totaled about $350 billion.[13] That same year, Forrester, a leading consumer market research firm, projected China's e-commerce market would reach $1 trillion by 2019.[14] It isn't necessary for the purposes of this discussion to provide a detailed explanation of all the factors and forces fueling the rapid expansion of China's e-commerce market, but I do want to sketch out the major features. They include: (1) the broader advances in manufacturing, retail, communication, and delivery systems (e.g., 3D printers, WiFi, social media, e-commerce, smart shipping containers, and automated distribution centers); (2) China's early adoption and development of mobile e-commerce platforms and services; and (3) state-driven initiatives and investments committed to giving China a stronger foothold in higher-value manufacturing and retail activities.[15]

Today, US media and popular discourse about Chinese retailers have rendered them practically synonymous with fake products and all the characteristics associated with them: intellectual theft, dishonesty, and laziness. But this stereotype is not an accurate representation of the actual state of Chinese e-commerce. What larger Chinese e-commerce firms (those able to conduct cross-border transactions) have done exceptionally well is to build and maintain a fluid and hybrid marketplace. Alibaba—a titan in the e-commerce world—boasts the most advanced logistics network in the world (a "just-in-time" auto-responsive management system) that can quickly stock, process, and deliver a mind-bendingly massive range and volume of items, from fake products that include legal and illegal copies to genuine luxury products that are legally imported as well as smuggled into the country (to avoid China's high import taxes). Alibaba's market dominance is one reason Western brands are pursuing cooperative relationships with it. For example, prestige brands like Burberry, Coach, and Louis Vuitton and popular mass-market brands Clinique and Clarins have set up virtual storefronts on the Alibaba-owned TMall site—a business strategy to edge out Chinese competitors selling look-alike products but also to gain access to Chinese customer support services, payment platforms (e.g., UnionPay and Alipay), and the all-important Chinese luxury consumer.

Finally, no contextual account of *Looking Glass* would be complete without mentioning the broader emotional climate surrounding China and fashion design. In contrast with (but not contradictory to) the exhibition's feel-good orientation toward China, the US public sentiment about China has been generally negative—panicky, to be more precise. Stories that paint China as "the world's leading counterfeiting superpower"[16] are common occurrences in the media and are routinely shared and consumed in social media. Often, these stories and their social media commentary are rendered with as much emotional intensity as the Orientalist fantasies that inspire the *Looking Glass* garments. Chinese fake products are not just a problem, they are a "mind-blowing,"[17] "staggering,"[18] or "colossal"[19] problem. The television documentary *Counterfeit Culture* (2013) may take the prize for the most sensationalizing overstatement about the counterfeit economy (it blames China), calling it "a crime wave unprecedented in human history."[20] Contemporary expressions of anti-Chinese panic are also invoked in official and informal campaigns against piracy in which a "made in China" label has come to be viewed as an indicator of fake fashion. In the "how to spot a knock-off" news article, think piece, and Internet forum discussion that now constitute a genre of ethical consumption discourse, comments like "if it made in china you know it's fake fashion for sure [*sic*]" and "most counterfeits are made in Asia so a 'Made in China' label is highly suspect" exemplify the commonsense racial logic about fashion property and impropriety.[21]

In describing some of the shifting terrain of the global cultural economy, the point I am making is this: The *Looking Glass* exhibition opened at the same time that the hegemonic whiteness of luxury fashion was being seriously challenged by Chinese consumers, e-tailers, manufacturers, and, yes, counterfeiters, as well as their cutting-edge merchandising systems—not to mention a wave of Chinese fashion designers (beneficiaries of China's economic and political investments in its creative industries) who were becoming more visible on fashion's global stages. The general response to China's emergence as a fashion retail superpower has been to disparage Chinese people as congenitally uncreative and Chinese products as fake, cheap, and unethically, if not illegally, produced. The anti-Chinese rhetoric, though, has done little to slow China's retail growth. Taking a contextual perspective of the *Looking Glass* exhibition, then, what we see is a prominent US fashion institution in a prominent US fashion city deliberately installing an Orientalist exhibition at the very moment when there is widespread moral and economic panic about the locus of fashion value shifting to Asia.

The exhibition's romantic Orientalism, I suggest, does not just reflect Western fashion's nostalgic desire for a racially normative relationship with China—one in which China's role in global fashion is limited to servicing the West's creative output and capital accumulation (whether as a resource of cheap physical labor or unrestricted creative inspiration). It functions here as a tactic for reconstituting that relationship, for reasserting a very specific authorial labor relationship where the West is the authorial source of global fashion—and thus, in the Lockean tradition, has a natural entitlement to all the property rights, resources, and privileges that come with authorship—and China is its primary resource (an open reserve of raw materials for fueling US and European property accumulation). The exhibition's positioning of Western designers' authorial/authoritative relation to Asian aesthetics is not based on any legal doctrine but instead on a hegemonic feeling that, in this exhibition, goes by the name romantic Orientalism. Romantic Orientalism is an appealing and thus powerful emotional strategy precisely because, rather than drawing on the negative feelings of Orientalist panic and anxiety, it is inspired by their equal and opposite counterparts, the positive feelings of Orientalist "romance, nostalgia, and make-believe." A contextual analysis of *Looking Glass* brings into focus how fashion's Orientalist productions are not just isolated moments of cultural insensitivity but a practice linked to a broader property grab that has resulted in the uneven development of the global economy. What *Looking Glass* brings to the fore is how racialized feelings, specifically "white feelings," are assets in the property grab process.

I take the *Looking Glass* exhibition as an illustrative case of how race and property rights and relations are constructed and enacted beyond the law and within the domain of public sentiment. My discussion draws on but also departs from important scholarship by Derrick Bell, Cheryl Harris, Nancy Leong, and George Lipsitz, which focuses on the role the law plays in constructing and maintaining "a property interest in whiteness." A key insight from this scholarship is that the law recognizes and reinforces the value of whiteness by vesting it with a wide range of material, social, and cultural benefits, privileges, and protections. Harris describes whiteness as "a type of status property."[22] Like property, whiteness is an asset that produces value in the form of material and nonmaterial resources and whose value is protected through legal and social norms and practices. *Looking Glass* demonstrates that whiteness and fashion property are also linked. But this relationship is not articulated through the law since US law does not recognize fashion design as property.[23] Instead, social and cultural norms, practices, and their public expressions (e.g., romantic Orientalism) determine property definitions, entitlements, and the distribution of value derived from these property rights.

My examination of *Looking Glass* draws most directly on Lipsitz's research on "the possessive investment in whiteness" because he explicitly addresses the relationship between property rights, wealth accumulation, and racialized feelings that I argue is *Looking Glass*'s central organizing framework. (Lipsitz focuses on different histories and expressions of white feelings, especially white guilt, resentment, shame, and solidarity.) As Lipsitz explains it, emotional and economic investments in whiteness have created "a world where the advantages of whiteness [are] carved out of other people's disadvantages."[24] For example, "residential segregation and home-loan discrimination skewed life chances along racial lines and inhibited opportunities for asset accumulation among members of aggrieved 'minority' groups."[25] For Lipsitz, though, emotional and economic investments belong to two different though mutually constitutive social spheres, an interior world of private prejudice and an external world of public policy. Moreover, he prioritizes the significance of public policies in the perpetuation and maintenance of white supremacy. "[W]hite supremacy is usually less a matter of direct, referential, and snarling contempt than a system for protecting the privileges of whites by denying communities of color opportunities for asset accumulation and upward mobility."[26]

Where my analysis diverges from Lipsitz's is in my focus on public feelings rather than private ones. I understand the exhibition's romantic Orientalism as an articulation of a set of white feelings that are institutional and pervasive rather than individual and private. This isn't to say that romantic Orientalism is never a personal or private feeling. Certainly designers, curators, and consumers possess personal feelings about the idea of the Orient—for example, as an unrestricted and unlimited reserve of creative "inspiration." The internalization or personal investment in these racialized feelings is why challenges to Orientalist appropriations are often taken so personally. To challenge Orientalist feelings is tantamount to robbing that individual of a long-privileged source of social, cultural, and economic capital. (NB: The exhibition organizers never use the terms Orientalist appropriation or cultural appropriation.)

But white feelings are not only (or even most importantly) personal feelings. They are public feelings that neither belong to nor are restricted to any one individual or group of people. They constitute a collective mood in much the same way that Jonathan Flatley describes the social and historical forces of shared experience and emotions shaping modern life. "We find ourselves in moods that have already been inhabited by others, that have already been shaped or put into circulation, and that are already there around us."[27] I understand white feelings to be structurally embedded public feelings of entitlement to and priority for white creative expression constituted by institutions, norms, and practices that reproduce and reinforce the value of that sense of entitlement under the rhetorical covers of creativity, genius, and innovation.

One example of the structural function of white feelings is the widespread convention of assigning unequal status to Western and non-Western fashion designs and dress styles. The exhibition's introductory wall informs visitors from the outset: "High fashion is juxtaposed with Chinese costumes." While Chinese garments are presented as the primary source material for Western designers, the feelings white designers derive from these cultural sources (e.g., as "inspiration," "lush and forbidden sensuality that made their work more intellectually daring") are what determine authorship. The exhibition labels grant white designers authorial agency and intention over the garments (e.g., "Ralph Lauren jacket" or "Valentino evening dress"). In contrast, the exhibition, like the designers, treats Chinese garments as authorless forms and therefore free and open resources (e.g., "Women's court robe—Chinese, 19th century" and "Cheongsam—Chinese, 1932").[28] The media coverage of the exhibition shows the same tendency to erase Chinese authorship. A *New York Times* review of the exhibition initially credited Andy Warhol for the Mao portraits seen on Vivienne Tam's famous Mao dresses. The actual artist is Zhang Hongtu.[29] (While a correction notice was posted to the online article shortly after it was published, the print version, published one day later, still credits Warhol.[30] In the exhibition catalog, Zhang is listed as "unidentified artist.")[31] Such carelessness when taken together demonstrates a pattern of citational colonialism. That is to say, these examples reflect something more than just an absence of source information, they are active erasures of authorship that maintain and reproduce the prevailing, if implicit, assumption that fashion is a normative white authorial enterprise.

Throughout the exhibition, creative agency and control are organized around the primacy of white feelings of inspiration, forbidden sensuality, intellectual boldness, and so on. The creative expressions of the handful of Asian designers featured in the exhibition are either glossed over or treated superficially.[32] Anna Sui, for example, is inadvertently omitted from the exhibition list of designers published on the museum's website and in the exhibition catalog. Meanwhile, Guo Pei's designs are characterized as derivative. The organizers describe her design as "an act of Occidentalism" and "a practice . . . of assimilation" (not an act of cultural inspiration).[33] For the organizers, Occidentalism represents a different—but equal—practice with Orientalism. It's a calculated rhetorical move intended to cancel out the asymmetrical structure of race and cultural production. But this is a false equivalence. If Pei's design is influenced by the West, it is not because she is drawing on cultural myths that reduce the West to a set of aesthetic signs but because the long and ongoing history of Western cultural, economic, and political imperialism in Asia has made the West an inextricable part of the East. To be sure, none of the garments created by Asian/North American designers fit the romantic Orientalism theme since the designers themselves cannot be said to share in the collective fantasy of China. For them, China is not a fantasy but a real place in which four of the five Asian designers were born and/or raised. The exhibition's asymmetrical treatment of Asian designers is consistent with the broader Western fashion industry and culture in which Chinese, black, and other nonwhite designers' feelings of cultural inspiration are routinely undervalued or not valued at all.[34] As we've seen, Chinese designers inspired by European and US designs are routinely branded as copycats and intellectual property thieves (whether the copy is legally infringing or not). Cultural inspiration, like romantic Orientalism, is a white feeling, an emotional property of whiteness.

But the expression and experience of white feelings is not limited or localized to the exhibition's wall text or object labels. The mood and orientation to white feelings begin well before visitors reach the exhibition itself. What *Looking Glass* shows so well is how white feelings permeate and structure fashion institutions in ways that naturalize the hegemonic everydayness of their whiteness. In what follows, I describe the perceptual factors that give the exhibition what British *Vogue* calls its "oriental feel"[35] and what the Fashionista website promises will give visitors "a palpable feeling of zen."[36] Not surprisingly, we find them first in the contextual features of the exhibition.

Getting in the Mood for Orientalism

To reach the *Looking Glass* exhibition from the museum's main lobby, visitors walk up the Met's grand stairway to the second floor and turn right. Three-quarters of the way up the stairs the distinctive sound of Chinese music fills the air. It is playing from speakers located in the museum store (directly to the right at the top of the staircase). *Looking Glass* is one of 31 exhibitions the Met is running concurrently, but throughout the exhibition's run the store's playlist comprised only the music from this, its most popular exhibition. Each of the three days I visited, my first physical encounter with the exhibition was the upbeat sound of a woman's voice singing what sounded like Chinese popular music of an earlier decade. The salespeople working in the store at the times of my visits could not identify the songs, much less the singers, but I'm relatively certain I never heard the same song twice.

The museum store stands at one end of the Great Hall Balcony, a wide hallway leading to the museum's Asian galleries where part of the *Looking Glass* exhibition is displayed. On the left side of the hallway is a wall of glass cases filled with Chinoiserie-style porcelain and ceramic vases, teapots, and plates made by potters throughout Europe (see figure 2.3). Chinoiserie represents a European aesthetic tradition of imitating or evoking Chinese design motifs that dates back to the seventeenth century. The objects displayed here are part of the Asian galleries' permanent collection. Turning left toward the entrance of the exhibition, another wall of glass cases features Chinese and Japanese ceramics from the late nineteenth and early twentieth centuries. At the end of this hallway and just outside the entrance to the Florence and Herbert Irving Asian Wing is an information desk. On my first visit, a senior white woman was sitting at the desk. She stood out to me because, unlike the museum staff in the main lobby, she wore a silk Chinese-style jacket in cobalt blue with pink, white, and yellow floral embroidery and a "mandarin collar" neck.

Passing the information desk and heading into the Irving Asian Wing's first room, the cinematic surround sound effects of thumping Chinese drums and whistling flutes rush the senses. The music is the soundtrack accompanying film clips being projected on the wall opposite the entrance. The clips are taken from two popular *wuxia* or martial

Figure 2.1. The glassy bamboo forest. Photo by author.

arts films: *A Touch of Zen* (1971) directed by the Hong Kong–based film-maker King Hu [the original Chinese title 英文 (Xiá Nǚ) translates to something closer to *Hero Woman* or *Knight Woman*] and *House of Flying Daggers* (2004) directed by Zhang Yimou and starring one of China's most famous and beautiful actors, Zhang Ziyi. While the soundtrack is intensely audible, views of the film clips are obstructed and—frankly—overtaken by an incandescent bamboo forest made from what looks like glass but is probably a transparent thermoplastic acrylic material (figure 2.1). Somewhat hidden between the tall, glassy stalks of bamboo are three warrior mannequins.

Set around part of the perimeter of the bamboo forest are several large sandstone sculptures of highly adorned bodhisattvas. These are also part of the museum's permanent collection. Behind one bodhisattva sculpture—identified by the museum as created in the Shanxi Province (China) sometime around 550–560—is a large, flat screen showing scenes of bamboo forest fights from the films mentioned above. Such battle scenes are characteristic of *wuxia* films, a contemporary iteration

Figure 2.2. Bamboo forest fight scene from King Hu's 1971 film, *A Touch of Zen*. Photo by author.

of a millennia-old Chinese martial arts fiction genre known for its acrobatic fight scenes. Only since about the early 1990s, with films like Tsui Hark's *Swordsman* (1990) and *Once Upon a Time in China* (1991)—which includes a bamboo fight scene that pays homage to *A Touch of Zen*— have these films had a US audience of any significant size. In this exhibition, though, the short clips of classic *wuxia* films serve as a backdrop (physical and cultural) for the museum's own bamboo forest scene.

Past the *wuxia* section of the exhibition is the Arts of Ancient China room, or Gallery 206, where the first of "more than 140 examples of haute couture and avant-garde ready-to-wear"[37] outfits is displayed: an Yves Saint Laurent red silk coat with gold metallic brocade and a gold leather conical hat from his famous "Chinese" collection (autumn/winter 1977–1978). (See figure 2.4.) Standing at the entrance to this room, visitors get a side view of the outfit. To see it from the front, visitors must enter the room and look left. From this point of view, the exhibition's introductory wall text (posted directly perpendicular to the mannequin) is visible.

The text prepares visitors for an experience to match the likes of Lewis Carroll's famous heroine, Alice, who "enters an imaginary, alternative universe by climbing through a mirror in her house. In this world, a reflected version of her home, everything is topsy-turvy and back-to-front." "Like Alice's make-believe world," the wall text explains, "the China mirrored in the fashion in this exhibition is wrapped in invention and imagination." This formal introduction to the exhibition includes acknowledgments of Edward Said's theoretical framework of Orientalism, the exhibition's Orientalist relation to China, and the Orientalist style of the garments on display. At first glance, it may be surprising that the organizers acknowledge Said's critiques, but they recognize it in order to disavow romantic Orientalism's continuity with Said's Orientalism. Said's work, the wall text specifically points out, is from 1978. The designers' approaches to Orientalism "encourage *new* aesthetic interpretations and broader cultural understandings" (emphasis added).

So to sum up, then, the first impressions visitors are provided of this exhibition are: the Chinese-language singing and music coming from the

Figure 2.3. Chinoiserie from the Met's permanent collection. Photo by author.

Figure 2.4. The first outfit displayed in the *Looking Glass* exhibition, from Yves Saint Laurent's "Chinese" collection (1977–1978). Photo by author.

museum store and later the bamboo forest room; centuries-old Asian and pseudo-Asian porcelain, ceramic, and sandstone pieces; acrylic and filmic bamboo forests and supernaturally moving bodies in impossibly effortless fight scenes; an outfit (or two, for some visitors) that simultaneously articulates the West's fascination with and fabrications of Orientalism; and finally a discourse on the delightfully dizzying "Alice through the looking glass" stylistic approach to Orientalism that visitors are about to experience.

None of the objects described above are the exhibition's main attractions. More than three-quarters of a million visitors did not travel to

New York City's Upper East Side to see the Chinoiserie collection, listen to the music, or watch film clips. Certainly some visitors stop and admire the complementary and supplementary museum objects, but they are not the audience's main focus. The exhibition's high fashion and its promise of a transcendent view and experience of Orientalism are the real draws for what is at present the largest number of visitors the Costume Institute has seen. Yet the complementary and supplementary museum objects cannot be divorced from the *Looking Glass* exhibition.

As with all museum exhibitions, the complementary and supplementary objects do the important work of creating a general mood that permeates and shapes the exhibitionary experience. In the *Looking Glass* exhibition, the extra-exhibition objects and the structural arrangements they implicate (from the physical arrangements of the exhibition objects to the institutional arrangements between the fashion industry, fashion press, and art museum to the social arrangements of race, power, knowledge, and emotion) do this work and more. They operate in a systemized way to produce and circulate an air of romantic Orientalism, an amorphous and non-specific feeling of Chineseness. Framed by this decontextualized and flattened out concept of racial difference, the extra-exhibition objects are not there to be comprehended but to be intuited by visitors who may or may not stop to look and listen as they pass by on their way to the main exhibition galleries and objects.

The extra-exhibition objects prime audiences to experience a general sense of Chineseness (even when it is represented by Japanese- and European-made ceramics) from the distancing position of Orientalist spectatorship. Their presentations and arrangements position audiences at a physical, social, and historical remove from them so that music is heard but does not need to be understood, cinematic spectacles of racial bodies in action are enjoyed without the meaningful frameworks of plot or character development, and aesthetic constructions of Chineseness like conical-shaped hats and Chinoiserie patterns and colors provide the frisson of racial exoticism while still being familiar and comforting. In short, the extra-exhibition objects are organized from the perception of what the Council of Fashion Designers of America astutely, if accidentally, calls "the American side of China," a Western perception of Chineseness that can be included in the category of white feelings.[38]

Orientalist feelings, sensations, fantasies, and needs are the points of reference for experiencing this exhibition.

The extra-exhibition objects create an atmosphere in which feelings of entitlement to and priority for white creative expression predominate. The overall treatment of the extra-exhibitionary objects—the lack of identifying information, the curatorial and historical decontextualization, and the peripheral placement of the music, film, martial choreography, porcelain, embroidery, and religious iconography just outside the exhibition's main gallery spaces—indicates (whether intentionally or not) that their inclusion is merely incidental. The hodgepodge of Chinese and pseudo-Chinese arts that make up the exhibitionary experience do not demand slow, deliberate, serious contemplation but a tacit knowing of them, a sense or vibe about them. They evoke an appreciative mood for the Orient as a resource "of infinite and unbridled creativity" for the West, attuning visitors to feel toward the Orient as the curators and designers already do.

This air of Chineseness is not limited to the extra-exhibitionary objects but persists throughout the actual exhibition as well. It surrounds, for example, the Philip Treacy "Chinese Garden" carved headdress that curiously features Japanese bonsai trees and the Dior dress made of a calligraphy textile print that, it turns out, is "from an eighth-century letter by Zhang Xu in which the author complains about a painful stomachache." Dior's blind copying of a not so charming Chinese text ends up inadvertently reasserting the material and banal realities of ordinary Chinese life into an exhibition premised on Orientalist fantasia. Tellingly, Treacy's and Dior's gaffes do not cost them their privileged place in the exhibition or Western fashion. Much the opposite is true, since they are fully in keeping with the exhibition's approach to representing Chineseness as a set of undifferentiated and decontextualized aesthetic forms and practices. A docent giving a tour of the exhibition provides a tellingly casual (but knowing) explanation for the discrepancy of the Japanese bonsai trees in the "Chinese Garden" headdress: "So China and Japan are brought together here—sort of classic thinking about these things."[39] We see the evidence of this "classic thinking" throughout the exhibition. For example, in one room of the exhibit named the Astor Garden Chinese Court, Dior pieces inspired by Japanese Kabuki theater are presented next to pieces by Maison Martin Margiela inspired by the Beijing opera—presented without comment, much less explanation. This Orientalist logic also shapes audience's responses to the exhibition—recall Fashionista's promise that visitors to an exhibition about China will experience "a palpable feeling of zen."

By mixing or mistaking Chinese, Japanese, and other Asian aesthetic referents in "Chinese-inspired" designs, white Western designers are, in effect, making bad copies. Yet Chinese- and Asian-inspired garments are rarely perceived as "copies"—and some even win accolades such as a featuring role in a major fashion exhibition. The difference between a US or European garment inspired by China (or somewhere imagined to be like China) and a Chinese garment inspired by a US or European design is that one is vested with white feelings and the cultural and social value ascribed to and embedded in this property of whiteness. Again, white feelings of inspiration (or correspondingly, white indignation at being copied, a variant of white fragility) are not just the designer's personal feelings. They find their basis and legitimacy in cultural and social norms about what constitutes creativity and who looks like a designer as well as in legal norms about authorship and traditional culture. These structural factors, which shape the public consciousness about legality— even the legality of things that are not copyrightable—give white feelings their property status.

If the *Looking Glass* extra-exhibitionary objects materialize white feelings, giving them form and dimension, then the Internet has provided a way to virtualize these feelings. The exhibition's website shows images of several of the complementary and featured museum objects as well as a selected collection of tweets that bear the museum-suggested hashtag #ChinaLookingGlass. Not surprisingly, all of the tweets shared on the exhibition's "Social Media" webpage are positive (in fact, most are adoring). The website effectively expands the extra-exhibitionary experience to museum non-visitors. In so doing, it expands the circuits of white feelings of creative authority and priority into and through the Internet. The "Social Media" webpage virtualizes the public feelings that give meaning to romantic Orientalism. It reproduces and transmits romantic Orientalism as both a digital experience and one that can be experienced vicariously through multiple layers of mediation (cultural, social, curatorial, and technological). In effect, the website carries Orientalism to its logical conclusion. The Orient has always been virtual, never actual, though the feelings attached to it have acquired real tangible and intangible outcomes. In fashion, these include employment opportunities; institutional/industrial recognition in the form of media coverage, design awards, and museum exhibitions; and public recognition. But, as I'll elaborate later, perhaps the most crucial benefit that public investments in white feelings provide is the racial presumption of authorial power, without which none of the resources, opportunities, and rewards mentioned above would be possible.

The Value of White Feelings

Romantic Orientalism is a compelling force of public feeling. It is compelling because it offers the alluring prospect of a new post-Orientalism era where old racial problems are apparently resolved by a more worldly, high art attitude toward difference. This utopian politics of feeling is premised on a highly appealing liberal progressive narrative in which the West has progressed beyond the history of oppression and discrimination. From this liberating, more tolerant place beyond or outside history, we are free to enjoy symbols, images, objects, and lifestyles without credit or compensation. Thus, what seems like a strange decision on the curators' part to mention Said's criticism of Orientalism at all in this exhibition is actually strategic. The organizers must concede (old) Orientalist racism in order to disavow it in the fashion present. By demonstrating their awareness of bad Orientalism, the organizers place themselves in the position of being able to assure audiences that the exhibition's romantic Orientalism is not only *not* bad Orientalism but that romantic Orientalism does away with bad Orientalism. The (old) bad feelings attached to Orientalism put into sharp relief the legitimacy of (new) romantic Orientalism and the exhibition's racial progressivist message that Western fashion transcends old historical problems—that Western fashion is timeless. This is cultural appropriation's tacit presumption and task: to raise up (or "elevate" in popular fashion-speak) "ethnic" garments generally perceived as stuck historically in time, meaning, and design into the higher-order temporalities of the modern West and of Western fashion capitalism.

Romantic Orientalism is also compelling in another way. It compels or pushes to silence critical perspectives about the very historical inequalities that underpin this exhibition—namely, the persistence of Western fashion's hegemonic relationship to Asia. The exhibition disregards and, in some cases, erases the historical and ongoing inequality between Western fashion and China, the result of labor-related exploitation in terms of human and environmental devastations; unequal trade and intellectual property terms and, with them, asymmetrical structures of capital accumulation; as well as the continual racial and gender discrimination on the runway, in the apparel factory, shop floor, and the media. All of these inequalities persist even as China is gaining influence and power in the global fashion market. But, as I've suggested earlier, I see the exhibition as part of a larger campaign to redraw, not erase, the boundary between Western fashion and China at the point of authorship. At a time when China's power as a lucrative consumer market and as a leading producer of clothes at all price points is on a rapid rise (trends that threaten to destabilize the United States' and Europe's dominance), the cultural construction of fashion authorship is a key site of struggle over cultural economic power especially for designers in the United States, where legal protections for fashion design are comparatively weak.

The *Looking Glass* exhibition exemplifies the role racialized feelings play in creating the conditions for the popular understanding of the relationship of fashion, property, and impropriety. Recall that nearly all the luxury brand garments featured in the exhibition—a vital means and source of the museum's funding—are the results of copying: whether blindly copying Chinese calligraphy, copying Orientalist design motifs that are themselves bad copies of a Western idea of China/ Asia, or copying actual Chinese, Japanese, and, in the case of Galliano's Dior collection, Russian aesthetics[40] and German copies of Orientalist representations.[41] Yet white designers who copy are still able to assume the very lucrative mantle of fashion designer and the authority for representing and selling "Asia" on global platforms. Some of the "Looking Glass" designers receiving the most curatorial and media attention, like Paul Poiret, Tom Ford, John Galliano, Jean Paul Gaultier, Marc Jacobs, and Philip Treacy, are treated much like grand couturiers. White designers' capacity to copy Chinese designs and aesthetics with impunity (under the rhetorical-emotional guise of "inspiration") while moralizing against Chinese designers and companies that copy

Western designs indicate that they already enjoy exceptional authorial status. In the absence of and perhaps unfettered by legal processes, racialized feelings serve as a means of creative control—of controlling the norms, behaviors, and meanings around what constitutes fashion authorship, especially the racialized delineation of fashion copying as a creative act (of cultural inspiration) or a criminal act (of piracy). (More on this later.)

Western designers' authorial control over Asian and Asian-like aesthetics through branding and intellectual property rights (even the presumption of intellectual property rights) serves the museum as well. The brand names enhance the prestige of the museum's exhibition, a key factor for attracting its two most important financial resources: tourists and investors. In recent years, the Met, like other top US museums, has focused its efforts on drawing Asian and especially Chinese tourists and investors. In addition to installing exhibitions like *Looking Glass*, the Met now has Mandarin-language audio and book guides, mobile web apps, Mandarin-speaking tour guides, and a social media presence on China's popular Weibo platform. In addition, "[b]oth the Met and the Museum of Modern Art participated in promotional missions . . . to mainland China, visiting Guangzhou, Shanghai, Nanjing and Tianjin in November [2014]."[42] In June 2015, the museum began accepting the Chinese UnionPay credit card. For all their efforts, the Met has seen a steep rise in Chinese tourists—now its largest segment of foreign visitors. According to the *New York Times*, Chinese visitors to the museum "more than quadrupled over five years, from 50,000 in fiscal year 2009, to 209,000 in fiscal year 2014."[43] So closely linked are intellectual property rights with boosting investments that financial analysts consider IP a form of investment.

By the time visitors move from Gallery 206 (the bamboo forest room) to Gallery 207 where the exhibition of Orientalist fashions is in full display, the intensity of white feelings is at a high Orientalist fever pitch—or at least this is the organizers' hope. In the words of one exhibition label, the Orientalist fashions aim to create "an alternate reality with a dream-like, almost hallucinatory, illogic." The exhibition's sensorial and experiential world of white feelings intends to draw visitors into a pervasive and powerful fashion myth about the exceptional status of cultural appropriation as a mode of copying that is legitimately original creative work.

The most salient benefit produced by the possessive investment in white feelings is the racialized presumption of authorial positionality and power. This presumption can be understood as part of fashion Orientalism's imagined geography and its distinction between the West/Occident as a site of creative agency and the East/Orient as an open resource there for the free use and benefit of Western creative activity. This imagined geography of creative agency and creative inspiration provides the basis on which another racialized boundary can be drawn between supposedly post-Orientalist or post-racist practices of fashion copying that are accepted, even lauded, as creative acts and other practices of fashion copying that are racially framed as noncreative and, in more extreme cases, criminally liable acts. The possessive investment in white feelings confers an extra-juridical advantage for US fashion designers, one that is just as valuable as (and, as I've argued elsewhere, more effective than) legal protections.

As the history and current reality of Western fashion bear out, fashion authorship is not based or even necessarily linked to what Rosalind Krauss identifies, in a different context, as a "myth of originality." In her landmark study, Krauss shows that early twentieth century avant-garde art- and artist-making (she sees the two processes as mutually constitutive) is premised on a conceptualization of originality "as a literal origin, a beginning from ground zero, a birth."[44] In contrast, Western fashion's construction of authorial originality does not preclude repetition, replication, and copying, although not all copying is valued equally. Where the copy is located on or outside fashion's spectrum of originality is coded in different ways. An original creative work of copying is often described as an homage, a reinterpretation, an inspiration, or an adaptation. These terms are most often applied to modes of top-down fashion copying in which blue chip designers copy the work of those who have fewer resources, status, and power. They see themselves and are seen by others in the media and public as "elevating" or "refining" the original design model. An unoriginal creative work that is the result of bottom-up copying is generally disparaged as a counterfeit, a knockoff, and a fake that degrades the original.

The issue in fashion is not whether a particular design is an absolute original with no historical precedence. The variety and frequency of sayings, parables, and jokes in Western fashion popular discourse disputing the idea of originality suggest that it is a rather well-established truism that all fashion is copied. But if all fashion is copied—based on and driven by trends, fads, and basic utilitarian design considerations (the very reason for fashion design's exclusion from US copyright law)—only some copied fashions are recognized as original works of authorship. Determinations about the originality of a fashion copy are not based on any essential property of the garment or some inherent nature of its production but, as I've been suggesting, on emotional and economic cultural constructions of authorial status and value.

Media and public debates about fashion copying practices provide clear examples of the possessive investment in white feelings. These debates typically turn on whether the copy was a (legitimate) expression of "cultural inspiration" or an (illegitimate and possibly illegal) instance of "plagiarism." Unifying these two poles of debate is a frame of reference in which the white Western designer's authorial intention is central. White Western designers' personal and professional feelings about their fashion copying supersede and are valued above non-Western ones. It's worth noting that even in cases of bottom-up copying, Western designers' hurt feelings about the "theft" of their creative work remain at the center of the media and public discourse. The possessive investment in white feelings is a structural mechanism that benefits white designers whether they are the ones doing the copying or being copied.

If cultural inspiration is a structurally embedded force that enables white Western fashion designers to construct and maintain an authorial identity, it is also a force divesting racialized and indigenous creative communities of authorial power and the cultural, social, and economic benefits that accrue to it. That is to say, cultural inspiration practices are better understood not so much as drawing on "authorless" creative works but as effecting the de-authorization or de-propertization of these works. When fashion designers and the fashion public talk about "cultural inspiration," about transforming racially marked designs and aesthetics into "Fashion," they are expressing the colonialist idea that non-white, non-Western things are *terra nullius* ("empty land")—that they are uncultivated and unrefined ideas and objects belonging to no one and so free for the taking. Because racially marked aesthetics are considered authorless, they are also excluded from US and Western campaigns to protect fashion design as intellectual property.

Looking Glass exposes Western fashion's contradictory relationship to Asia and its contradictory position on fashion copying. Copying that facilitates or perpetuates Western fashion's authorial claims to unregulated access to Asia as a site of free resources (of everything from cultural objects to cultural inspiration) is celebrated in rhapsodic terms such as "romantic Orientalism" and post-racism. Copying that reverses the direction of access, that forges a path from Asian designers, manufacturers, and retailers into European and US markets, is met with panic and defensiveness. Daily, instances of bottom-up fashion copying are constructed as threatening acts of all kinds of boundary crossing (up to and including terrorism) whereas practices of fashion copying classified as cultural inspiration are constructed as positive expressions of cultural appreciation, cultural mixing, and creative transcendence. The possessive investment in white feelings creates and sustains conditions of accumulation (of authorial power, status, and rewards) that benefit Western fashion economies—while encouraging us to feel good about Western hegemony.

The possessive investment in white feelings of entitlement to and priority for white creative expressions of fashion design secures the kind of exclusivity of authorship for US-based designers that the law has so far denied them and in ways that are faster and more effective than legislative and juridical processes. As the *Looking Glass* exhibition illustrates, authorial rights and privileges are not simply matters of the law. In the US fashion context, they are almost not at all about the law. And they don't need to be. Intellectual property scholars like Ann Bartow and Kal Raustiala and Christopher Jon Sprigman have shown that the US fashion industry has not just survived but thrived without copyright protections.[45] Indeed, luxury copies spur interest and brand familiarity and recognition to luxury brands—generating potential new markets that create more desire for these products.

If weak legal protections have not hindered the US industry, copyright's expansion to include fashion design would almost certainly not help those most vulnerable to copying either. Current copyright law includes a number of statutory exceptions such as educational exemptions or "fair use"; critical commentary in the forms of parody, satire, scholarship, and news reporting; public domain works whose copyright has expired or was never protected by copyright such as traditional knowledge. Under the traditional knowledge exception, objects and ideas that don't have a traceable and recognizable author—like those classified as "ethnic costume"—are not legally protectable. Traditional knowledge, "a living body of knowledge that is developed, sustained and passed on from generation to generation within a community," is also at odds with Western intellectual property rights systems that typically grant protections for limited periods of time.[46]

An effect of the traditional knowledge exception is that racial, ethnic, and indigenous communities are structurally disadvantaged when it comes to seeking legal protection for their cultural works compared to fashion designers who can copyright the copy they make of that work. For example, the Oaxacan Mixe people in Mexico cannot (easily) legally protect an embroidery pattern they created and have worn for more than 600 years, while others who copy the pattern are entitled to legal protection. Today, Italian designer Gabriella Cortese (creator of the Antik Batik label, a name inspired by her trip to Asia) holds the patent for the Mixe embroidery pattern—a fact that came to light when the Mixe community accused French designer Isabel Marant of copying its design. Months later, a French court cleared the French designer of any legal wrongdoing, a decision based on Marant's defense of cultural inspiration.[47] The court also revoked Antik Batik's patent but maintained the embroidery pattern's traditional knowledge/public domain status, leaving the pattern vulnerable to other designers' use of the pattern and property claims to the work on which the pattern appears. This is not at all uncommon in fashion. Legally, the eco-fashion label Feral Childe is the owner of a (Lakota) teepee design it once accused the clothing chain store Forever 21 of copying. Numerous powerful brands like Louis Vuitton have copied the distinctive red plaid pattern that characterizes the Maasai shuka, and by virtue of trademark laws, own the rights to the copied products. One estimate holds that six companies including Ralph Lauren, Calvin Klein, and Diane von Furstenberg "have each made more than $100 million in annual sales during the last decade using the Maasai name," while the Maasai people (of Tanzania and Kenya) have received no monetary compensation.[48]

Absent a legal framework, an extra-juridical system of race, knowledge, power, and emotions effectively licenses and legitimizes the most profitable and powerful kinds of fashion copying. This system protects the privileged position of white Western designers by maintaining the hierarchical classifications of fashion copying through creating consensus around a hierarchy of feelings in which white feelings are the most valued emotionally, culturally, socially, and monetarily. As the *Looking Glass* exhibition demonstrates, the possessive investment in white feelings that go by many names, such as romantic Orientalism, cultural inspiration, and so on, is a primary means by which Western fashion designers are publicly endowed with the power to create clothes and to control their circuits of production and distribution but most crucially, to control the meanings of design, aesthetic representation, race, and value.

The *Looking Glass* exhibition illustrates how fashion design is a key site where emotion, capitalism, and race are fused. As we've seen, white feelings define property and allocate property rights even for things not legally considered property. The exhibition's theme and message depend on an unquestioned, unexamined, and so normative construction of property and property relations. As *Looking Glass* demonstrates so clearly, it hardly matters when white US and European designs are products of outright copying or a practice of fashion copying usually described as cultural appropriation. They are nevertheless credited to white designers. More specifically, they are credited to white feelings of enchantment, inspiration, and nostalgia about racialized difference. As such, the featured garments are presented, on one hand, as individual designers' property and on the other hand, as the materialization of the essential racial property of creative genius and inspiration. In a strange twist of irony—but one that perfectly encapsulates the illogic of the inverted worldview through the looking glass—Western fashion's use of Orientalist reproductions of "China" and "Asia" has enabled it to both draw and blur the lines between authors and copyists.

NOTES

1 See, for example, Maxine Builder, "Why the 2015 MET Gala Is Making Me Nervous—On How 'China: Through The Looking Glass' Could Go Horribly Wrong," February 19, 2015, https://www.bustle.com/; and Connie Wang, "The Met's New Exhibit Is About Orientalism, Not China," May 4, 2015, http://www.refinery29.com/.

2 See Builder, "Why the 2015 MET Gala Is Making Me Nervous," and "It's Fashionable, But Does Met Gala's China Theme Make a Fantasy of the Far East," May 5, 2015, http://www.scmp.com/.

3 Izzy Grinspan and Julia Rubin, "The Met's China Exhibit: Thoughtful, Beautiful, and Surprisingly Respectful," May 4, 2015, https://www.racked.com.

4   I have written about both the Poiret collection and the Lagerfeld film. See Pham, "Paul Poiret's Magical Techno-Oriental Fashions (1911): Race, Clothing, and Virtuality in the Machine Age" in *Configurations: A Journal of Literature, Science, and Technology* 21.1 (2013): 1–26, and Pham, "The Truth of Lagerfeld's Idea of China," December 7, 2009, https://iheartthreadbared.wordpress.com/.

5   Andrew Bolton, "Toward an Aesthetic of Surfaces," *China through the Looking Glass* (exhibition catalog). (New York: Metropolitan Museum of Art New York, 2015), 17.

6   Ibid.

7   "Emperor to Citizen" label, *China: Through the Looking Glass.*

8   Bolton, "Toward an Aesthetic of Surfaces," 18.

9   "China Through the Looking Glass," May 7–September 7, 2015, https://www.metmuseum.org/.

10 "815,992 Visitors to Costume Institute's China Exhibition Make It Fifth Most Visited Exhibition in Metropolitan Museum's History," September 8, 2015, http://www.metmuseum.org/.

11 Erwan Rambourg, "Meet the Chinese Luxury Shoppers Who Are Taking Over the World," January 13, 2015, http://www.businessinsider.com/.

12 "China's eCommerce Revolution," March 13, 2015, https://www.morganstanley.com/.

13 Frank Tong, "China's Online Retail Sales Grow a Third to $589 Billion in 2015," January 27, 2016, https://www.digitalcommerce360.com/.

14 Catherine Shu, "E-commerce Sales in China Will Reach $1 Trillion By 2019 Thanks to Mobile, Says Forrester," February 4, 2015, https://techcrunch.com/.

15 Thuy Linh N. Tu provides a detailed discussion of the development of creative economies in China and elsewhere in Asia in her book, *The Beautiful Generation: Asian Americans and the Cultural Economy of Fashion* (Durham, NC: Duke University Press, 2010).

16 Mark Turnage, "A Mind-Blowing Number of Counterfeit Goods Come from China," June 25, 2013, http://www.businessinsider.com/.

17 Ibid.

18 Steve Hargreaves, "Counterfeit Goods Becoming More Dangerous," September 21, 2012. http://money.cnn.com/.

19 Brian W. Lewis, Nicole Nocera, and E. Tim Walker, "Stop Counterfeiters from Jeopardizing Your Brand and Bottom Line," September 15, 2008, http://www.industryweek.com/.

20 *Counterfeit Culture* documentary, dir. Geoff D'Eon and Jay Dahl, Telltale Productions, 2013.

21 "How to Spot a Fake Lacoste?" September 4, 2010, http://forums.redflagdeals.com/, and Meaghan Thomas, "How to Spot Fakes & Get Real Designer Goods Online from the USA for Less," May 16, 2016, https://www.myus.com/.

22 Cheryl I. Harris, "Whiteness as Property," *Harvard Law Review* 106.8 (1993): 1714.

23 While some features of a garment are protected—logo, unique textile prints, and decorative embellishments, for example—the overall shape and construction of a garment have never been protected under US copyright law despite the fashion industry's numerous efforts. Since 1914, more than 80 proposals to amend the Copyright Act to include fashion design have been introduced. The latest one, the Innovative Design Protection Act (S.3523), was introduced in September 2012. None has passed. Consistently, the law and the courts have held that fashion design is a "useful article" since it serves the useful purpose of covering the body.

24 George Lipsitz, *The Possessive Investment in Whiteness* (Philadelphia: Temple University Press, 1998), xiii.

25 Ibid.

26 Ibid., viii.

27 Jonathan Flatley, *Affective Mapping: Melancholia and the Politics of Modernism* (Cambridge, MA: Harvard University Press, 2008), 8.

28 Quoted from some of the labels in the "Looking Glass" exhibition.

29 Holland Cotter, "Review: In 'China: Through the Looking Glass,' Eastern Culture Meets Western Fashion," May 7, 2015. https://www.nytimes.com/.

30 Holland Cotter, "West Meets East, and Wears It Well," *New York Times*, May 8, 2015, C19.

31 *China through the Looking Glass* (exhibition catalog), 242.

32 All of the *Looking Glass* designers are white except five who are Asian or Asian North American: Anna Sui (Chinese American), Guo Pei (Chinese), Laurence Xu (Chinese), Vivienne Tam (Chinese American), and Jason Wu (Taiwanese Canadian).

33 Exhibition label.

34 There are too many examples to name, but the recent example of Pakistani designer Nida Khurram's pillorying by the fashion press and public (via social media) for using fashion illustrations created by European and American artists in her designs despite her defense that she was inspired by these artists' work provides a good illustration. Unlike Western designers' copying, Khurram's was seen as casting a pall over the entire Pakistani fashion industry. See Maliha Rehman, "Fashion Scandal: Why Target Nida Khurram When We All Plagiarise?" June 4, 2015, http://www.dawn.com/.

35 Suzy Menkes, "China's Moon in the Water," May 6, 2015, http://www.vogue.co.uk/.

36 Alyssa Vingan Klein, "Inside the Met's Spring Exhibit, 'China: Through the Looking Glass,'" May 4, 2015, https://fashionista.com/.

37 Press release, Metropolitan Museum of Art.

38 Marc Karimzadeh, "The American Side of China: Through the Looking Glass," May 5, 2015, http://cfda.com/.

39 Overheard while walking through the exhibit, July 4, 2015.

40 "John Galliano: In Conversation with Andrew Bolton," *China through the Looking Glass: Fashion, Film, Art*, edited by Andrew Bolton (New York: Metropolitan Museum of Art, 2015), 234.

41 Ibid., 233.

42 Jane L. Levere, "Making Chinese Tourists Feel at Home," *New York Times*, March 19, 2015, F12.

43 Ibid.

44 Rosalind Krauss, *The Originality of the Avant-garde and Other Modernist Myths* (Cambridge, MA: MIT Press, 1986), 157.

45 See Ann Bartow, "Counterfeits, Copying and Class," *Houston Law Review* 48 (2012): 707–749, and Kal Raustiala and Christopher Jon Sprigman, *The Knockoff Economy: How Imitation Sparks Innovation* (New York: Oxford University Press, 2012).

46 "Traditional Knowledge and Intellectual Property—Background Brief," World Intellectual Property Organization, http://www.wipo.int/.

47 Paulia Szmydke, "Isabel Marant Cleared of Plagiarism Allegations," December 7, 2015, http://wwd.com/.

48 Stephan Faris, "Can a Tribe Sue for Copyright? The Maasai Want Royalties for Use of Their Name," October 24, 2013, http://www.bloomberg.com/.

3

Beauty between Empires

Global Feminisms, Plastic Surgery, and the Trouble with Self-Esteem

S. HEIJIN LEE — what do you do, when people go too far

Since 2012, when Korean rapper PSY's "Gangnam Style" dominated US airwaves, television, and computer screens, the popularity of K-pop has created renewed interest among American media outlets and netizens in the topic of South Korean (hereafter Korea or Korean) plastic surgery consumption. *The Atlantic* featured a story on "The K-Pop Plastic Surgery Connection," while *Bloomberg News* published on medical tourism in Korea: "Gangnam Style Nip and Tuck Draws Tourists to the Beauty Belt."[1] *Buzzfeed*'s story was more provocative, if strangely Eurocentric, asking, "When Does Plastic Surgery Become Racial Transformation?"[2] And most recently a *New Yorker* piece asks, "Why Is Seoul the World's Plastic-Surgery Capital?"[3] Other, much more sensationalized reporting has produced images such as the "Miss Korea gif," which went viral in less than 48 hours, appearing first on a Japanese blog, then Reddit, and then in national and international newspapers in April 2013. The gif (officially, graphics interchange format), which compresses several still photos (jpegs) into moving images such that the beauty contestants' faces morph one into the next at rapid speed, was meant to illustrate visually what *Jezebel*'s headline summed up as "Plastic Surgery Means Many Beauty Queens but Only One Kind of Face."[4]

The gif—posted and reposted on social media sites such as Facebook, Twitter, and Reddit and reported upon by countless outlets—signified "Korea's plastic surgery mayhem," as one Reddit user described it.[5] Such characterizations pathologize Korean cosmetic surgery consumption as a push toward racialized uniformity defined by a singular national beauty aesthetic across diverse Korean women's faces.[6] For US feminists, however, the gif took on particular salience. Mainstream feminist sites such as *Jezebel* offered the gif as evidence of a bizarre form of racialized patriarchal oppression happening abroad, making it distinct from, and exotic in relation to, forms of heteropatriarchal violence in the United States. As such, *Jezebel* reported on the Miss Korea gif, and Korean plastic surgery consumption more generally, at least four times in the spring and summer months of 2013, in articles such as "I Can't Stop Looking at These Korean Women Who've Had Plastic Surgery." As it turned out, however, the individual images making up the viral gif were photoshopped.[7] What was issued as objective visual evidence of Korean women's fanatic obsession with plastic surgery instead reveals a fanatic obsession on the part of Americans for producing and consuming Korean women as such.

Just a couple of months after the Miss Korea gif went viral in the United States, a Korean feminist nonprofit organization, *Yŏsŏng Minuhoe* (한국여성민우회), known in English as Korean Womenlink (hereafter Womenlink), widely publicized a forum called "*Apkujeong Station Exit #4: Let's Talk about It.*" A follow-up to their 2003 nationwide "Love Your Body" campaign, which sought to curb dieting and plastic surgery consumption among women, the forum's title references the fact that nearly half of Seoul's plastic surgery clinics are located in the Gangnam district (made world-famous by PSY's viral hit song), many of which can be accessed via the *Apkujeong* subway station and, more specifically, via the #4 exit from that stop.[8] The forum was held in Seoul's congressional building and sought public policy alternatives to curb a problem that the group asserts "has only gotten worse" since 2003.[9] Besides Womenlink activists, the event featured a panel including a doctor, professor, television director, and lawyer, with a congressional representative making closing remarks.[10] The specialists provided insights into what they saw as the major factors fueling the cosmetic surgery industry as well as possible solutions to the problem. For Womenlink activists, it was a time to reflect on the ten years since their "Love Your Body" campaign.

That Korean plastic surgery consumption would occupy the minds of *Jezebel* writers, editors, and millions of readers as well as Womenlink's members, panelists, and forum attendees at roughly the same time—feminists from opposite ends of the world, so to speak—illuminates several key issues. First, such interest attests to the new visual economies arising through blogs and social media sites that have renewed fetishized interest in Korean bodies and fuel cosmetic surgery consumption in Korea itself. As exemplified by PSY's YouTube phenomenon, "Gangnam Style," these visual economies have been part and parcel of Korea's global, and federally funded, projects of pop culture and plastic surgery—the former serving as global advertisements for the latter. Second, that both groups take a feminist interest in the topic deserves more attention. Both groups agree that Korean plastic surgery consumption is a feminist "problem." Given this, then, how do these women's differing geopolitical locations and political investments affect their articulation and understanding of this problem? What does feminism mean in these particular contexts and in relation to this topic? How might we think about these two feminist groups relationally?

Using a transnational feminist practice, then, that privileges "an attention to the linkages and travels of forms of representation as they intersect with movements of labor and capital in a multinational world," this chapter offers a consideration of feminist assumptions not only about the politics of beauty but about how it circulates and how to organize around it.[11] Using Jezebel's coverage of Korean plastic surgery consumption and the Miss Korea gif as a starting point, I examine beauty at the intersection of social media, feminism, and geopolitics in order to illuminate the contours of a highly accessible global feminism that takes white Western women's experiences as the telos of modernity. As a counterpoint to Jezebel's obsession with the Miss Korea gif, a fabricated cultural production about Korea, I then examine Womenlink's feminist organizing in Korea in order to show that beauty is mediated through variously structured fields of power specific to the geopolitical context. Finally, after providing a sketch of the contemporary landscape of Korean plastic surgery consumption today, I argue that these seemingly disparate feminisms are tied together in their valuation of the self as a locus of liberation. Ultimately, juxtaposing feminisms in these ways provides us with an understanding of how local and global feminist politics both intersect and diverge through transnational industries, in cybercultures, and as everyday politics.

"It Scares the Shit Out of Me": *Jezebel* and the Spread of Global Feminism

While the interest in Korean bodies that the global popularity of K-pop has engendered and the issues the gif and other similar social media representations raise may seem new, these types of discourses have been circulating in US media since the 1990s, when Korea itself was making headlines as an "economic miracle." In November 1993, for instance, the *Wall Street Journal* ran an article titled "Cosmetic Surgery Goes Hand in Glove with the New Korea."[12] The subhead read: "What Would Confucius Say about the Westernization of Eye, Nose and Breast?"[13] Nearly a decade later Oprah Winfrey did a segment on Korean women and plastic surgery, likening it to Oprah having surgery "to not look black."[14] Occurring during what many characterized as Korea's "miraculous" emergence as an "industrial tiger," these discourses from the 1990s through the first decade of the 2000s, found in myriad national and international news outlets, are concerned with two things. First, and perhaps most obviously, these discourses characterize Korean plastic surgery as a desire to appear more "Western" or white. Much as the burqa has come to symbolize Middle Eastern women's oppression in both popular and academic discourses, cosmetic surgery—and more specifically the double eyelid surgery, as it is colloquially known—has come to signify Korean (and in many instances, Korean and Asian American) women's acquiescence not only to patriarchal oppression but to racial oppression as well. Second, as the *Wall Street Journal* article clearly exemplifies, these discourses allude to anxieties around a "New Korea," the emergence of which is signified by the conspicuous consumption of its citizens. In other words, these older discourses indexed US anxieties concerning the possibility of a Korean competitive force in the Asiatic region alongside Japan, where the "bubble economy" was at its peak at the time and posed a threat to US economic dominance. Then, as now, US obsessions with Korean cosmetic surgery, as a primary avenue through which to contend with Korea's newfound affluence (and influence), came at a time when US economic global dominance appeared most threatened, which bespeaks an anxious Western gaze desiring to see itself in places where its hegemony is on the wane.

Today, however, Korea is no longer thought of as "new" but is regarded as an established economic and political actor on the global stage, as evidenced by the fact that Korean products are now household names—Hyundai, Kia, Samsung—and its cultural products are known worldwide—Girls' Generation, the Wonder Girls, Rain, and 2ne1, to name just a few. In fact, as literary scholar Jin-Kyung Lee has shown in *Service Economies: Militarism, Sex Work, and Migrant Labor in Korea*, Korea can no longer simply be considered a neocolony of the United States but has emerged as a capitalist sub-empire in its own right, demonstrated in part by its exploitation of cheap labor from Southeast Asia and Mexico.[15] Pop culture has been part and parcel of Korea's newfound hegemony and soft power. Dubbed *Hallyu* or "the Korean Wave" by Chinese reporters in the late 1990s for its rippling popularity among Chinese teens (the first besides Japanese pop culture to gain such popularity in the region), Korea's "sub-empire" status and soft power rankings have been further solidified by its increasing pop cultural hegemony throughout Asia in particular but also to varying degrees in the Middle East, Europe, Latin America, and among a diversity of communities within the United States.[16]

Moreover, both the Miss Korea gif and PSY's record-breaking viral music video, "Gangnam Style," are part of the new visual economy that popular social media sites have created, setting contemporary discourses on Korean plastic surgery apart from those of an earlier era. On the one hand, South Korea is the most wired nation globally, with the highest number of DSL connections per head worldwide, and these levels of connectivity are reflected in South Korean marketing, music, and business campaigns. Korean entertainment companies themselves leverage their stars' pop music on social media sites as their main platform for launching and sustaining the popularity of their global pop stars. According to cultural studies scholar Stephen Epstein with James Turnbull, "Korean popular music is driven by the visual. . . . The savvy use of YouTube, literally and figuratively a key 'site' for the experience and distribution of music at a mass level, has now become a core component of Korean entertainment companies' promotion strategies, especially at the international level."[17] That is to say, visuality both in the sense of pop music's tendency toward spectacle and in the emphasis on pop stars' aesthetic appeal, has become a key factor in K-pop's global production and distribution, if not the key factor. As such, K-pop stars' "looks" are micro-managed by entertainment companies and then commodified alongside their music and dance.[18] As a package, then, these are promoted abroad to international fans via YouTube and other visually driven sites.

On the other hand, Korean entertainment companies' emphasis on the visual is buttressed by the work of netizens who manipulate and mash, post, and collect visual images, creating a synergistic relationship between the two. As digital studies scholar Lisa Nakamura points out in *Digitizing Race: Visual Cultures of the Internet*, social media's visual economy and its emphasis on sharing, tweeting, and tumbling exemplifies the interactivity and blurring of the line between producer and consumer that sets new media apart from old media.[19] In other words, netizens are not merely passive recipients of K-pop stars' self-promotion but rather themselves become producers, depending on what they do with such images (or others like them). As such, Internet users' dual roles as producers and consumers have renewed fetishized interest in Koreans' cosmetically enhanced bodies, creating a cyber stage for the spectacle of the commodified body, and at the same time making these bodies—as symbols of an emerging sub-empire—widely available for mass consumption. Such interest manifests both as fans who seek to emulate the Korean aesthetic through fashion, style, and plastic surgery and also as voyeurs who seek to analyze, critique, and display Korean aesthetics as exemplified by the Miss Korea gif.

One zone for such scrutiny has been US mainstream feminist blogs, since headlines like "I Can't Stop Looking at These South Korean Women Who've Had Plastic Surgery" and their accompanying visuals are surefire ways to encourage blog traffic. In recent years we have witnessed a marked increase in reporting on the topic in feminist blogs such as *Jezebel*—reports that then get shared over and again, making the consumer herself a producer and disseminator of knowledge through the acts of retweeting, reposting, and resharing. Critical analyses of outlets like *Jezebel*, its authors, and readership are especially crucial because *Jezebel* is considered a mainstream feminist news source, and as such it operates and sees itself as a form of highly accessible feminism that puts forth its own set of racialized and politicized ideologies. Founding editor Anna Holmes, who worked at women's magazines such as *Glamour* and *InStyle* before being tapped by executives to start a "girly Gawker," intentionally set out to make *Jezebel* the anti-women's magazine.[20] As *Jezebel*'s manifesto outlines, the blog refuses the usual tactics of women's magazines encompassed by "The Five Great Lies of Women's Magazines," which include airbrushing, must-have product promotion, profiling of the celebrity-sartorial complex, and the heightening of women's insecurities vis-à-vis their weight, sexual prowess, self-confidence, and more.[21]

Notably, the manifesto never mentions "feminism" or self-describes as "feminist." As media studies scholar Susan Douglas has argued, since the 1990s feminism has become an "f-word" of a different sort, heard mostly in the declaration: "I'm not a feminist, but . . ."[22] The ambivalence in the statement illuminates how women in the United States understand it as a philosophy from which they have benefited and might continue to benefit but with which they do not desire the consequences of affiliating. As Douglas explains, the statement also "identifies the speaker as someone who both acquiesces to and resists media representations of women and of feminism."[23] That is to say, while young women today are perhaps conscious that they enjoy the legislative and social gains made by second-wave feminists, images of feminists themselves have been reduced to angry, man-hating women such that these same women steer clear of such identifications. It is precisely such ambivalent readership that *Jezebel* seeks to attract. The blog began its tenure using a method that has been described as "a sort of stealth feminism," which Holmes explains involves writing "about celebrities, fashion, lifestyle and popular culture, but through a feminist lens" with "a healthy dash of social justice too."[24] Although Holmes left the blog in 2010, according to the *Guardian* in 2013, "there's little argument today that *Jezebel* fits on the list of mainstream, popular feminist blogs," while National Public Radio (NPR) has characterized it as "jolly feminist commentary."[25] If blogs such as *Jezebel* are considered the mainstays of Internet feminism, as attested to by the *Guardian* and NPR's characterizations of it, then it is critical to analyze the kind of feminist thinking that is being promoted on the site. In other words, mainstream feminist blogs act as one-stop shops for feminist viewpoints that are easily accessed and have an interface promoting easy consumption. Given the multiplicity of feminisms and feminists, when Holmes explains that *Jezebel* covers a variety of topics "through a feminist lens," through what lens are *Jezebel* readers indoctrinated? And what kinds of feminists make up *Jezebel's* readership?

These questions become even more crucial when one considers the blog's traffic. During a one-month period between July and August 2014, *Jezebel* reached 8,601,906 people, from 25,706,148 visits to the site spread over 54,901,656 page views.[26] As these numbers attest, like K-pop, mainstream feminism is reaching an unprecedented number of people, not only through site visits but also through social media sharing.[27] While it would be difficult to generalize about *Jezebel's* writers since there are many and they are varied, mainstream outlets such as the *New Yorker* have characterized at least some of the blog's contributors as the voices of "young feminism."[28] In the instances mentioned in the following discussion and in nearly all the articles on the blog relating to Korean plastic surgery, however, *Jezebel* promotes a brand of easily consumable global feminism. As transnational feminist scholar Mimi Nguyen asserts, global feminism, "in its claim to universal applicability, comprises a set of discourses and practices that elide the structuring violences of geopolitics and transnational capital in favor of a liberal ideal of women's freedom that celebrates individuality and modernity."[29] In so doing, global feminism equates oppression with poor self-image, offering self-esteem and empowerment as individualized solutions and Western women as exemplars of such right living. As Nguyen goes on to note, it is precisely this "politics of comparison" that constructs Western women as "ethical and free and as saviors of oppressed women around the world."[30] To be sure, global feminism is not new and not solely the domain of *Jezebel* or its writers. Yet what is significant about blogs like *Jezebel* is how the medium of the Internet facilitates the quick and accessible dissemination and consumption of global feminism. That is to say, if *Jezebel*, as an interface, "compels particular sorts of identifications, investments, ideological seductions, and conscious as well as unconscious exercises of power," as Nakamura has argued, then these identifications coalesce around a feminist lens informed by global feminism as a political and racial project that takes white liberal American women as its subjects.[31]

While Korean plastic surgery consumption no doubt raises many questions with regard to how neoliberal self-management of the body is coded as necessity yet signified as choice, and more specifically, ethical

BEAUTY BETWEEN EMPIRES | 77

questions regarding medical interventions in the realm of the aesthetic, these discursive formations reveal more about a US empire in relative decline than they do about Korean women. More specifically still, these discourses reveal more about mainstream American feminism than they do about Korean women. For example, in "Plastic Surgery Means Many Beauty Queens but Only One Kind of Face," deputy editor Dodai Stewart, in an attempt at balanced reporting, suggests that the Korean beauty queens' uniformity of looks is no different from the way that US pop culture celebrities such as Britney Spears and Taylor Swift are similarly coiffed. To further the point, Stewart includes pictures of the entertainers side by side. In the comments section, commenter Carlotta79, who identifies herself as white, disagrees:

> I still see a lot of variation in the latter group of women [US pop stars]. I wouldn't confuse them for each other—each woman is still very *individual* with distinctive features when you compare them. I can't say the same of the sampling of Korean women shown here. I find it very Brave New World. It scares the shit out of me (emphasis mine).[32]

Indeed, Carlotta79's comments expose key assumptions about the positioned differences between white American women and Korean women, particularly since we know that the gif was visually contrived. Carlotta79's declaration that she sees "a lot of variation" among the white women because they are "still very individual" in comparison to the fabricated production of Korean women's uniformity of looks reveals how white women are often granted the privilege of being individuals such that their experiences stand in as universal, while women of color are not. As transnational feminist scholar Chandra Mohanty has argued, the discursive self-representation of "other" women as unenlightened, ignorant, and victimized helps construct white women as "educated, as modern, as having control over their bodies and sexualities and [exercising] the freedom to make their own decisions."[33] In the digital realm, such self-representations are solidified by the fact that "the woman of color in the integrated circuit of information technology production is framed as an object rather than a subject of interactivity."[34] That is, *Jezebel*'s article and Carlotta79's reactions to it exemplify how the Internet facilitates the deployment of women of color as objects in the self-construction of white personhood.

Far from being a space free from the constraints of race, gender, or sexuality, then, the Internet allows for this dynamic through an arrangement organized around what Nakamura cogently points out is nothing short of digital capitalism. Following this logic, raced and gendered bodies are organized such that the user need only "click on a box or link . . . to acquire it, to choose it, to replace one set of images with another in a friction-free transaction that seems to cost nothing yet generates capital in the form of digitally racialized images."[35] As mentioned earlier, the visual currency of Korean bodies and their accompanying headlines help generate traffic to *Jezebel*'s site because they are sensationalized and thus easily consumable. Lured by the visual, Internet users simply click on the highly racialized, gendered, and sexualized images and in the case of the gif, the capital accrued is a feminist sensibility of which Nguyen's "politics of comparison" is central. *Jezebel* readers thereby bolster their own sense of feminist empowerment knowing that they, like Britney Spears, Taylor Swift, or Carlotta79, are not these Korean women. Whether or not they have had plastic surgery themselves becomes moot since, as Carlotta79's comments suggest, they would have done so for more individual reasons and more individual outcomes. Whether articulated in the digital realm or vis-à-vis the power relations of the quotidian, such thinking is part and parcel of global feminism, which positions white Western women's experiences as the telos of feminist modernity.

Accordingly, fashion and beauty stand in as signifiers for the "choices" offered by liberal democracy and consumer culture. Nowhere, perhaps, has this been more visible in recent years than in US discourse surrounding Middle Eastern women's veiling practices. Since the George W. Bush administration launched a military campaign after September 11, 2001 using the language of global feminism to justify war, Middle Eastern women's oppression (and their seeming liberation from it) is measured in popular US discourses by their ability to make choices about their style and dress, namely in ways that mirror Western fashions. Ostensibly, the journey from burqa to Barney's parallels the journey from tradition to American-style modernity and from oppression to freedom. In her insightful essay, "The Biopower of Beauty: Humanitarian Imperialisms and Global Feminisms in an Age of Terror," Nguyen cogently explains how beauty is mobilized in national and transnational contests of meaning and power:

Beauty bears the weight of what Minoo Moallem calls "civilizational thinking," a "powerful modern discourse influenced by the Enlightenment and the idea of progress dividing the civility of the "West" from the barbarism of the "Rest." In the familiar oppositions that organize such thinking, the burqa operates as anticivilizational, a life-negating deindividuation that renders the Afghan woman passive and unwhole, while beauty acts as a life-affirming pathway to modern, even liberated, personhood.[36]

One can see traces of such "civilizational thinking" in the Korean War as well, when the double eyelid procedure was made available to the masses as its own "life-affirming pathway" to liberated personhood through the US military's efforts to build public relations between Koreans and Americans. Akin to the chocolate and soda the soldiers regularly passed out to ameliorate bonds, the double eyelid procedure was made available to the masses when US military doctors performed the cosmetic procedure along with the free reconstructive surgery they offered Korean War victims.[37] Medical services as humanitarian efforts not only facilitated public relations but did the work of empire-building through a regime of morality that cemented the liberated-liberator, colonized-colonizer relationship as well as setting into motion a hierarchy of racialized looks. Indeed, plastic surgery in Korea is an afterlife of the Korean War and in many respects we can say that the plastic surgery consumer—as alluded to over and again on social media sites—was born in and of the Korean War and US involvement there.[38] Much as Nguyen argues about the imperialist attachments to beauty as it intersects with humanitarianism in Afghanistan, beauty at the end of the Korean War, too, was also deployed as a "war by other means."[39]

While possessing its refractory imprint, cosmetic surgery in Korea has taken on new meanings since its (neo)colonial origins. In the sixty years since the armistice was signed and as a result of Korea's neoliberal reforms, plastic surgery has been produced as economically necessary in Korean culture. In this way, cosmetic surgery is a form of "body work" that encapsulates both work performed on the body through surgeries and the work the altered body is readied to perform, or perform better, in a national market economy.[40] Given its ubiquity—Koreans consume plastic surgery at the highest rates per capita globally—and that Korea is home to one of the leading plastic surgery industries as well as its own medical tourism program, we see the "civilizational thinking" outlined in this discussion at play in contemporary discourses on Korean cosmetic surgery, only in reverse. The proliferation of Korean products globally, and Korean cultural products in particular, indexes Korea's current position in the global order. As such, contrary to discourses on Middle Eastern women's fashion and style, which measure their freedom based on their proximity to the choices of Western women, discourses on Korean beauty practices can be understood as disciplinary discourses that chastise Korean women for having gone too far beyond the limits of morality and modernity embodied by and embedded in Western fashion and beauty.

Given this, we might better understand Carlotta79's reference to *Brave New World* as a techno-orientalist critique of Korean women's beauty practices. Using the genre of science fiction, *Brave New World*, Aldous Huxley's 1931 dystopian novel, takes place in the future but contends with the contemporary issues of the early twentieth century, including the industrial revolution and the subsequent mass production and availability of technologies such as cars, telephones, and radios. Most notably, *Brave New World* expresses Huxley's own views on the United States from the standpoint of the English, who at the time were worried about the Americanization of Europe. In Carlotta79's formulation, however, Korean women's seemingly excessive consumption of plastic surgery and their resulting uniformity of looks embody the dystopian future outlined in Huxley's novel. As cultural studies scholar Jane Chi-Hyun Park has outlined in *Yellow Future: Oriental Style in Hollywood Film*, since the 1980s East Asian peoples and places have become intimately linked with technology to produce a collective fantasy in which East Asia signifies the future. Such techno-orientalist imaginings are a manifestation of the West's resentment of the East for its ability to appropriate and improve on Western technology and started with stereotypes of the Japanese as an economic and technological yellow peril, but have since extended to other East Asian groups.[41] Much as the United States signified the potential erosion of traditional values at the hands of technological advancement in Huxley's day, in this instance Korea signifies technology's anti-civilizational potential when developed and consumed incorrectly. While global feminist discourses often operate along a North-South axis, depicting the global South as "backward," Korea's history as a former colony of Japan and current status as a burgeoning sub-empire under the tutelage of the United States eschews simple classification within such categories. Accordingly, Korea—as with East Asia more generally—is depicted as a place where technology has run amuck, which often gets recoded as perverted excess. Carlotta79's position on the matter is more than clear when she says, "It scares the shit out of me." That this particular form of visuality offers Korean women as a spectacle through which to work out anxieties about the future of white life, as opposed to holding any journalistic integrity, can be illustrated by the fact that very few news outlets, including *Jezebel*, corrected their reports retroactively once the gif was found to contain photoshopped images.

In contrast to the way that Middle Eastern women are framed as having limited choices, then, Korean women are framed as choosing in excess, exemplifying the mismanagement not only of technology but of liberal democracy and its attendant capitalist freedoms. That is, Koreans have mishandled the gift of freedom already bestowed upon them by the United States. Stewart's article "I Can't Stop Looking at These Korean Women Who've Had Plastic Surgery" instantiates such logics. In one portion of the article, Stewart writes:

If you have a limited ability to see beauty in someone who is not big-eyed and small-faced and straight-nosed, do you also have a limited ability to understand, empathize, sympathize and relate to that person, as well? Do you become intolerant of those who don't meet your lookist standards? It wasn't that long ago that Western society practiced Physiognomy, making correlations between physical features and character traits, making things like large jaws and hooked noses—common among certain races—shorthand for evil or deceitful. It was racism and xenophobia disguised as science, and persists when it comes to Disney villains. In fact, we still use phrases like "baby-faced killer," as if one thing has anything to do with the other. Is the penchant for surgery in Korea a simple matter of self-improvement, or is something more cultish going on here?[42]

Ironically, Korean feminists identify "lookism" as one of the central causes for plastic surgery consumption, which I expand upon in the following section. Yet rather than interrogate or even gesture toward how lookism might be institutionally structured, thus catalyzing the discourses and logics of "self-improvement," Stewart's formulation employs a politics of comparison to paint instead a picture of the United States as again, not Korea. As such, Korean beauty practices themselves are not only oppressive but a system of oppression, one that, despite a heightened surveillance security state premised on racial profiling, a more enlightened United States has now surpassed. While Stewart herself may not intend it as such, her article reads as if xenophobia is no longer an issue in the United States save its persistence among cartoon villains, and presumably Stewart's own positionality as a black woman, though she never mentions it in her article, gives her the authority from which to discuss such matters and to deem them a thing of the past. Accordingly, what is unquestioned is the Western episteme shaping Stewart's gaze as well as her ability to presume to be the ultimate arbiter of whether Korea is truly free and, more specifically, whether Korean women are liberated feminist subjects. Ultimately, Stewart characterizes Korean plastic surgery consumption as "cultish" and "herd behavior," which we might construe as "a life-negating deindividuation" that, like the burqa for Afghan women, also renders Korean women "passive and unwhole." That is to say, despite the excesses characterizing techno-orientalist thinking, Korean women and Middle Eastern women's beauty practices are similarly constructed as affronts to the liberal personhood exemplified by white American women.

Apkujeong Station Exit #4: Let's Talk about It

On July 11, 2013, just a couple of months after the Miss Korea gif went viral, Womenlink, the largest and most active feminist organization in Korea, with more than 9,000 members, held a public forum in Seoul's congressional building to discuss plastic surgery consumption as a social issue. According to the event's program booklet, despite the fact that women's beauty practices seem voluntary, there are "cultural, social and economic issues within Korean society that are creating body dysmorphia and standards of beauty."[43] As such, the forum sought to raise these issues as a first step toward the eventual goal of lobbying for a law provisionally titled the "Body Diversity Guarantee" that would regulate the media and medical market in order to encourage a diversity of appearances and bodies.[44] Rather than solely focusing on and thus pathologizing Korean women as individual patients—which as Victoria Pitts-Taylor has written, "decenters other actors: the surgeons, the psychiatrists, the technologies, the media, the ideologies, the structure of medicine"—Womenlink's feminist organizing highlights "cultural, social and economic issues within Korean society." As such, in the following section I offer an analysis of these issues in order to start to untangle the "structuring violences of geopolitics and transnational capital" of the local context and to serve as a counterpoint to *Jezebel* writers' and readers' global feminist narratives that pathologize Korean women as individual patients.[45]

The 2013 forum was not Womenlink's first foray into organizing around the issue. In 2003, Womenlink initiated what was formally known as the "Women's Bodies Are Beautiful as They Are: The Lookism Perception Reform Project"—a yearlong series of educational events and programming that reached out to women and sought institutional reform. It was known for short as the "I Am the Owner of My Body" campaign and most commonly as "Love Your Body." Womenlink identified lookism as the major social problem driving plastic surgery consumption and attempted to curb it, as the formal title suggests. Although a full accounting and analysis of Womenlink's campaign is beyond the scope of this chapter, the "Love Your Body" campaign was composed of a wide array of activities and actions both to stymie the multiple industries sustaining and benefiting from lookism and to educate women, the latter to which I return at the end of the chapter.[46] These programs included public rallies, petitions, and performances, a mother-daughter overnight camp, media monitoring that yielded published statistics on gendered representations on television programming, legal action against plastic surgery clinics violating medical law by using before and after advertising, and producing and publicly airing an educational satire that approaches the plastic surgery industry through the mockumentary genre. Indeed, Womenlink cast a wide net in 2003 in order to address what they viewed as a primary obstacle to gender equality.

As already noted, Stewart also mentions lookism in her article. Although in the preceding paragraphs Stewart mentions that photographs required on university and job applications are a major impetus for surgery, her focus shifts from the structures that institutionalize lookism to the individuals who must contend with it. Stewart asks, "What would the average South Korean teen think about some so-called 'unconventional beauties' such as Frida Kahlo, Rossy De Palma and Grace Jones?"[47] She follows this question with: "If you have a limited ability to see beauty in someone who is not big-eyed and small-faced and straight-nosed, do you also have a limited ability to understand, empathize, sympathize and relate to that person, as well? Do you become intolerant of those who don't meet your lookist standards?" Though subtle, it is critical to highlight how the positioning of Stewart's series of questions makes South Korean teens the key actors motivating and perpetuating lookism despite her mention of both university admissions and career concerns as major reasons for surgery. In other words, Stewart's modification of "lookist standards" with the possessive second person pronoun "your" shifts the responsibility for the standards onto South Korean teens as well as the South Korean women of whom she writes. This sleight of hand pathologizes Korean women in a way that paints them as conformist and intolerant dupes rather than providing a deep analysis for their beauty practices, something Womenlink's organizing around lookism as a social problem seeks to do.

By centralizing the concept of lookism, Womenlink's campaign attempts to address the material consequences of women's everyday concerns as well as the capitalist practices (and the profits they engender) that produce them. Although Womenlink attributes the term lookism to the *New York Times Magazine* columnist William Safire and his column "On Language: Lookism" on August 27, 2000, Safire actually traces the word to a *Washington Post Magazine* article in 1978, when it was used by the Fat Acceptance Movement to describe both what their members experience and what they oppose.[48] Today in the United States, lookism is associated with Nancy Etcoff, a psychologist at Massachusetts General Hospital and faculty member at Harvard Medical School whose book *Survival of the Prettiest: The Science of Beauty* argues that human propensity to favor beauty is biological and a product of human evolution.[49] Her book brings together numerous scientific studies, including one she conducted in conjunction with other researchers at Massachusetts General Hospital, Harvard Medical School, and Massachusetts Institute of Technology who used magnetic resonance imaging (MRI) technology to analyze men's brain activity as they viewed photos of beautiful women. The researchers found that the images triggered the same parts of the brain that alcohol triggers for alcoholics, food triggers for hungry people, and money triggers for gamblers. In other words, beauty elicits the same chemical reactions in the brain as addiction. Because humans are hardwired toward beauty, Etcoff reasons, insistence that beauty is socially constructed is counterproductive and actually serves to entrench the beauty hierarchy further. Many critics understand her book as a direct response to feminists such as Naomi Wolf who argue that beauty is not only socially constructed but also premised on misogyny.[50]

Womenlink's use of the concept of lookism derives from the US context but also significantly departs from it as they identify it as "one of the causes of unequal relations in human history along with race, religion, sex and ideology."[51] While Etcoff would certainly agree with this definition, Womenlink's similarities with Etcoff in their use of the term end there. Although none of their materials indicate whether Womenlink members believe the propensity toward beauty is biologically driven, this seems to fall outside their major concern. In addition to a patriarchal analysis, Womenlink understands beauty through a capitalist framework that interrogates the material consequences of lookism and also who benefits from it. In other words, Womenlink asserts that Korean women are increasingly seeking body work because lookism affects their job and marriage prospects, as Stewart briefly mentions, and further asserts that the beauty industry sustains these social circumstances to its benefit.

While lookism creates a society stratified by a hierarchy of looks, it operates on the level of the day-to-day through the internalization of neoliberal mandates for self-management—neoliberal governmentalities—that have become imperative to economic success since the Asian Debt Crisis, also known as the IMF Crisis. Korea became the subject of IMF bailout in 1997 because it lacked the American dollars necessary to pay back loans from foreign financial institutions. Under the neoliberal regime of Kim Dae Jung, Korea's first civilian president, who took office but a month after the crisis began, Korea restructured its economy, and unemployment rates went from as low as 3 percent to as high as 20 percent. At the same time the government also decreased spending in the areas of social services, leaving many people to fend for themselves in a fiercely competitive economic environment.⁵² Such competition has fostered neoliberal mandates for self-management that operate in such a way that individuals are controlled through their freedom and the myriad choices they make toward their personal success, which are coded as the results of their self-entrepreneurship. According to feminist scholar Cho Joo-Hyun, in Korea's neoliberal regime "the most successful self-entrepreneurs . . . will be those who faithfully internalize the neoliberal logic, subjugating themselves to the techniques of biopower with no intention of activating their own critiques or initiating their own forms of subjection."⁵³ Thus, body work and the success it represents encompass the neoliberal logics of competitiveness, self-management, and entrepreneurship to the exclusion of all else. Such changes are the consequences of new gender norms and shifting social realities in post-IMF, neoliberal Korean society. While marriage has been considered most important to women's success, in the last decade job security has begun to displace marriage in its salience, with marriage becoming optional. At the same time divorce rates have increased and on average, women stay unmarried for far longer than in the past. Moreover, rapidly decreasing birthrates have caused a crisis of the middle class, leading the Korean government to enact numerous policies—such as improving maternity leave—as incentives for childbearing. These social changes signal significant ruptures in a culture where motherhood traditionally has been the only ideal role for women. While neoliberal imperatives push women toward methods of self-care, these rationalities dovetail with traditional notions of motherhood.

Notably, Womenlink put neoliberal imperatives for self-management at the forefront of their 2003 campaign by contextualizing it within these shifting identifications with the body. Their "Love Your Body" campaign proposal describes the situation as such:

> As women's participation in society has increased, women's bodies have increasingly been seen as objects. In the past, women's bodies were focused on a mother's role of having, then raising children. Now, however, the body is a site for raising one's self-value and is a symbol of one's position or lifestyle. As such, a well-maintained appearance is not only a marker of her self-satisfaction but is an avenue to attaining social status. Thus, many women are aggressively managing their bodies.⁵⁴

While identification with motherhood has changed, the body has become a site for "raising one's self-value and has become a symbol of one's position or lifestyle." As a result, the neoliberal rationale of investing in one's own body becomes all the more imperative since one's body is an "avenue to attaining social success." That is to say, because of the body's increasing social importance and visibility, women's choices to manage their bodies are all the more constrained even as they are narrated as liberatory. Significantly, Womenlink's 2013 interviews, published in the forum's program booklet, confirm that the pressures of the labor market continue to be major factors in Korean women's beauty choices. For example, one interviewee who works as a flight attendant states explicitly the connection between work and self-management: "Ten years ago appearance helped a little in getting a job. English language, physical fitness and academic achievement were the most important qualities and appearance was secondary but these days, almost everyone gets plastic surgery before their job interview."[55] Womenlink organizers thus conclude: "Neoliberalism justifies the acceleration of competition and women's deepening worries about employment make their bodies a site for the evaluation of their self-management, indoctrinating them into the idea that self-management of their bodies is inevitable."[56] As these quotes indicate, ten years after the "Love Your Body" campaign, women continue to internalize neoliberal mandates for self-management as imperative to their economic success and understand lookism to be a part of everyday work life.

These structures of lookism and the neoliberal governmentalities bolstering them signal a shift in the way gendered power disciplines women's bodies in Korean society.[57] Womenlink's "Love Your Body" campaign proposal's reference to the ways in which Korean women identified with their bodies, as mothers, does not celebrate or romanticize the past but rather points out that new, gendered mechanisms for control are in place. According to Kim Sang-hŭi, executive director of Womenlink, in a self-written editorial for JoongAng Ilbo, "In traditional society, a woman's body was completely controlled by male-centered society, especially because of the ideology of staying a virgin, which was a strict controlling tool of women's bodies. But now, lookism has replaced that ideology."[58] Kim points out that lookism is a mechanism of control that, like chaste ideologies in centuries prior, discipline women's behaviors and relationships to their own bodies. Moreover, lookism is powerful precisely because there are negative consequences for not participating in addition to perceived benefits for doing so: "In a lookist society, it is not just about self-maintenance, it's that unbeautiful women are seen as lazy and as incapable. Lookism discrimination is pervasive in job hunting and marriage and such discrimination based on 'looks' is deemed ok by this society."[59] In other words, women who choose not to invest in themselves are seen as not fulfilling their potential. As such, beauty ads for cosmetic surgery, dieting, skin and body care literally use the neoliberal language of "self-management" (자기 관리), "self-development" (자기개발), and "self-investment" (자기투자) to describe their products, goods, and services.

Although Womenlink asserts that the body has not only displaced motherhood as women's primary vehicle for social success but is the central locus of neoliberal identification, I would argue that motherhood is not outside neoliberal rationale creating a situation in which both types of neoliberal identifications are happening simultaneously. Accordingly, mothers must act upon their own bodies as self-entrepreneurs as well as those of their children as extensions of themselves. That is to say, traditional emphases on mothers to sacrifice everything for the success of their children have combined with neoliberal rationalities urging parents to the consumer market to purchase advantages for their children in a highly competitive post-IMF society. In addition to plastic surgery for their children, typically given as high school or college graduation presents, Korean children notoriously attend academies or hagwon (학원) to improve their skills in English, math, and science. The *Washington Post* reports that Korean parents spent $15.6 billion in 2006 on English-language tutors alone, and at least 24,000 children in the first to twelfth grades left the country to study English abroad.[60] In 2011, nearly 72 percent of all elementary, junior, and high school students attended private academies costing their parents a total of US$17.8 billion.[61] Since *Hallyu*'s global popularity, these academies are no longer entirely academic or artistic in the classical sense. As sociologist Swee-Lin Ho has shown, K-pop academies have emerged to provide alternative forms of mobility to children who are not academically inclined. These professional training programs, which provide training not only in singing and dancing but also in personality, appearance, and even manners, cost up to US$20,000 to complete just three years.[62] To be sure, Korea's highly competitive society engenders conformity to trends and neoliberal (and highly costly) solutions that interpellate mothers as self-entrepreneurs who act not only for the benefit of their children but for themselves in the hopes that through their children's success they might affirm their own "self-worth" and gain "recognition by the wider Korean society that they are 'good parents.'"[63]

As the growing popularity of K-pop academies today suggests, major developments occurred in the ten years between the "Love Your Body" campaign and the 2013 forum that dramatically changed the landscape and scope of plastic surgery in Korea. First, *Hallyu* became a global phenomenon, and second, Korea launched its medical tourism industry with cosmetic surgery as its largest market in 2007. As transnational industries, the two work hand in hand. *Hallyu* in its various genres— film, dramas, and K-pop—enacts aspirational desires on the part of viewers in other locations such as Japan, China, and Southeast Asia as well as in the diaspora through its glossy depictions of Koreans' capitalist consumption mediated through traditional tenets of Confucianism. In the particular realm of bodily aesthetics, these cultural productions proliferate a standard of beauty deemed particularly Korean and associated with Korea's seemingly successful forms of consumerist modernity. As sociologist Kimberly Hoang has shown in *Dealing in Desire: Asian Ascendency, Western Decline, and the Hidden Currencies of Global Sex Work*, Vietnamese sex workers catering to elite Vietnamese businessmen construct themselves as pan-Asian modern subjects whose "looks" conform to regional standards of beauty taking K-pop stars as a sought-after beauty ideal.[64] In addition to wearing makeup and clothing styled after the stars, these women also modify their bodies through rhinoplasties, double eyelid surgeries, breast augmentation, and liposuction surgeries.[65] Anthropologist Dredge Kang has illuminated similar dynamics in Thailand in his examination of transgender performance in K-pop cover dance and calls this privileging of light-skinned Asians from developed countries such as Japan, Korea, Singapore, and Taiwan a desire for and to be like "white Asians."[66] In other words, *Hallyu*'s regional popularity in Asia is not merely about pleasure and pop but rather points to new formations of modernity in Asia that defy east-west binaries and are creating regionally specific cultural and social meanings through tangible practices of consumption and embodiment.

According to my interview with a representative of South Korea's tourism board, this connection between popular culture, beauty, and marketing is not lost on South Korean governmental agencies. In fact, Korea's medical tourism industry spends very little, she told me, on advertising for its biggest market, cosmetic surgery—*Hallyu* is their global advertising.[67] As a result, *Hallyu* fans travel across the world to Seoul in order to look just like their favorite Korean actors or pop stars while embarking on *Hallyu* tours during recovery. Such global advertisements have been so successful that 30 percent of all cosmetic patients in Korea are Chinese, and of medical tourists, Japanese patients are the second largest group, with Singaporean and Indonesian numbers not far behind.[68]

The opening remarks at Womenlink's 2013 forum addressed these changes since 2003 by acknowledging that the relationship between media and the medical market shape beauty practices as self-management.[69] Given that the panel featured several speakers in addition to Womenlink representatives, including a doctor, professor, television director, and lawyer, the panel had a hard time reaching any unified conclusions. Womenlink's Media Division did have a concrete position, however, that the "problem is not surgery" but rather "the media broadcasting and promoting what surgeries celebrities have had"—promotion both on television and on the portal sites.[70] In other words, Womenlink, understanding the connection outlined in the previous section between K-pop, plastic surgery, and digital media, contends that media reform is key to distancing women from the pressures of beauty ideals. To these ends, the group presented five proposals: first, that celebrity plastic surgery no longer be the subject of programming or television reporting of any kind; second, that the media no longer produce programs that foster lookism, such as the "Baby Face Contest," which rewards people for the most youthful appearance; third, that a variety of actors and especially actresses are cast to show a diversity of body types; fourth, that media programming not make light of plastic surgery; and last, that new plastic surgery techniques are not introduced as part of programming.[71] The forum concluded with the remarks of a congressional representative who proposed the ambiguous concept of "health" as the most critical component to the discussion.

That a congressional representative would end the day's events points to a central contradiction: namely, that the very government that provided Womenlink with three-quarters of their funds for their "Love Your Body" campaign is the same government that promotes both *Hallyu* and medical tourism.[72] After the 1997 IMF Crisis, when Korea was in need of new industries, President Kim Dae-jung allotted US$50 million to create the Cultural Content Office. Today the office has a budget of US$500 million for its four divisions: video games, television, cultural industry policy, and cultural technology, and it expects to double the size of Korea's cultural industry exports to US$10 billion by 2019.[73] That the government considers its cultural products a lucrative investment is evidenced by the fact that current president Park Geun-hye created a US$1 billion for-profit investment fund aimed at making high returns.[74]

Medical tourism, on the other hand, has a more recent beginning. The Bureau of Korean Tourism established medical tourism as one of its main areas for growth and as one of the country's strategic products in 2007.[75] After Korea recovered from the 1997 IMF Crisis, plastic surgery as an industry experienced a boom, since improved looks were believed to provide an advantage in South Korea's highly competitive society. By 2009, however, patient visits declined as much as 40 percent, with a number of clinics closing their doors.[76] In addition, South Korea's currency depreciated enough for procedures to be cheaper than in other currencies at the same time that medical tourism was identified as one way to bring demand to South Korea's oversupply of clinics. According to Samuel Koo, president and CEO of Korea's Tourism Board in 2010, 7.8 million tourists visited South Korea in 2009, of whom 60,000 were medical tourists seeking mostly cosmetic and dental procedures.[77] This is a staggering increase from the fewer than 20,000 foreign patients South Korea saw in 2007. Just five years later, Korea welcomed 150,000 medical tourists, and in 2014 the medical tourism industry generated US$349 million in revenue.[78]

As these numbers suggest, the Korean government has invested in the three projects of *Hallyu*, medical tourism, and Womenlink without contradiction. As such, Womenlink is one of the many feminist activist nonprofits today that are tasked with managing women as a population. As states increasingly enact neoliberal policies that privatize or disregard welfare concerns, feminist nonprofits and NGOs have become central to such management as they are "understood as less corrupt, more efficient, and more closely attuned to needs on the ground than states are" and "claim an organic connection to the populations who are the objects of their welfare and feminist work."[79] But this connection is far from natural and in neoliberal Korea, Womenlink provides services the government itself has outsourced to mitigate circumstances its industries have created and to produce certain kinds of self-governing subjects. We see this fluidity between feminist activism and state government in Congresswoman Nam Yoon In Sook's comments, published in the forum's program booklet, when she calls the event a "meaningful next step" in her collaboration with Womenlink against "distorted body images and enforced beauty standards" that "threaten the health of the Korean public and require at least minimal measures and regulations."[80] She goes on to acknowledge that "federal and local governments use plastic surgery and enhancing appearance as the main products of medical tourism to stimulate the economy" and that this contributes to the "diffusion of distorted body images."[81] Kim concludes: "We must stop discrimination . . . based on appearance and begin discussions about the problems of the plastic surgery industry . . . to correct distorted views of the body."[82] As her comments illustrate, the government does not eliminate opposition to its federally funded projects but rather works through it by representing the counter-narrative in a way that works on behalf of hegemonic norms. That is to say, although Kim cursorily acknowledges the government's role, the government is not framed within these discussions as either generating or benefiting from the twin industries of medical tourism and *Hallyu* but instead primarily stands in as part of the solution, through her participation and collaboration with Womenlink, to what critics frame as Korea's plastic surgery epidemic. In this way, we see what Nguyen, engaging the work of Sonia Alvarez, describes as the troubling relationship into which "feminist organizations are increasingly drawn . . . with state powers: as gender experts, providing knowledge about the biopolitical category of 'women' . . . and as service subcontractors, advising and executing government or independent women's programs."[83]

Although the specific ways in which Womenlink's 2003 campaign interacted with or acted upon women has been beyond the scope of this chapter, focusing instead on the social, economic, and cultural issues the organization lays out as the landscape for Korean women's surgery consumption, I return to it here as a way of tying together *Jezebel's* and Womenlink's seemingly disparate feminisms to argue that perhaps they are not so disparate after all. Toward the end of her article, "I Can't Stop Looking at These Korean Women Who've Had Plastic Surgery," Stewart offers this piece of wisdom to young people considering body modification: "True beauty is on the inside!"[84] While *Jezebel* writers, editors, and millions of readers as well as Womenlink's members, panelists, and forum attendees can perhaps be characterized as feminists from opposite ends of the world, so to speak, and as I have shown, they understand, articulate, and analyze Korea's plastic surgery consumption in vastly different ways, it is critical to identify the unifying logic that undergirds both the idea that "True beauty is on the inside!" and the command to "Love Your Body." As mottos and maxims, these posit self-love or self-esteem as alternatives to surgeries and as antidotes to social problems. In so doing, both feminisms are complicit in the logics of the self-esteem movement that began in the 1980s and has taken on global dimensions today, feminist politics notwithstanding.[85] By 1992, self-esteem became enmeshed with mainstream global feminist politics when Gloria Steinem published her book, *Revolution from Within: A Book of Self-Esteem*, which calls for an internal revolution to address external barriers to gender equality, going so far as to say that self-esteem is a prerequisite for democracy and equality. As political scientist Barbara Cruikshank cogently argues, Steinem's book and the self-esteem movement it represents "does not so much avoid 'real' political problems as transform the level on which it is possible to address those problems."[86] As such, the self-esteem movement seeks to wage "a social revolution not against capitalism, racism, and inequality, but against the order of the self and the way we govern ourselves."[87] In other words, while our inner selves are painted as paths to liberation waiting to be unlocked within us, such self-making is itself a way of becoming a self-governing subject, able to govern where the state cannot.

Moreover, these slogans implicitly assert that loving your body or cultivating your inner beauty is the individual agency necessary to eschew cosmetic surgery or to counter the seductive practices of the industry when paradoxically, plastic surgery as a field has historically used the acquisition of self-esteem to justify its existence as a medical science.

Borrowing from psychoanalysis and psychology, the importance of appearance was first tied to the "inferiority complex," which then gave way to the larger and more flexible notion of self-esteem, which anthropologist Alexander Edmonds notes, "is important for cosmetic surgery because it enables surgeons to argue they are healing a psychological complaint. In the notion of low self-esteem one might say aesthetic surgery found a treatable condition."[88] Thus, self-esteem is packaged by the cosmetic surgery industry as its main product and by feminist movements as an antidote against that industry. Similarly, the campaign's other slogan, "I Am the Owner of My Body," also relies on neoliberal logics of self-possession that are not unlike the neoliberal governmentalities that push Korean women to the marketplace for forms of self-management and entrepreneurship as outlined earlier.[89] Such circular logic animates the ways in which, even in seeking to undo beauty, feminists rely upon its forms of governmentality. In this way, the logics undergirding Womenlink's feminist activities are perhaps not so different from those informing *Jezebel*'s writers, readers, and commenters in their emphasis of the self as a locus of liberation. That is to say, despite the fact that the two frame the problem quite differently, the global neoliberal discourses of self-esteem, empowerment, and ownership constitute powerful economic and social relations that bring their solutions into much closer proximity.

Conclusion

Social media has created new visual economies that have both increased the popularity of Korean popular culture and spawned fetishized interest in Korean bodies. On the one hand, the Miss Korea gif exemplifies the ways in which global feminist logics that celebrate individuality and privilege white and/or US women's experiences as universalisms undergird US discourses on the topic. Far from journalistic reporting, these stories are animated by US anxieties of an increasingly powerful Korea and use hollow appeals to morality to discipline Korean women in proper modes of consumption and beauty. While the gif was circulated and taken at face value, literally, as visual evidence of Korean modernity run amuck, I have offered Womenlink's activism as a counterpoint in order to outline the broader social, economic, and cultural issues that compose the landscape of plastic surgery consumption in Korea. Since 2003, Womenlink has identified lookism as an oppressive system that has material consequences vis-à-vis the marriage and job markets. In contrast to *Jezebel*'s global feminist politics, which pathologizes Korean women, Womenlink's activism takes Korean women's plastic surgery consumption as a result of a systemic problem that operates on the level of the everyday through neoliberal governmentalities that buttress myriad beauty industries.

Yet, as Womenlink's relationship to the Korean state and its reliance on discourses of self-possession and esteem suggest, in an age of neoliberalism, such forms of governance and personhood constitute the linkages that underwrite both groups' assumption that at least part of the solution to the "problem" of plastic surgery is self-love. Self-love, however, is itself a form of self-governance that parallels and thus cannot undo those forms espoused by the beauty industries feminists seek to stymie. Ultimately, the juxtaposition of the feminisms levied by *Jezebel* and Womenlink instantiates the ways in which neoliberal sentiments of self-possession, self-esteem, and empowerment have become part and parcel of feminist forms of resistance.

NOTES

1 Zara Stone, "The K-Pop Plastic Surgery Connection," *The Atlantic*, May 24, 2013, http://www.theatlantic.com/. Heesu Lee, "Gangnam Style Nip and Tuck Draws Tourists to the Beauty Belt," Bloomberg News, September 29, 2013, http://www.bloomberg.com/.

2 Chris Stokel-Walker, "When Does Plastic Surgery Become Racial Transformation?" *BuzzFeed News*, May 16, 2013, http://www.buzzfeed.com/.

3 Patricia Marx, "About Face: Why Is Seoul the World's Plastic-Surgery Capital?" *New Yorker*, March 23, 2015, http://www.newyorker.com/.

4 Marx, "About Face."

5 https://www.reddit.com/r/funny/comments/1d0784/koreas_plastic_surgery_mayhem_is_ finally/, April 24, 2013.

6 Dodai Stewart, "Plastic Surgery Means Many Beauty Queens but Only One Kind of Face," *Jezebel*, April 25, 2013, http://jezebel.com/.

7 David Ashcroft, "Blame Photoshop for Korea's Beauty Queen Clones," *Kotaku*, April 26, 2013, http://kotaku.com/. It was also later found that the women in the gif were not Miss Korea contestants but contestants for Miss Daegu, a province of Korea.

8 While the official McCune-Reischauer transliteration should be "Kangnam," I utilize "Gangnam" throughout to provide consistency with PSY's spelling in the title

of his song "Gangnam Style," to make clear that the same district is being referred to in various instances throughout the chapter.

9 "Opening Remarks," in Korean Womenlink, "*Apkujeong* Station Exit #4, Let's Talk About It: A Forum Seeking Alternatives to the State of Korean Plastic Surgery," Seoul, Korea, July 11, 2013 (hereafter cited as Womenlink, "*Apkujeong* Exit #4").

10 Congresswoman Nam Yoon In Soon, in Korean Womenlink, "*Apkujeong* Exit #4." The panelists included Kim Hee Young, Womenlink's Women's Health Division chair; Yoon Jung Joo, Womenlink's Media Division chair; Kim Jong Mi, professor of Media and Culture at Coventry University; Lee Sang Yoon, researcher for Health and Alternatives; Park Sang Wook, SBS director; and Lee Han Bon, lawyer from Lawyers for a Democratic Society.

11 Caren Kaplan and Inderpal Grewal, "Transnational Feminist Cultural Studies: Beyond the Marxism/Poststructuralism/Feminism Divide," in *Between Woman and Nation: Nationalism, Transnational Feminisms, and the State* (Durham, NC: Duke University Press, 1999), 357.

12 Steve Glain, "Cosmetic Surgery Goes Hand in Glove with the New Korea," *Wall Street Journal*, November 23, 1993.

13 Glain, "Cosmetic Surgery."

14 *The Oprah Winfrey Show*, "Around the World with Oprah" (syndicated, October 6, 2004). For my article on this episode of *The Oprah Winfrey Show*, see Sharon Heijin Lee, "Lessons from Around the World with Oprah: Race, Neoliberalism and the (Geo)Politics of Beauty," *Women and Performance: A Journal of Feminist Theory* 18 (2008): 25–41.

15 Jin-Kyung Lee, *Service Economies: Militarism, Sex Work, and Migrant Labor in Korea* (Minneapolis: University of Minnesota Press, 2010).

16 For more in-depth analysis on K-pop's diversity of fans, see Crystal Anderson, "Who Can Speak for K-Pop?," High Yellow (blog), October 23, 2013, http://highyellow.me/. Crystal Anderson, "How Does It Feel to Be a Question?: That (Black) Girl and K-Pop," High Yellow (blog), September 22, 2013, http://highyellow.me/. Crystal Anderson, "Of Misconceptions about Cultural Appropriation in K-Pop," High Yellow (blog), January 12, 2013, http://highyellow.me/.

17 Stephen Epstein with James Turnbull, "Girls' Generation? Gender (Dis)Empowerment, and K-Pop," in *The Korean Pop Culture Reader*, ed. Kyung Hyun Kim and Youngmin Choe (Durham, NC: Duke University Press, 2014), 316–17.

18 Such micro-managing of looks is exemplified in the documentary, *9 Muses of Star Empire*, directed by Hark Joon Lee (Seoul, Korea, 2012), a year-long chronicle of an all-girl K-pop group training before their debut. Several scenes instantiate the way in which body management and looks are just as important as talent, as several scenes show the stars and their management team dissecting their physical flaws and discussing ways to improve them.

19 In "The Popular Economy," John Fiske, writing against the idea that people are merely passive recipients of popular culture, argues that consumers of old media (he is mainly theorizing about television) are also producers in that they make

meanings that cannot be controlled by the producers of pop culture: "The power of audiences-as-producers in the cultural economy is considerable. . . . This power derives from the fact that meanings do not circulate in the cultural economy in the same way that wealth does in the financial"; John Fiske, "The Popular Economy," in *Cultural Theory and Popular Culture: A Reader*, ed. John Storey (New York: Pearson Longman, 2009), 540, 564–80. Since Fiske was writing in the 1980s before the development of the Internet, I see Nakamura and other digital humanities scholars as building upon his theorizations about how consumers interact with popular culture products in unexpected ways. As Nakamura points out, although early predictions of such lines blurring to the extent that everyone has a homepage have not proven true, platforms such as blogs and vlogs and social networks such as Facebook have manifested this somewhat; Lisa Nakamura, *Digitizing Race: Visual Cultures of the Internet* (Minneapolis: University of Minnesota Press, 2008), 18.

20 Jill Fillipovic, "Jezebel: From Blog to Book," *Guardian*, October 28, 2013, http://www.theguardian.com/.
21 "Jezebel Manifesto: The Five Great Lies of Women's Magazines," http://jezebel.com/.
22 Susan Douglas, *Where the Girls Are: Growing Up Female with Mass Media* (New York: Crown, 1994), 270.
23 Douglas, *Where the Girls Are*.
24 Fillipovic, "Jezebel: From Blog to Book."
25 Maureen Corrigan, "If You're Looking to Read Lady Things Choose Jezebel over Jones," *NPR Book Reviews*, October 21, 2013, http://www.npr.org/.
26 https://www.quantcast.com/jezebel.com.
27 *Jezebel* is also reaching readership in book form. In 2013, Anna Holmes published *The Book of Jezebel*, an anthology of the most popular articles on the site during her tenure there.
28 "The Rebirth of the Feminist Manifesto," *New York Magazine*, October 30, 2011, http://nymag.com/.
29 Mimi Thi Nguyen, "The Biopower of Beauty: Humanitarianism, Imperialism and Global Feminisms in an Age of Terror," *Signs* 36 (Winter 2011): 370.
30 Nguyen, "The Biopower of Beauty."
31 Nakamura, *Digitizing Race*, 17.
32 Stewart, "Plastic Surgery."
33 Chandra Mohanty, "Under Western Eyes Revisited," in *Feminism without Borders: Decolonizing Theory, Practicing Solidarity* (Durham, NC: Duke University Press, 2003), 227.
34 Nakamura, *Digitizing Race*, 20.
35 Nakamura, *Digitizing Race*, 20.
36 Nguyen, "The Biopower of Beauty," 366–67.
37 David Palumbo-Liu, "Written on the Face: Race, Nation, Migrancy, and Sex," in *Asian/America: Historical Crossings of a Racial Frontier* (Stanford, CA: Stanford

University Press, 1999), 81–115; Eugenia Kaw, "Medicalization of Racial Features: Asian American Women and Cosmetic Surgery," *Medical Anthropology Quarterly* 7, no. 1 (1993): 82; Nadia Kim, *Imperial Citizens: Koreans and Race from Seoul to LA* (Stanford, CA: Stanford University Press, 2008), 53.

38 Elsewhere I argue that the plastic surgery consumer and the *yanggongju* (military sex worker) emerged out of the Korean War and are distinct instantiations of the ways that capitalism has mobilized gendered bodies; Sharon Heijin Lee, "The (Geo)Politics of Beauty: Race, Transnationalism and Neoliberalism in Korean Beauty Culture," PhD diss., University of Michigan, 2012.

39 Nguyen, "The Biopower of Beauty," 364. As Nguyen outlines, beauty's involvement with war is not merely discursive but intimately tied to humanitarian imperialisms and global feminisms. For example, the nongovernmental organization (NGO) Beauty without Borders, consisting of North American and European fashion industry and nonprofit professionals, opened the Kabul Beauty School in Afghanistan in 2003 to teach Afghan women, as their website describes it, "to do hair." As Nguyen explains, the women who started the NGO acted "on the hope that beauty can engender a new world order" (360). That is to say, these women— Vogue's Anna Wintour among them—imagined not only that an education in hair and cosmetics would bring Afghan women into modernity by giving them new skills but also that these skills and the Western (read: modern) styles they engendered would bring Afghan women a new sense of self and self-esteem and bring them closer to the promises of liberal democracy that are signified by the promises of beauty.

40 According to sociologist Debra Gimlin, "body work" is "work on the self. By engaging in body work, women are able to negotiate normative identities by diminishing their personal responsibility for a body that fails to meet cultural mandates"; Debra Gimlin, *Body Work: Beauty and Self-Image in American Culture* (Berkeley: University of California Press, 2002), 6. Gimlin's "body work" is a method for reconciling the separation between "the body" and "the self" and takes place in aerobics classes, weight control organizations, and beauty salons in addition to plastic surgery clinics. While my use of the term body work builds on Gimlin's, I depart significantly from her definition because I use the term to suggest both the work that women do to their bodies and the labor performed by their bodies.

41 Jane Chi-Hyun Park, *Yellow Future: Oriental Style in Hollywood Film* (Minneapolis: University of Minnesota Press, 2010), 8.

42 Dodai Stewart, "I Can't Stop Looking at These Korean Women Who've Had Plastic Surgery," *Jezebel*, January 16, 2013, http://jezebel.com/.

43 Korean Womenlink, "*Apkujeong* Exit #4."

44 Korean Womenlink, "*Apkujeong* Exit #4."

45 Victoria Pitts-Taylor, *Surgery Junkies: Wellness and Pathology in Cosmetic Culture* (New Brunswick, NJ: Rutgers University Press, 2007), 184.

46 For a fuller accounting and analysis of Womenlink's 2003 programs, events, and actions see Lee, "The (Geo)Politics of Beauty."

47 Stewart, "I Can't Stop Looking at These Korean Women."

48 Korean Womenlink, "여성건강[여성의 몸, 그대로가 아름답다(가칭)회의,"
March 11, 2003; William Safire, "The Way We Live Now, On Language: Lookism,"
New York Times, August 27, 2000. That William Safire coined lookism seems to be
a widely held belief in Korea, appearing on multiple blogs and Internet videos on
the topic. Whether this can be attributed to Womenlink's educational campaigns
cannot be ascertained, although they alone seem to have raised awareness around
the idea. Safire's weekly column "On Language," where "On Language: Lookism"
appeared, focused on linguistics and grammar in playful and insightful ways.
Thus, his column on lookism actually traces the origins of the word and its usage
while satirizing the concept by likening it to other "politically correct" terminology. Womenlink's citation of Safire's article may well point to the politics of
(mis)translation and their need to ground their concept in a Western"-ism" akin
to racism and sexism. Another possibility, however, is that Womenlink aligns
with Safire precisely because of his satiric use of the term. As briefly mentioned,
Womenlink produced a mockumentary called *Knifestyle*, satirically critiquing the
cosmetic surgery industry.

49 Nancy Etcoff, *Survival of the Prettiest: The Science of Beauty* (New York: Anchor
Books, 2000).

50 While lookism in and of itself is not a major concern for feminists in the United
States, it was a topic of concern within the mainstream media around the time
that Etcoff published her book and Safire published his column. ABC News, for
example, conducted experiments for which they hired actors, "some great looking, some not," and compared them in various situations such as applying for
jobs, soliciting for charitable donations, and asking for help along the road. In all
these situations, the better-looking actors were treated more favorably compared
to their average-looking counterparts—they got the job, made more in donations,
and got more help. The report ends with the suggestion: "We should add the
bias of 'lookism' to sexism and racism. It's just as bad but we don't need a federal
program." John Stossel, "The Ugly Truth about Beauty—ABC News," ABC News,
http://abcnews.go.com/; Karen Lehrman, "The Beautiful People," *New York Times*,
March 21, 1999, sec. Books, http://www.nytimes.com/; Naomi Wolf, *The Beauty
Myth: How Images of Beauty Are Used against Women* (London: Vintage Press,
1991).

51 Korean Womenlink, "여성건강[여성의 몸, 그대로가 아름답다(가칭)회의,"
March 11, 2003. Although Womenlink uses the Korean term for lookism,
oemochisangjuŭi (외모지상주의), interchangeably with the English word, in
most of their campaign materials, they use the term lookism.

52 Jesook Song, "Family Breakdown and Invisible Homeless Women: Neoliberal
Governance during the Asian Debt Crisis in South Korea, 1997–2001," *positions*
14, no. 1 (2006): 40–42.

53 Cho Joo-Hyun, "Neoliberal Governmentality at Work: Post-IMF Korean Society
and the Construction of Neoliberal Women," *Korea Journal* 49, no. 3 (Fall 2009): 37.

54 Korean Womenlink, "여성건강[여성의 몸, 그대로가 아름답다(가칭)회의,"
    March 11, 2003.
    In writing about the increase in breast augmentation surgeries and con-
    sumption of enhancement products and treatments, Laura Miller has noted
    this same shift in Japan: "the body has become central to capitalist expansion,
    and women are urged to seek surfaces through which to frame their now more
    assertive personalities. In earlier decades, clothes and hairstyles were sufficient
    to announce one's modernity, but today it is breasts and other parts of the body
    around which calculations about gender and identity are fashioned"; Laura
    Miller, *Beauty Up: Exploring Contemporary Japanese Body Aesthetics* (Berkeley:
    University of California Press, 2006) 295.
55 Korean Womenlink. "*Apkujeong* Exit #4."
56 Korean Womenlink. "*Apkujeong* Exit #4."
57 Not only are Korean men increasingly seeking plastic surgery, also citing employ-
    ment as a major motivator, but Korea is now the largest market for men's skincare
    in the world. Korean men's cosmetics consumption illustrates how neoliberal
    mandates for self-management are not limited to women but interpellate men
    as well, albeit in a distinct way that deserves its own attention. Nadine DeNinno,
    "The Korean Men Makeup Fad: South Korea Is Largest Market for Men's Skincare
    in the World," *International Business Times*, September 18, 2012, http://www
    .ibtimes.com/.
58 Kim Sang-hŭi, "Society Incites Cosmetic Surgery," *JoongAng Ilbo* (Seoul, Korea,
    n.d.), sec. Minority Voices.
59 Sang-hŭi, "Society Incites Cosmetic Surgery."
60 Johee Cho, "English Is the Golden Tongue for S. Koreans," July 2, 2007, http://
    www.washingtonpost.com/.
61 As cited in Swee-Lin Ho, "Fuel for Korea's Global Dreams Factory: The Desires
    of Parents Whose Children Dream of Becoming K-Pop Stars," *Korea Observer* 43
    (Autumn 2012): 486.
62 Ho, "Fuel for Korea's Global Dreams Factory."
63 Ho, "Fuel for Korea's Global Dreams Factory."
64 Kimberly Hoang, *Dealing in Desire: Asian Ascendency, Western Decline, and the
    Hidden Currencies of Global Sex Work* (Oakland: University of California Press,
    2015), 130–31.
65 Hoang, *Dealing in Desire*, 135.
66 Dredge Kang, "Idols of Development: Transnational Transgender Performance in
    Thai K-Pop Cover Dance," Theme issue: "Trans* Cultural Production," *Transgen-
    der Studies Quarterly* 1, no. 4 (2014): 559–71.
67 Eun Mi Kim, personal interview, March 10, 2010.
68 Bae Ji-sook, "Cosmetic Surgery Emerges as Export Product," *KoreaToday*, January
    27, 2010.
69 Opening Remarks, Korean Womenlink, "*Apkujeong* Exit #4."
70 Korean Womenlink, "*Apkujeong* Exit #4."

71 Korean Womenlink, "*Apkujeong* Exit #4." Womenlink has successfully organized around media in the past. In 2009, Womenlink's Media Division requested that telecom corporation KT pull its "Olleh!" campaign because it featured women in supporting roles only that reproduced gendered stereotypes. When KT refused, Womenlink went on national television to announce a boycott of KT until the campaign was stopped. Not only were the ads withdrawn but in its next campaign series, KT featured an ad that promoted women's equality by ridiculing patriarchal norms. Olga Federenko, "South Korean Advertising as Popular Culture," in *The Korean Popular Culture Reader*, ed. Kyung Hyun Kim and Youngmin Choe (Durham, NC: Duke University Press), 347–48.

72 Korean Womenlink, "국비보조금 교부신청서," February 11, 2003.

73 Euny Hong, *The Birth of Korean Cool: How One Nation Is Conquering the World through Pop Culture* (New York: Picador, 2014), 101.

74 Hong, *Birth of Korean Cool*, 101–A102.

75 Yoon Hyung Ho, (윤형호), 서울시 의료관광 현황과 방, 서울시정개발연구원 (Seoul, Korea: Seoul Development Research Institute, 2010), 25.

76 Martin Fackler, "Economy Blunts South Korea's Appetite for Plastic Surgery," *New York Times*, January 1, 2009, http://www.nytimes.com/.

77 Samuel Koo, "Korea in the Global Village and the Effort to Strengthen Its Brand Power," lecture presented at Yonsei University, Seoul, Korea, May 20, 2010.

78 Peng Qian, "Feature: South Korea's Medical Tourism Revenue Slips Amid Growing Malpractice," Xinhua Net Asia&Pacific Edition, February 10, 2015, http://news.xinhuanet.com/; "South Korea: Korea Increases Number of International Patients," *International Medical Travel Journal*: News, June 4, 2014, http://www.imtj.com/.

79 Nguyen, "The Biopower of Beauty," 373.

80 Nam Yoon's comments also mention her previous collaboration with Womenlink in October 2012 co-hosting a debate titled "Planning the Future of Korean Society through Gender Equality and Welfare," which included a discussion on a "Society That Allows Various Bodies and Considers Lifelong Health." Korean Womenlink, "*Apkujeong* Exit #4."

81 Korean Womenlink, "*Apkujeong* Exit #4."

82 Korean Womenlink, "*Apkujeong* Exit #4."

83 Nguyen, "The Biopower of Beauty," 373.

84 Stewart, "Plastic Surgery."

85 As Cruikshank notes, the self-esteem movement began in 1983 with the California Task Force to Promote Self-Esteem and Personal and Social Responsibility, who promised to deliver programs that would solve social problems such as crime, poverty, and gender inequality. Barbara Cruikshank, *The Will to Empower: Democratic Citizens and Other Subjects* (Ithaca, NY: Cornell University Press, 1999), 88.

86 Cruikshank, *Will to Empower*, 88.

87 Cruikshank, *Will to Empower*, 88.

88 Alexander Edmonds, *Pretty Modern: Beauty, Sex, and Plastic Surgery in Brazil* (Durham, NC: Duke University Press, 2010), 78. The "Love Your Body" campaign

did not end in 2003 but was relaunched in 2006. The project, officially called "Seeing Lookism through the Eyes of Teens," sought to empower teenage girls by giving them the opportunity to use media on their own terms. The result was a DVD featuring four short films that interrogate the issue of lookism from the girls' perspectives. Having already produced *Knifestyle*, their educational satire, and screened it in women's education health classes throughout South Korea as well as on the national television network KBS, Womenlink took a different approach to media organizing that continued to prioritize women's everyday lives, but this time from the perspective of the consumers most targeted for self-management through the economic necessity of plastic surgery as well as those most targeted by the effect of pop culture generally and pop music in particular. Korean Womenlink, "10 대들의 눈으로 보는 외모지상주의 여상제작" (Seoul, Korea: Korean Womenlink, 2006).

89 The campaign also had a third slogan, "No Diet, No Plastic Surgery." The campaign was called either of these slogans for short, depending on the event and the emphasis of the message, but "Love Your Body" was the most popular and seems to be the most remembered of the slogans.

4

Beauty Regimens, Beauty Regimes

Korean Beauty on YouTube

EMILY RAYMUNDO

In the film *Celeste and Jesse Forever*, protagonist Rashida Jones encounters a young, newly viral celebrity in the bathroom. The young woman is complaining about her skin breaking out and blames it on her "new skin regime." Rashida Jones can't help herself and corrects the celebrity: "It's regimen." The woman stares at her blankly, and Rashida continues, "Regime is a system of government . . . you mean skin regimen." "Thanks, Scrabble," the celebrity replies.[1]

This wordplay has stuck in my head ever since seeing that scene, and I've taken up referring to my own daily and nightly beauty routines as "beauty regimes." During my almost daily routine of applying makeup, I'm reminded of Lisa Rofel's description of capitalism as a world-building project that "has the capacity to reach into the sinews of our bodies and the machinations of our hearts."[2] Applying makeup is an often visceral pleasure, as the kinetic motion of the movement of my hand and the brush on my face ignites the surface of my skin, while simultaneously, my skin is itself resurfaced—color corrected, smoothed, and shaded. Yet such pleasures are informed by, and respond to, cultural imperatives that dictate what a face—my face, a woman of color's face, a professional's face, etc.—should look like. And so I'm also constantly reminded of Mimi Thi Nguyen's description of beauty as a form of biopower, a normalizing and often moralizing form of "right living" that is equally useful at the micro level of policing individuals' appearance *and* the macro level of distributing life and death chances throughout populations.[3] Thus, Rashida Jones isn't totally correct when she corrects the young celebrity. The woman might have meant to say beauty regimen, but beauty regimens are never separable from beauty regimes.

This chapter examines the tension between these two concepts: regime as a system of government, and regimen as a regulated course of behavior designed to produce health. This tension rises to the surface in the ever-more-popular genre of beauty YouTubing, a genre that has, in the last few years, come to dominate the site, spawning a total of 45.3 billion video views, 123,164,115 total channel subscriptions, and 182,621 makeup- and beauty-related channels in 2015 alone.[4] Like other YouTube genres, beauty on YouTube is populated by a dizzying array of diverse content makers, but also like other YouTube genres, it is marked by the popularity and visibility of Asian and Asian American vloggers—a visibility even more noticeable for its contrast to the lack of Asian and Asian American–centric television and film in the United States, YouTube's largest content producer and audience. This is partially the result of the Asian American youth community's relative virtuosity with social media; yet, in terms of beauty YouTubing in particular, it is also influenced by the beauty industry's larger turn toward Asia, particularly Japan, Hong Kong, and, increasingly, South Korea.[5] Beauty YouTube's intersection with both domestic racial and economic schemas *and* the vicissitudes of the global beauty market make it, I suggest herein, a unique archive of the operations of global neoliberalism as it articulates through social media and, particularly, through raced and gendered ideas about beauty, makeup, and self-care.[6]

Reading a series of Korean and Korean American YouTube makeup tutorials and beauty videos, I argue that these videos reveal a map of connectivities between seemingly disparate global economic and social structures. In particular, they reveal how two striking features of global neoliberalism—the centralizing of women as a global labor and consumer force, and the "globalization" of capital as marked by the rise of capitalism in Asia—converge to remap and remake race and gender as global biopolitical schemas. I examine three scales of this network of connectivities: neoliberalism as a global ideology that centralizes women consumers and laborers; neoliberalism as a color-blind discourse in the domestic United States, that depends on yet obscures its production of racial difference; and global neoliberalism as a market system that facilitates transnational flows of commodities and cultural ideologies, sometimes to unruly effects. These scales are not separate but related phenomena; rather they interlock, each depending on and shaped by the others, and together they reveal the complexity discussing race and gender within global systems of consumption and (uneven) cultural exchange.

Throughout, these videos index a specific imperative within neoliberalism to master and manage the self as simultaneously both normalized and individualized—a tension crystallized in the non-distinction between individual beauty regimens and national or global beauty regimes. That is, they show the ways in which neoliberalism deploys a constrained vision of individualization, crystallized within a personalized beauty regimen, to channel impulses of self-making back into a global system of consumption and normalization—a beauty regime. In doing so, these videos also mark potential flaws in the system; places where neoliberalism's deviousness at containing difference sometimes threatens to undo the system itself. These flaws are quickly concealed, but they yet leave behind traces and potentialities that cannot quite be buffed away. At the same time, they reveal how beauty, as a neoliberal technology that functions to produce, contain, and make useful racial and gender difference, works to contain the inevitable spillover of potentially disruptive difference and channel it back into capital, so that the site of neoliberalism's potential undoing is also always the site of its redoing.

Making (Up) the Self

While makeup has a history that extends far beyond the historical bounds of neoliberalism, I argue in the following section that it takes a particular place of prominence within the social schema that neoliberalism coheres and dictates. Correspondingly, I also argue that makeup, as a racialized and gendered technology of self-fashioning, reveals how neoliberalism both produces and harnesses difference through multiple modes of subjectification, marketization, and normalization.

Makeup is often figured as a coextension of "fashion," part of a broader range of discourses of "beauty" and of technologies of bodily adornment and self-fashioning. Recently, scholars have pushed back against the notion that fashion is trivial or an epiphenomenon of larger sociocultural forces. Instead, fashion is revealed to be a key site of negotiation between the psychic and the social, which, as part of an individual's *habitus*, both is shaped by and shapes personal and social modes of being.[7] Fashion also operates as a mode of governance that functions alongside discourses of human rights, dignity, and morality to extend Western military power and distribute life and death chances throughout national and global populations.[8]

Makeup, is, however, distinct from fashion as a technology, and serves a unique function within neoliberal markets. Makeup uniquely coarticulates with multiple neoliberal imperatives, including self-expression through consumption, self-management through bodily health, and the proliferation of difference in the name of expanding consumer markets. While makeup is a medium of self-expression, that is, it is simultaneously a medium of bodily management and perfection, coextensive with discourses of technology, science, and medicine. Within neoliberalism, self-management in the form of bodily health increasingly dovetails with self-management in the form of bodily "perfection": in the latter half of the twentieth century, Nikolas Rose argues,

> The very idea of health was refigured—the will to health would not merely seek the avoidance of sickness or premature death, but would encode an optimization of one's corporeality to embrace a kind of overall "well-being"—beauty, success, happiness, sexuality, and much more. It was this enlarged will to health that was amplified and instrumentalized by new strategies of advertising and marketing in the rapidly developing consumer market for health.[9]

This will to optimization is compounded by both the ever-expanding pressure to correct new areas of the body—from armpit coloration to eyebrow shape—and the increasing entwining of the physical and psychic dimensions of makeup. Unlike fashion or plastic surgery, that is, makeup is financially accessible to almost everyone and does not discriminate between desirable and undesirable bodies; makeup can correct any and every body. Exhortations to "love the skin you're in" and ad slogans like "you are more beautiful than you think" frame makeup as a means of self-love and self-care, conflating "looking good" and "feeling good."[10] Recasting beauty as a "state of mind," Ana Elias, Rosalind Gill, and Christina Scharf argue, does not alleviate makeup's "punishing appearance standards for women," but rather extends and aids "capitalism's move to colonise all of life—including our deepest feelings about ourselves."[11] Thus, makeup's utility as a technology of self-fashioning vacillates between imperatives of self-expression (individualization) and imperatives of self-*correction* (normalization).

Makeup is also a unique beauty commodity because it can proliferate difference—and thus multiply markets—far beyond the capacity of fashion, plastic surgery, and other beauty technologies. A key feature of neoliberalism is that it coerces not through discipline, but through a careful cultivation of a dizzying array of differentiated "choices" between styles of individualized consumption—rendering consumption itself a *precondition* of self-making. Where fashion inevitably attempts to eliminate bodily difference by standardizing its shapes and sizes, and while makeup ad campaigns might centralize white or thin bodies, makeup product lines themselves feed on racial and other bodily difference to reproduce: skin tones, for instance, can be endlessly differentiated based on undertone, shade, moisture level, discoloration and acne scarring, and more. Most prominent makeup brands, for example, carry multiple foundation lines, each with their own specific formulation (moisturizing; age defying; sun protecting; matte; heavy coverage; etc.), and each with anywhere between 5 and 35 shades. Even individuals who don't purchase or apply "makeup" consume commodities like shampoo, sunscreen, lotion, and lip balm, for example, and the infinite range from "high end" to drugstore or "low end" cosmetic lines extends makeup's accessibility through virtually any and every global market.[12] And whereas fashion is associated with "taste," which is relatively unteachable, makeup is associated with "skill," which anyone can acquire with practice—hence the proliferation of makeup tutorial videos across the Internet. Makeup can then instantiate and channel consumption habits more efficiently and more widely than other beauty commodities, while still elaborating the discourses that fuel the beauty industry as a whole.

The vacillation between regimen and regime allows makeup to become a neoliberal technology par excellence. That is, neoliberalism ruthlessly exploits the productive tension between individualized expression (regimen) and corrective normalization (regime). The successful application of makeup—according to beauty bloggers and their transnational fandoms—requires an intense and practiced knowledge of the self. "Good" makeup—either convincing in its corrective capacity or spectacular in its artistic virtuosity—requires that the person applying it know their own face in incredible specificity. Most beauty bloggers often start videos with a clean, makeup-free face, in part to demonstrate that everyone has an assortment of flaws that need to be addressed. Skin, eyes, lips, noses, cheekbones, eyebrows, eyelashes, and more can each be a "problem" on an individual face, and each need an assortment of products (or surgeries) to either be accentuated or hidden, depending on that face's particular structures and needs. The recent US trend in color-correcting and contouring, for example, has revealed a new way to map skin flaws based not on shapes or scars but on irregular coloring, all of which needs to be corrected and concealed to produce what is often referred to by beauty bloggers as "natural."

For example, Korean American beauty blogger Morgan Stewart, who blogs under the title "TheBeautyBreakdown," has posted several "every day makeup" videos over the course of her YouTube career. In each, she begins with a bare face and proceeds through her beauty routine, making sure to highlight each product she uses for the camera. The name and brand of each product is displayed in the video itself and also included in the video's description on YouTube. In her video "My Every-day Natural Pretty Makeup," Stewart displays and applies 26 different products. These products include sunscreen, eyebrow gel and powder, five different shades of eyeshadow, concealer, foundation, setting powder, bronzer, blush, and lipstick. When she mentions a product she has discussed before, a link to the other video appears in the corner of the current video.[13] In more recent videos, created as her prominence as a blogger has grown, she has shifted to a "one-brand" model of blogging, where videos like "Effortless Spring Makeup" or "My Everyday Summer Day to Night Makeup" are dedicated to a singular brand or store, with whom, presumably, Stewart has a promotional relationship.[14] Avid viewers or subscribers to her video feed will recognize her preference for matte "air cushion" foundations or her occasional struggle to find Korean foundations dark enough to match her skin tone.

In each of these videos, consumption of and participation in "makeup" as a self-fashioning technology is assumed; it forms the unspoken background from which specific products, looks, or effects can emerge as particularly useful or desirable. The amount of products used is unremarkable, except by virtue of being relatively little in comparison to other beauty bloggers; because this is an "everyday" look, for instance, only three to five eyeshadows need to be applied. That defined eyebrows and cheekbones, lighter and blemish-free skin, and bigger eyes are desirable is also unstated; the videos merely demonstrate more efficient ways to achieve these effects, which are both "pretty" and "natural."

Thus, the economic logic and activity that fuel beauty blogging at large disappear into the background. Prices are never listed, nor is much, if anything, made of the fact that most successful beauty bloggers receive the products they use in their videos for free. The videos provide a dizzying array of looks, effects, or technologies from which to choose—hence the need, ostensibly, to narrow one video's focus to a singular brand or purpose ("summer" or "night time" makeup), yet the desire for, participation in, and capital and labor needed to achieve these looks go unremarked upon, instead becoming part of the video's framing conditions.

To be successful at applying her own makeup, then, every individual is invited first to catalogue each and every idiosyncrasy of her own face. Then, she has to purchase a wide array of personalized and individualized products to counteract or highlight each of those idiosyncrasies in turn. These products may only be useful in certain seasonal conditions or on certain occasions, or only during the upswing of a particular market trend. The markets and commodities that makeup can produce are, in this way, almost unlimited, capable of infinite reproductions and proliferations that yet leave little room for what Judith Butler calls "reproduction with a difference."[15] That is, by combining the neoliberal imperatives to fashion the self—through consumption choices that define the individual—and to perfect the self—through "corporeal optimization" that ostensibly extends health and life throughout populations—makeup can endlessly multiply its markets and extend its reach without leaving much, if any, room for dissent or non-engagement.

It is no coincidence that neoliberalism has found an ideal vehicle in cosmetics. Makeup, though applicable to everyone conscripted by neoliberal market logics, is fundamentally a commodity market targeted at women. As Nancy Fraser explains, a key feature of neoliberalism is the centrality of women to the market, both as consumers and sources of labor. Indeed, Fraser suggests that second-wave feminism and neoliberalism shared an investment in a systemic critique of "traditional authority," leading the parlance of second-wave feminism—female autonomy,

an end to the "family wage" ideal—to be uniquely available for resigni-
fication under neoliberalism. The prominence of women laborers and
women consumers has come to signify a "moral" good of a neoliberal
system; women's freedom to participate in the market as active agents
who can make rational decisions that optimize their economic and social standing has been one ideological avenue through which neoliberal
economic and social systems have been enforced and validated by the
United States and the European Union.[16]

Developing beauty markets serves both domestic and transnational
needs; they can expand a country's soft power and validate their commitment to neoliberalism in the global arena, but are also a key tool
in domestic neoliberal governance. In post–Maoist China, for example,
women's bodies have become both symbols of and testing grounds for
"innovative technologies and new consumption patterns"; in the 1990s,
the Chinese state actively invested in cultivating the beauty market as a
way of encouraging consumerism and offsetting the economic effects of
massive layoffs at state-owned enterprises, which were mostly directed
at women workers.[17] Women's bodies underwent a similar shift in significance in South Korea during the 1980s transition to a postindustrial,
consumer society: "Women became more important as consumers than
as factory workers, shifting the utility of their bodies from national labour production to national consumption, becoming, in effect, [. . .]
the capitalist body."[18] South Korean women's participation in global
beauty markets then symbolizes South Korea's successful transition into
a postindustrialist, consumer society, and simultaneously solidifies a national aesthetic identity. Like self-care and the will to health, women's
active participation in the market is both a central moral imperative
and key technique of governance within neoliberalism; makeup as an
industry and market unites all of these mandates.

Makeup also serves a racial purpose within neoliberalism, one that
both stabilizes and disrupts neoliberal racial schemas. The popularity of
specifically Asian and Asian American beauty bloggers, as I suggested
in the introduction, reveals the racial function of supposedly color-blind
neoliberal commodities, as makeup produces racial differences that can
be contained and normalized within the spectrum of consumable products. At the same time, this unlimited production of racialized and gendered differences cannot help but produce surplus effects, particularly

in a global market in which Asian countries, particularly China, South Korea, and Japan, claim an increasingly larger portion—both of cultural consumption *and* production.

Dis/Embedding Racial Difference

Within the domestic racial schema of the United States, the popularity—even virality—of Asian and Asian American beauty blogs reveals the racial operations of supposedly color-blind neoliberalism. Makeup is extended throughout the population exactly through its capacity for simultaneously producing and managing difference, which is often racialized via shades of makeup, brands that specifically target non-white consumers, and even products that target racialized features (like "monolids") without ever explicitly stating their racial function. Color-blindness as a social ideal pledges to remove "race" from language, racial "difference" from perception, and thus "racial difference" as a tool of social hierarchy and division. Yet neoliberalism itself operates through differentiation, fragmentation, and multiplication; it's often *dependent* on racial difference as one way of proliferating labor and consumer markets. Color-blindness then helps to *manage* the excess racial difference *produced* by neoliberalism, even as it conceals this production of difference.[19] Thus, for example, monolids appear to be neutral features that "anyone" might have and want to correct, even as products (and surgeries) to correct them are specifically marketed toward Asian women.[20]

The tension between the production and management of racial difference is on display in one of the most popular makeup videos on YouTube—and so is that tension's unruly effects. "Taylor Swift transformation video," a video by Hye-min Park, aka Pony, a South Korean makeup artist hailed as "Korea's most famous beauty guru," gained almost 9.5 million views in the period between March and June 2016.[21] In the six and a half minute video, Pony silently applies 24 separate products to her face in order to "transform" into Taylor Swift, pausing, of course, to clearly display each product's name and brand.

The video begins with Pony in full "Taylor Swift" makeup, wearing a blonde wig, and making the wide-eyed, open-mouthed, head-tilted poses that often mark Swift's photos. After 20 seconds of posing, the video cuts to a shot of Pony's first product, and then, unceremoniously, to Pony's bare face (albeit with blue contacts) as she pats on the product just displayed. Pony proceeds to apply foundation, contour her jawline, nose, lips, and forehead, thicken and define her eyebrows, apply eyeshadow, eyeliner, and false lashes, and for the final touch, don Swift's signature red lipstick and blonde hair. Notably, she doesn't need to apply eyelid tape or glue (or does not do so onscreen); Pony's eyelids have visible creases, which could equally be a result of genetics, surgery, or unfilmed cosmetic interventions.

This video indexes the ways in which neoliberalism simultaneously embeds and disembeds racial difference in social relations.[22] Here, Pony's South Korean face proves the perfect medium for demonstrating makeup's transformative capacities, precisely because of her face's simultaneous distance from and proximity to the Western, white beauty norms metonymically symbolized by "Taylor Swift." In accordance with Swift's global pop star status and the global regime of Western beauty ideals that come attached to her celebrity, Swift's face is held up as a standard of beauty to which other women can (and should) aspire. Yet Pony's sublime capacity for transformation functions alongside her global audience to inject flexibility, multiplicity, and even instability into that standard of beauty.

YouTube no longer allows anyone to access the demographic data of each video's viewership, and accurate viewing metrics are frustratingly scarce for those who do not own the videos themselves (or pay for metrics services through third-party companies). Yet despite India, South Korea, and Japan's growing viewership and uploading activity on YouTube (representing the third, seventh, and ninth largest viewing markets in 2013), YouTube viewership is still largely dominated by the United States and the West. Although Pony is a South Korean makeup artist and her video is subtitled in Korean and English, it is probably safe to assume that least a third of the video's views come not from South Korea but from the United States, Europe, and Australia.[23] The growing US interest in South Korean beauty products, not to mention the gravitational pull of Taylor Swift herself, suggests that a not-insignificant portion of this Western viewership is "mainstream" white viewership.[24]

For this white, Western viewership, Pony's racial difference—her Asianness—is multiply dis/embedded in and from the spectacular nature of her "transformation." The video's viral spectacle depends on the tension between the visual "difference" and "sameness" of Asian and white faces, even as it erases that dependence by casting the transformation merely in terms of makeup products used and the virtuosity of Pony's skill.

On the one hand, race is embedded in the framework of the video. What makes this video spectacular—and worthy of 9.5 million views—is the way in which makeup transforms visual recognizable markers of racial difference into an illusion of racial sameness. With the use of colored contacts, contouring powder on her nose and jaw, and, potentially, eyelid surgery, Pony transforms a recognizable stable of "Asian" features— brown eyes, darker hair, round face, smaller lips, rounder nose—into a recognizable stable of white features, and this is indeed what draws viewers, if commenters can be believed: "this is incredible, she just went from asian to white in 6 minutes [sic]," one commenter wonders, and another one asks, "Why are Asian girls so good at makeup?"

This racial spectacle, however, depends not just on the racial crossing of any nonwhite face into whiteness; embedded within it is a specific visual history of Asian women in the West, which both naturalizes and amplifies Pony's spectacular transformation. Pony's transformation into Taylor Swift highlights Asian American women's ambiguous place in a spectrum of racialized femininities. Relative to white femininity, Asian American femininity is simultaneously *more than* and *too much*: despite, or perhaps because of, her seeming capacity for domestication and submission, "the Asian American woman cannot entirely displace the white woman, whose appeal is reinforced by racial privilege and the power of embodying the norm."[25] Thus are the supposedly typical features of the Asian woman desirable and sexualized, but rendered *less* desirable than the norms of white femininity embodied by Taylor Swift. The crowning moment of the video, after all, is when Pony contours her mouth (making her lips seem to protrude more from her face) and sharply overdraws her lip shape with Swift's signature red shade. Thus do the small, doll-like "Asian" lips—often shaded, in most Western representations of Asian women, a babygirl pink—transform into Swift's trademark well-defined, plump, large red lips. While sexual capital is not sacrificed or gained, the iconic status of Swift's lip shape and color secures it as both the norm and the ideal—that is, both what lips "should look like" and what women should *want* their lips to look like.

On the other hand, Pony's spectacular racial crossing is also not *so* spectacular; after all, the travel from Asian femininity to white femininity is not as far as other racialized crossings, which are less permissible and even less visually possible.[26] Here too, the spectacle of Pony's crossing is premised equally on Asian American and white femininity's relative distance between and *proximity to* each other. In other words, Asian women's faces are different enough to cause a spectacle when merged with white women's faces, but similar enough that the sight does not strike the viewer as excessive and boundary-crossing.

Thus, race is embedded in the foundations of Pony's video, at least for the white and Western portion of the viewing audience. Race simultaneously produces and contains the spectacle, in both instances reifying American white beauty ideals as the desired norm. And yet, simultaneously, race is disembedded from the video; the crossing is coded as race-neutral, the product of an arsenal of products well deployed. Pony's virtuosic skill with makeup then covers over the racial spectacle, which nonetheless drives the video's virality. This sleight of hand, to drive the point home, is foundational to the operations of neoliberalism, and, of course, to makeup itself as a technology of self-improvement: race here, like makeup itself, is meant to be seen but not noticed, drawing the eye and yet going unnamed.

Yet difference cannot be a closed system, endlessly multiplying in containment, without some kind of pressure building and, eventually, leaking out—or in the parlance of makeup, bleeding. Pony's video, then, also disembeds race in the sense that it destabilizes it, removes a little of its ground, as viewers watch racial difference literally disappear; by the end of the video, the distance between Swift's distinctive, and distinctly white, features and Pony's supposedly distinctly non-white features is virtually erased. While I suggested above that makeup leaves little room for "repetition with a difference," here racial phenotypes are performed with such *little* difference that their seeming fixity is itself disturbed.

Laura Kang has argued, for instance, the repetition of the term "yellow" in reference to Asian skin tones belies the fact that, visually, the pigmentation of Asian skin is actually difficult to discern from that of white Westerners. Instead, visual representations of Asians in Western cinema and art had to focus on "some other visible marker," namely, the monolid.[27] Yet even that most visible of racial differences is, in Pony's video, already erased: what might be the most spectacular feat of all—transforming a monolid into an illusion of a double lid with makeup rather than physical intervention—is never seen at all, but takes place off screen, if it takes place at all.

As a result, the disembedding of race is one of neoliberalism's central operations, but it can produce unruly surplus effects. Neoliberalism depends on race and its concealment, but the *erasure* of racial difference, or the destabilizing of race as a mode of physical difference, runs counter to neoliberal aims. In the context of the domestic United States, where the discourse of color-blindness is hegemonic, white consumption of the racial spectacle embedded in YouTube transformation videos highlights neoliberalism's deviousness, as its production of and reliance on racial difference is all but hidden—yet, like highlighter itself, is never able to disappear entirely.

But neoliberalism is not just a domestic phenomenon in the United States. Indeed, this is where the individualization of beauty regimens and the global reach and power of a singular, Western beauty regime come into conflict. While Western audiences may have been drawn to Pony's video because of Taylor Swift's star power, Korean audiences and other transnational fans of Korean beauty were drawn in by Pony's own considerable celebrity. In this framework, Taylor Swift's status as both norm and ideal is rapidly destabilized. Commenters speculate, for example, that by the end of the video, Pony resembles K-pop stars HyunA and Lee Hyori as much as Taylor Swift. What could be read, in a solely Western or US context, as a simple case of an approximation of Western whiteness, becomes something much more complex and fraught with power in the context of the video's global audience. Thus, in the final section of the chapter, I turn to a consideration of Korean and Korean American beauty blogging in the context not just of neoliberalism, but specifically *global* neoliberalism—wherein beauty, and its racial signifiers, is not just a domestic schema but part and parcel of a global regime.

Local Regimens, Global Regimes

Critics of the term "globalization" argue that the seeming democracy of the term obscures the ways in which global power is distributed unevenly, so that Western economic and cultural power—particularly

American power—retains its place of global primacy.[28] In light of the beauty market's central role in the spread of American standards of beauty during the Hollywood studio era in particular, it is tempting to read the global rise of beauty blogging and vlogging, in conjunction with the rise of Korean, Japanese, and other Asian beauty markets, as merely symptomatic of America's continued vice grip on global beauty regimes.[29] Yet cultural hegemony, even at the height of colonialism, never proceeded evenly and unchallenged at the scale of the local; in the age of social media, the introjection of the local into the global, as much as vice versa, can occur rapidly, spontaneously, and with surprising force.[30] The Korean American YouTube videos analyzed in this section highlight a porousness in the access to "culture" as a medium of soft power. That is, they reveal the ways in which transnational flows of commodities also necessarily result in transnational flows of cultural power; while these exchanges are certainly uneven, they are never solely unidirectional, and even point to potential futures in which global powers, cultural and capital, have been reshaped.

In "Korean vs. American Makeup," a video by US-based makeup artist Christina Suh, aka Suhrealmakeup, Suh goes "halfsies" to illustrate the differences between Korean and American beauty trends. That is, she styles one half of her face according to Korean trends, and one half according to US styles, in the same video. Dutifully displaying each product as the genre dictates, Suh does not merely demonstrate the country's differing aesthetics but also uses an entirely different stable of products for each side of her face; for foundation, for example, she applies US-based company Marc Jacobs's ReMARCable Foundation with a Morphe buffing brush on the American side, and Korean-based Innisfree's Longwear Cushion Foundation with the included cushion applicator on the Korean side. The differences between the two aesthetics range from the subtle (Korean women currently prefer thicker, straighter brows, while American women prefer high arches; Suh's Korean contouring is limited to her jawline in order to enhance her face's heart shape, while her American contouring cuts across her face to enhance her cheekbone) to extreme (when finished, Suh's eye makeup on the American side is markedly more intense and requires several more individual products than the Korean side). When she finishes both sides of her face, Suh covers each side with her hand in turn. When the Korean side is displayed, Suh flutters her eyelashes, smiles, squints her eyes, and flashes the peace sign. When she displays the American side, Suh flares her eyes, pouts with a half open mouth, and winks slowly at the camera. As one commenter succinctly puts it, "American: sexy, Korean: cute."

Historians of the globalization of American beauty standards regularly point to the emergence of Hollywood as a global cultural hegemon in the 1930s as American beauty's primary medium of dissemination.[31] *Hallyu*, or the "Korean wave" of culture that has dominated intra-Asian cultural markets since the early 2000s, is, similarly, the vehicle through which Korean beauty standards are spread.[32] Importantly, *hallyu* does not refer to any Korean cultural product, but only those products that have been exposed to a foreign market; the aesthetics of *hallyu*, then, are not primarily domestic aesthetics that secondarily leaked to transnational markets, but, like Hollywood aesthetics, are based in an intentionally transnational economy of consumption, celebrity, and desire.[33]

US media coverage of K-pop focuses exactly on this global intentionality. A 2012 *New Yorker* profile on K-pop—called, tellingly, "Factory Girls"—suggests that "*Hallyu* has erased South Korea's regional reputation as a brutish emerging industrial nation where everything smells of garlic and kimchee, and replaced it with images of prosperous, cosmopolitan life."[34] As this quotation suggests, analyses of Korea's growing cultural "soft power" are relentlessly accompanied by a whiff of US Orientalism; in one breath, journalist John Seabrook here assigns South Korea a "brutishness" that is presumably unique to it as a country and makes passing reference to how weird Koreans smell, all in an article whose title recalls "yellow peril" anxieties of an endlessly multiplying, undifferentiated horde.

Indeed, US coverage of *hallyu* has primarily dovetailed with a fixation on the seeming "factory" production of K-pop girl groups, and particularly the plastic surgery interventions used to homogenize each girl group's appearance. Seabrook describes "an idol making system" as a "Grand Guignol [. . . that] involves rigorous training in foreign languages, acting, and media presence," where "one in ten trainees makes it all the way to debut." He warns that the groups managed by S.M. Entertainment, like supergroup Girls' Generation, may be "too robotic" for the West, and describes the idols' physical attractiveness in literally science fiction terms: "Their faces, chiseled, sculpted, and tapering to a sharp point at the chin, Na'vi style, look strikingly different from the flat, round faces of most Koreans."[35] A piece in *The Atlantic* on "The K-pop Plastic Surgery Obsession" repeatedly refers to Korean women's faces as "identikit," a reference to computer-generated images of faces composed of different archived facial features, usually used to generate police projections of suspects that match witness descriptions.[36] These dehumanizing descriptions, coupled with an emphasis on the technological interventions needed to produce these idols, portray K-pop as an inhuman star-producing machine that is, implicitly, less "organic" and thus less deserving of global adoration than the likes of Taylor Swift, whose celebrity persona is crafted primarily around her "authenticity." Of course, despite K-pop's seeming alien nature, US media is sure to point out that it's still ultimately derivative of American pop music: at *Spin*, journalist David Bevan suggests that "even to a casual observer of turn-of-the-century American pop, the algorithms at work tonight are crystalline: Bigbang borrow from 'N Sync and Se7en channels Michael Jackson by way of Usher; 2NE1 bow at the altar of TLC and Gummy to Mariah Carey."[37]

The preoccupation about the apparent inauthenticity and replicability of K-pop idols is directed primarily, if not entirely, at K-pop girl groups— and by extension, the Korean and Korean American women who fall prey to the "K-pop package."[38] As noted above, US and Western conceptions of Asian and Asian American women have long fixated on their presumed pliability.[39] Yet despite the long history of the Western imagination of Asian women as dolls—infantilized, sexualized, and commodified at once—K-pop idol aesthetics are portrayed as endemic to South Korea in specific: "In Korea," says an interviewee for an ABC News story on Korean plastic surgery, "you go down the streets, you see this girl. And you walk down the street, and you see that girl again. It is actually a different person."[40] Another interviewee, this time in *The Atlantic*, gives an almost identical statement: "When you go to the Gangnam area in Seoul, may girls' faces are similar [. . .] Many people will look and say: I know that pretty girl. She did rotation cut, nose, and eye."[41]

These uncanny and inhuman descriptions of K-pop feminine aesthetics implicitly affirm old Orientalist binaries through neoliberal systems of value. On the one hand, Korean capitalism is characterized as both suspect and belated: The South Korean government's involvement in the transnational distribution and promotion of *hallyu*—its use of "soft power"—is characterized as sinister and exploitative, while descriptions of actual K-pop music and music videos always make reference to their American precedents. Implied in these descriptions of Korean capitalism, characterized here by apparently malevolent state planning and intervention, is a comparison to Western capitalism, with its more traditionally neoliberal relationship between state and capital flow. As Laura Kang suggests, this depiction "indicate[s] the specific impossibility of 'Asian capital' to lay claim to a 'global' status [. . .] because it will always be denoted and demoted by the West-centric teleology of capitalism."[42] On the other, K-pop feminine aesthetics are read as inherently antifeminist, as the culture's "far harsher" standards of beauty and apparent "obsession" with plastic surgery and medical intervention lead to an insidious climate where Korean women are forced to undergo plastic surgery because of self-hate and fear—"not like women who opt for surgery out of empowerment and choice."[43] Once again, the West here is the unspoken point of comparison, where standards of beauty are less harshly enforced and where, apparently, women undergo plastic surgery procedures "out of empowerment and choice" rather than in response to social coercion.

Yet in Christina Suh's video, Korean and American aesthetics are not presented unevenly, with emphasis on American empowerment and choice versus Korean compulsion. Instead, they are presented with parity: one half of her face, exactly, for each. When presented side by side, on the same face, Korean and American aesthetics don't look so different after all; neither can lay claim to some kind of organic, natural, or non-manufactured status, and both come embedded with layers of social meanings and strictures that determine the boundaries of the acceptably, and desirably, feminine. For the American side, Suh winks and pouts, sultry; for the Korean side, Suh "eye smiles" and giggles, cute. Both constructions of femininity are laid bare as equally performative and performable, equally manufactured and manufacturable. Suh's use of two completely different sets of products for each side similarly avoids portraying Korean cosmetics as somehow belated, that is, inferior to or dependent on US-branded products. Instead, the two systems are competing on a seemingly even playing field—her bare face. (Though even faces are never "bare" of signifiers—like Pony, Suh's ability to move flexibly between aesthetic regimes is underpinned by her racial, trans-national, and class positioning.)

Though the playing field is not, in fact, even—and may never be—Suh's video suggests that America, or even the West, is no longer the sole global exporter of cultural ideals, but rather one of many systems competing for global cultural and economic dominance. This is nowhere more clear than in another of Pony's videos, a video diary entitled "Hijab Beauty." In it, Pony dons a hijab and then begins to instruct her viewers on "interesting tricks to flatter the eyes."[44] The video, produced not on her own channel but by the YouTube channel of OnStyle, a South Korean cable and satellite TV channel, is performed completely in Korean, with English subtitles. Here, Pony and OnStyle actively court a trans-national, intra-Asian audience, acknowledging the growing presence of Muslims in Korea. Unlike the Taylor Swift transformation video, which, by using Taylor Swift, targets a "global," or Western, audience primed to consume Taylor Swift's features as both normal and ideal, "Hijab Beauty" seems primarily targeted at South Korean and other Asian consumer markets, like Malaysia and Indonesia, Muslim-majority countries that are also large consumer markets for K-pop and other *hallyu* products, where hijab makeup videos are popular. While there are, no doubt, American and European Muslim women watching hijab makeup videos, such videos could never be geared toward mainstream Western markets; in the United States and Europe, the hijab, and other iterations of the veil, are "implicated as the ultimate negation of life [. . .] a regressive and premodern remnant, a metonym for barbaric Islam, [and] a short-hand for the subjugation of women."[45] Thus "hijab beauty" is a paradox to mainstream US audiences; the possibility of infusing the face of a hijab-wearing woman with liveliness, worthiness, and dignity by beautifying it is already precluded by the fact that the woman is wearing a hijab.

Yet, though the video does not seem explicitly geared toward Western audiences, it nonetheless incorporates elements of American or Western-ized standards of beauty. Notably, Pony actually does apply eyelid tape in this video, even though her own eyes are already creased. She intro-duces the eyelid tape by saying, "For an exotic and defined eye makeup, I'll use the eyelid tape that comes in these fiber strings." Here, in a re-versal of Americans describing Asian aesthetics as "exotic," Pony por-trays double eyelids as inherently "exotic," presumably because of their relative rarity among the Asian audiences she addresses. She then proceeds to apply a "smoky" eye (typically at least three colors, with a dark color emphasizing the eyelid crease and outer corners of the eye), and adds dramatically "winged" liquid eyeliner, a signature Western makeup aesthetic—the one applied by Christina Suh on the "American" half of her face, in fact. In this video, then, Pony deploys Western aesthetics, alongside Korean aesthetics, to train hijab-wearing women in the act of self-beautifying—that is, to invite hijab-wearing women into the realm of the human, the lively, and the beautiful, an idea not only foreign but antithetical to Western aesthetics.

It's tempting to read Pony's video as heralding a future in which Western dominance over cultural norms—and therefore Western-developed and -defined understandings of the body, the individual, and even the human—has declined. But this chapter began with an invocation of neoliberal globalization's almost endless capacity for producing difference; a celebration of this seeming shift in beauty standards or consuming markets seems premature. If, within neoliberalism, the ability to flexibly manipulate legal, economic, and cultural systems across transnational boundaries is a marker of a new kind of globally privileged citizenship, Suhrealmakeup's video reveals that the ability to move fluidly and flexibly between beauty regimes might be another way that neoliberal citizens can access attributions of liveliness, worthiness, and dignity throughout the globe.[46] Here, Western aesthetics—which are always already collapsed with whiteness—are mimed, not as *the* ideal, nor even the norm, but as *an* ideal and *a* norm, which might already be waning in power and status.

These videos then reveal that neoliberalism does not need whiteness or Westernness itself to continue to proliferate; it only needs race or other broad categories of difference that can be exploited in the name of multiplying markets. Thus, the replacement of a Western beauty regime with a different regime of bodily and beauty aesthetics will not necessarily result in an end to neoliberalism itself. As Suhrealmakeup's videos reveal, the markers of humanity, dignity, worthiness, and liveliness can be shifted and resignified because they are fundamentally porous, but they are also resilient; they can be resurfaced and reshaped, individualized or differentiated, without losing their essential structure. Thus, though Pony's video might bestow worthiness and dignity on hijab-wearing women, it does not fundamentally adjust or rearrange those standards but merely extends them to include those who may not have been included before.

In these Korean beauty YouTube videos, Western whiteness's hegemony as the ne plus ultra of beauty is color corrected. That is, these videos each mark the ways in which a Western beauty regime can be and is undone by neoliberalism's reliance on individualization and fragmentation. Because the global spread of neoliberalism has been coded as a Western-centric phenomenon, reliant on Western ideas of empowerment, individualization, and choice, the destabilization of a Western beauty regime seems to signal a potential undoing of neoliberalism itself. But what these videos actually reveal is that neoliberalism's core functions—producing and managing difference—do not need to enshrine Western norms and ideals in order to perpetuate themselves. Instead, racial ideals and cultural norms are encouraged to proliferate, so long as the imperative to participate in consumer markets remains unchallenged. Individual beauty regimens across the globe, in other words, may continue to evolve, and may even move away from reliance on Western standards of beauty. Yet a change in beauty regimen does not mean a change in beauty regime; if neoliberalism is to be undone, it will not be through the proliferation of individual styles and choices, but rather through a radical unchaining of self-making, and "choice" itself, from the practices of consumption and normalization on which neoliberalism relies.

NOTES

1 Lee Krieger, *Celeste and Jesse Forever* (Sony Pictures Home Entertainment, 2013).
2 Lisa Rofel, *Desiring China: Experiments in Neoliberalism, Sexuality, and Public Culture* (Durham, NC: Duke University Press Books, 2007), 15.
3 Mimi Thi Nguyen, "The Biopower of Beauty: Humanitarian Imperialisms and Global Feminisms in an Age of Terror," *Signs* 36, no. 2 (2011): 359–83.
4 "Beauty on YouTube 2015," Pixability, 2015, http://www.pixability.com/.
5 Christine Bacareza Balance, "How It Feels to Be Viral Me: Affective Labor and Asian American YouTube Performance," *WSQ: Women's Studies Quarterly* 40, no. 1–2 (2012): 146; Kayleen Schaefer, "What You Don't Know About the Rise of Korean Beauty," *The Cut*, September 9, 2015, http://nymag.com/.
6 Christine Bacareza Balance and Minh-Ha Pham have both given nuanced accounts of the critical potentialities of Asian American YouTubers and fashion bloggers, arguing that while they are delimited by the systems of consumption

and representation upon which they depend, they are also capable of exploiting the Internet's status as an alternative cultural space in order to contest hegemonic notions about Asian and Asian American bodies and subjectivities. These are necessary and urgent analyses of the eruptive or radical potential of social media in the shadow of global capitalism, but my chapter does not think through how Asian and Asian American beauty YouTubers contest hegemonic norms and structures—something they no doubt both do and do not by varying registers and degrees. Balance, "How It Feels to Be Viral Me"; Minh-Ha T. Pham, "Blog Ambition: Fashion, Feelings, and the Political Economy of the Digital Raced Body," *Camera Obscura* 26, no. 176 (January 1, 2011): 1–37.

7 See, for example, Jennifer Craik, who draws on Pierre Bourdieu to make this argument. Jennifer Craik, *The Face of Fashion: Cultural Studies in Fashion* (New York: Routledge, 2003).

8 Pham, "The Right to Fashion in the Age of Terrorism"; Nguyen, "The Biopower of Beauty."

9 Nikolas Rose, "The Politics of Life Itself," *Theory, Culture & Society* 18, no. 6 (December 1, 2001): 18.

10 Ibid., 31.

11 Ana Sofia Elias, Rosalind Gill, and Christina Scharff, "Aesthetic Labour: Beauty Politics in Neoliberalism," in *Aesthetic Labour: Rethinking Beauty Politics in Neoliberalism*, ed. Ana Sofia Elias, Rosalind Gill, and Christina Scharff (London: Palgrave Macmillan, 2017), 33.

12 For more on the difficulty of defining the "beauty" market exactly because of this ubiquity, see Geoffrey Jones, "Globalization and Beauty: A Historical and Firm Perspective," *EurAmerica* 41, no. 4 (December 2011): 885–916.

13 TheBeautyBreakdown, *My Everyday Natural Pretty Makeup Tutorial*, YouTube, 2016, https://www.youtube.com/watch?v=7TeOInzBp_0.

14 TheBeautyBreakdown, *Effortless Spring Makeup | Tony Moly One Brand Korean Makeup Tutorial*, YouTube, 2016, https://www.youtube.com/watch?v=gu02t054 _KQ; TheBeautyBreakdown, *My Everday Summer to Night Makeup Tutorial | Ft. Korean Makeup from Aritaum*, YouTube, 2016, https://www.youtube.com /watch?v=f4KxRyEdJXo.

15 Judith Butler, *Gender Trouble: Feminism and the Subversion of Identity* (New York: Routledge, 2006).

16 Nancy Fraser, *Fortunes of Feminism: From State-Managed Capitalism to Neoliberal Crisis* (Brooklyn, NY: Verso, 2013), 221–223; see also Inderpal Grewal, *Transnational America: Feminisms, Diasporas, Neoliberalisms* (Durham, NC: Duke University Press, 2005).

17 Jie Yang, "Nennu and Shunu: Gender, Body Politics, and the Beauty Economy in China," *Signs: Journal of Women in Culture and Society* 36, no. 2 (January 1, 2011): 341, 346.

18 Taeyon Kim, "Neo-Confucian Body Techniques: Women's Bodies in Korea's Consumer Society," *Body & Society* 9, no. 2 (June 1, 2003): 97–113.

19 See Eduardo Bonilla-Silva, *Racism without Racists: Color-Blind Racism and the Persistence of Racial Inequality in America*, 4th edition (Lanham, MD: Rowman & Littlefield, 2013).

20 Monolids, also known as epicanthic folds, are a facial feature typically associated with people of Asian, particularly East Asian, descent.

21 Maxine Builder, "Who Is Pony Makeup? 7 Things to Know About Korea's Most Famous Beauty Guru," *Bustle*, November 3, 2015. http://www.bustle.com.

22 A standard descriptor of the intent of neoliberal globalization is the desire to "disembed" markets from any political or social constraint. Developed in part to distinguish neoliberalism from its Keynesian predecessor—also known as "embedded liberalism"—the language of "disembedding," or otherwise freeing markets from government intervention (or social and moral codes) in the name of efficiency and accumulation, is frequently deployed to characterize neoliberal ideology and policy. In reality, however, neoliberalism actually relies on and actively develops both state institutions and social structures that work to further its aims. See Martijn Konings, "Neoliberalism & the State," *Alternate Routes: A Journal of Critical Social Research* no. 23 (2012): 85–98; Wendy Brown, "Neo-Liberalism and the End of Liberal Democracy," *Theory & Event* 7, no. 1 (2003); Aihwa Ong, *Neoliberalism as Exception: Mutations in Citizenship and Sovereignty* (Durham, NC: Duke University Press, 2006).

23 "The Top 10 Countries in YouTube Viewership Outside the USA [INFO-GRAPHIC]," *New Media Rockstars*, March 18, 2013, http://newmediarockstars.com.

24 US beauty giant stores Sephora and Ulta have both added "Korean Beauty" sections to their stores in recent years. According to NY Mag, in the first half of 2015, the total export value of Korean beauty products to the United States was $52 million, already a 60% increase from the previous year. Schaefer, "What You Don't Know About the Rise of Korean Beauty."

25 This portrayal, Koshy reminds us, builds on a long history of "Asia" being figured as an extraterritorial site of desire for white American men; this racialized erotic, based on tropes of the perpetual foreignness and exoticness of Asian women, nonetheless resulted in thousands of Asian women entering the United States as wives of American military men during the mid-twentieth century. Post–second-wave feminism, the same trope of the sexual allure of Asian feminine submissiveness, was revived in juxtaposition to the unruly white American feminist. "Thus by a long circuitous route we arrive at a postmodern American moment when Asian American women's sexuality—earlier defined as extraterritorial because the sexual license it represented had to be excluded from the moral order of the nation and marriage—is by the late twentieth century domesticated to mediate a crisis for the white bourgeois sexual order." Susan Koshy, *Sexual Naturalization: Asian Americans and Miscegenation* (Stanford, CA: Stanford University Press, 2004), 37.

26 These other, *un*visible racial crossings haunt the visible: one commenter wondered, "Would people call it blackfacing if she would recreate a black celeb's face

[*sic*]?" Gina Marchetti has argued that, in the history of American cinema, "Hollywood used Asians and Asian Americans [. . .] as signifiers of racial otherness to avoid the far more immediate racial tensions between blacks and whites or the ambivalent mixture of guilt and enduring hatred toward Native Americans and Hispanics." Gina Marchetti, *Romance and the "Yellow Peril": Race, Sex, and Discursive Strategies in Hollywood Fiction* (Berkeley: University of California Press, 1994), 6.

27 Laura Hyun Yi Kang, *Compositional Subjects: Enfiguring AsianAmerican Women* (Durham, NC: Duke University Press, 2002), 104.

28 Political theorists Leo Panitch and Sam Gindin have argued that despite claims that American hegemony has waned in the era of globalization, the United States maintains an "informal empire" by positioning itself as the superintendent of global finance, leaving America central to both the making and the sustaining of global capitalism. Leo Panitch and Sam Gindin, *The Making of Global Capitalism: The Political Economy of American Empire* (Brooklyn, NY: Verso, 2013).

29 Jones, "Globalization and Beauty."

30 Genevieve Clutario reveals that even in the Philippines, during the period in which US empire was not "informal" but literal, American beauty standards were not hegemonic; instead, they unevenly interacted with local histories and structures to shape distinctively Filipino standards of beauty. Sharon Heijin Lee, similarly, cautions against reading Korean beauty standards—even those that seem to favor typically white or Western features, like the preference for double-lidded eyes—solely within a framework of American global dominance. Genevieve Clutario, "The Appearance of Filipina Nationalism: Body, Nation, Empire" (PhD diss., University of Illinois at Urbana-Champaign, 2014); Sharon Heijin Lee, "Lessons from 'Around the World with Oprah': Neoliberalism, Race, and the (geo)politics of Beauty," *Women & Performance: A Journal of Feminist Theory* 18, no. 1 (March 1, 2008): 25–41.

31 Kathy Peiss, "Educating the Eye of the Beholder: American Cosmetics Abroad," *Daedalus* 131, no. 4 (2002): 102; Jones, "Globalization and Beauty," 893.

32 *Hallyu* is broadly characterized in waves; the first wave was defined largely by the surprise success of Korean televisions dramas, like *Winter Sonata*, sold for the highest price Japan had ever paid for a Korean dramatic import in 2003. The second wave, or *hallyu* 2.0, is characterized simultaneously by the success of Korean pop groups and the use of social media as a medium of transmission. Jeongmee Kim, "Why Does *Hallyu* Matter? The Significance of the Korean Wave in South Korea," *Critical Studies in Television: An International Journal of Television Studies* 2, no. 2 (January 1, 2007): 50; Dal Yong Jin and Kyong Yoon, "The Social Mediascape of Transnational Korean Pop Culture: *Hallyu* 2.0 as Spreadable Media Practice," *New Media & Society*, October 16, 2014, 6.

33 Kim, "Why Does *Hallyu* Matter?," 49–50; see also Stephen J. Epstein and Rachael M. Joo, "Multiple Exposures: Korean Bodies and the Transnational Imagination," *Asia-Pacific Journal* 10, no. 33.1 (August 13, 2012): 1–19; Youngmin Choe, *Tourist*

Distractions: Traveling and Feeling in Transnational Hallyu Cinema (Durham, NC: Duke University Press, 2016).

34 John Seabrook, "Factory Girls," *New Yorker*, October 8, 2012, http://www.newy orker.com.

35 The Na'vi are a fictional race of alien creatures, featured in the film *Avatar*, directed by James Cameron (Hollywood, CA; 20th Century Fox, 2010), theatrical release.

36 Zara Stone, "The K-Pop Plastic Surgery Obsession," *The Atlantic*, May 24, 2013, http://www.theatlantic.com.

37 David Bevan, "Seoul Trained: Inside Korea's Pop Factory," *Spin*, March 26, 2012, http://www.spin.com.

38 Stone, "The K-Pop Plastic Surgery Obsession."

39 This submissiveness, as Aljosa Puzar reminds us, is not just imagined as a suppleness of personality, but also of body and face. Puzar highlights the usage of "doll-related imagery and metaphors in regard to Asian femininities" in both the United States and Asia, arguing that the common confluence of the phrase "Asian doll" "in the English-speaking world is indicative of the preserved Western employment of centuries-old orientalist motifs: dollified Asian femininity is the old co-product of Western gaze acting together with various local patriarchal circumstances based on the image of docile and malleable yet exotic and eroticized femininity." Aljosa Puzar, "Asian Dolls and the Westernized Gaze," *Asian Women* 27, no. 2 (June 1, 2011): 90.

40 Juju Chang and Victoria Thompson, "South Korea's Growing Obsession with Plastic Surgery," *ABC News*, June 23, 2014, http://abcnews.go.com.

41 Stone, "The K-Pop Plastic Surgery Obsession."

42 Laura Hyun Yi Kang, "Late (Global) Capital," in *The Routledge Companion to Asian American and Pacific Islander Literature*, ed. Rachel C. Lee (New York: Routledge, 2014), 307.

43 Stone, "The K-Pop Plastic Surgery Obsession."

44 Pony, *Pony's Beauty Diary—Hijab Makeup*, YouTube (OnStyle, 2014), https://www .youtube.com/watch?v=xqbqgfjn3Ic.

45 Nguyen, "The Biopower of Beauty," 365.

46 See Aihwa Ong, *Flexible Citizenship: The Cultural Logics of Transnationality* (Durham, NC: Duke University Press, 1999); Jodi Melamed, *Represent and Destroy: Rationalizing Violence in the New Racial Capitalism* (Minneapolis: University of Minnesota Press, 2011).

5

Fashioning the Field in Vietnam

An Intersectional Tale of Clothing, Femininities, and the Pedagogy of Appropriateness

ANN MARIE LESHKOWICH

In Vietnam during the 1990s, the rapid expansion of a market economy led to dramatic social and cultural transformation, particularly in urban areas such as Ho Chi Minh City. The growing visibility of a conspicuously consuming middle class sparked vociferous debates about morality and national identity that often focused on claims about proper femininity. Public concern, sometimes rising to the level of moral panic, typically centered on younger women whose limited experience of revolutionary values made them seem vulnerable to the decadence of the marketplace. But the character and comportment of older women warranted scrutiny as well. Having experienced war and a decade of high socialist restructuring in Vietnam's southern region, women in midlife provided fertile ground for claims-making about the relationship between a national revolutionary past and a global market future.

These issues came into sharp relief during "Fashion for the Forties" (Thời Trang Tuổi 40), a state-sponsored show held in March 1997 that focused on styles for women in their forties. The event depicted an appropriate midlife Vietnamese femininity as mature, attractive, self-confident, and modest. More subtly, the show's vision of midlife called upon a generation of wives, mothers, and workers at the height of their productivity and family responsibilities to model for younger and older cohorts how Vietnamese might appropriately engage with an individual-ized, globalized, and sexualized marketplace in ways that would preserve their moral and cultural values. Fashion for the Forties also spoke back to racialized global fashion hierarchies by highlighting Vietnam as a source of stylistic creativity. As such, the show contributed to a budding trend throughout the region in which Asian governments promoted development policies to move "up the value chain" by establishing Asian cities as hubs of design innovation in a knowledge economy, rather than simply reserves of inexpensive labor for producing others' designs in a manufacturing economy (Tu 2011, 12). Fashion for the Forties suggested that Vietnamese fashion was on the cusp of receiving international attention—a metaphor for Vietnam's development more broadly—and that what women wore and how they behaved were central to the attainment of this recognition.

By exploring the background context for, organization of, and public reaction to Fashion for the Forties, this chapter analyzes how fashion in Vietnam during the 1990s had become what Bourdieu (1977) terms a field: a system of social positions in which agents vie for various forms of capital. In this case, the competing forms of symbolic and economic capital associated with what Vietnamese officials call a "market economy with socialist orientation" (*kinh tế thị trường định hướng xã hội chủ nghĩa*)—market socialism for short—were being fashioned through the bodies and aspirations of women in midlife. This fashioning explicitly centered on a concept of the "appropriate" (*phù hợp*) in which Vietnamese women's bodies would display a form of proper femininity that would judiciously mediate between traditional cultural values and transnational modernity. Fashion shows, especially state-sponsored ones such as Fashion for the Forties, served as key training sites in this emerging pedagogy of the appropriate.

The Fashion for the Forties show was a field in a second sense of the term: a site in which I conducted ethnographic research. My interest in the show had developed from my primary fieldwork with cloth and clothing traders in Ho Chi Minh City's central marketplace (Leshkowich 2014). Eager to find out how market stallholders, most of them women, learned about style trends and determined which merchandise to sell, I frequently attended fashion shows and related events. Sometimes a market trader accompanied me, and we could discuss what styles were attractive or potentially lucrative. Other times, such as the Fashion for the Forties show, I went alone. I was part of the first generation of postwar, non-Vietnamese researchers to conduct intensive participant observation, and my endeavors occasionally generated suspicion or confusion. Far more often, however, interlocutors enthusiastically embraced the opportunity to have me bear witness to individual experience. Days in the marketplace rushed by, as the briefest question or slightest show of interest in an episode caused stories to tumble forth. As Paul Rabinow (1977) has argued, such stories were not direct reports of what had happened, nor were they raw snapshots extracted from memory, but rather, intersubjectively crafted tales constructed through the give and take of conversation with the ethnographer. I came to see that my identity mattered greatly. To my interlocutors, mostly middle-aged women from southern Vietnam whose families had been on the losing side of the war, it was significant that the audience for their stories was a white American woman then in her late twenties: old enough to have memories of that time, but too young to be personally implicated in her own country's experiences. My status as "younger sister" to my informants lent their stories a didactic cast, yet my being a graduate student at a prestigious foreign university also imparted the authority that, through a dissertation and subsequent publications, I could carry their stories to a wider global audience. My interest served as a sign of validation: In suggesting that individuals' stories mattered, I prompted those stories to be told in new ways.

We have, then, two fields, each constructed through narrative: the field of a fashion show through which culture brokers made didactic claims about appropriate femininity to stake positions as arbiters of Vietnam's present and future, and the field site of a marketplace in which traders voiced their experiences to a graduate student in the hope that they might be related to a broader audience in the United States—a geopolitical power that many traders felt had abandoned their families two decades earlier, even as it had since offered a new home to many of their friends and relatives.[1] These fields operated on seemingly distinct scales: one national, significant, and public, the other located in one marketplace, mundane, and relatively private. To the extent that they intersected, it seemed largely unidirectional, with authoritative ideas about appropriate Vietnamese femininity providing a field in which traders attempted to position themselves through their daily activities.[2]

What I did not expect in conducting ethnographic fieldwork at the Fashion for the Forties show was that my own position as a (then) young, foreign woman and PhD candidate would itself also become part of the field in Bourdieu's sense. In an unexpected turn of events detailed below, my presence at the event generated national press coverage. Much to my own discomfort, my act of fieldwork rather briefly played a role in bolstering a designer's and a reporter's claims to expertise about Vietnamese fashion and femininity—a field that I otherwise thought myself merely to be documenting. For a fleeting moment, my words and, even more important, my raced and gendered embodiment were deployed to validate state-sponsored construction of fashion through its pedagogy of appropriateness. Although particular to the novelty of foreign research about Vietnamese culture and society in the 1990s, this episode highlights the dialogic, intersectional, and embodied politics of knowledge production and circulation that shape the political economy of fashion—and research on it—in Vietnam and other globalizing contexts.

A Successful Fashioning of Vietnamese Femininity

"As Vietnam becomes integrated into ASEAN and the world, the behavior and comportment of women, especially the task of carefully preserving the *áo dài* of our ethnic group, is an issue of the utmost importance" (Thúy Hà 1997, 9). Phan Lương Cẩm, the wife of then Prime Minister Võ Văn Kiệt, made these remarks to the press at the Fashion for the Forties show. Her comments succinctly captured both the headiness and peril of that particular moment in Vietnam. After a decade of steady growth resulting from market-oriented policies, Vietnam finally seemed ready to take its place in a global community of nations. Standards of living had risen dramatically, and a growing urban middle class embraced the spirit of a popular saying, "Eat deliciously, dress beautifully" (*ăn ngon mặc đẹp*). Ho Chi Minh City was in the throes of what newspapers and cultural critics dubbed a "fashion craze" (*cơn sốt thời trang*). Thousands of people flocked to runway shows, beauty and dress contests, and variety productions that highlighted recent collections by domestic and foreign designers. Many more turned to newspapers and magazines for expert advice about which styles were most chic, modern, and appropriate for different social situations and types of people. In the midst of such great optimism, commentators ranging from journalists to government officials to academics nonetheless expressed fears that in the rush to become part of the "modern world," Vietnam might lose a sense of the identity and independence that it had spent most of

Figure 5.1. Amateur models in business attire at the Fashion for the Forties show
(photo by Ann Marie Leshkowich).

the twentieth century fighting to achieve. Fashion shows became pedagogical venues to craft women whose appropriate embodied femininity
would represent the future envisioned by state-affiliated cognoscenti.

By all accounts, Fashion for the Forties, featuring creations by Minh
Hạnh, noted designer and director of the national Fashion Design Institute (FADIN), achieved its goal of "encouraging and orienting" middle-
aged women at the peak of their careers to choose clothing "appropriate
[phù hợp] for their age and work circumstances, lifestyles . . . fashions
that are modern [hiện đại], worldly, yet rich in traditional color" (B.T.
1997). One journalist described the event, held on International Wom-
en's Day, as "One of the liveliest activities of this year's March 8th celebration" (Thúy Thúy 1997). Sponsored and highly publicized by the Ho
Chi Minh City Women's Newspaper (Báo Phụ Nữ), the event had quickly
sold out.

The models for this fashion show were amateurs: regular women from
different walks of life selected and trained by Minh Hạnh especially for
the evening. In the audience, smiling husbands and children clapped as
their wives and mothers radiantly moved across the stage in business

Figure 5.2. Eveningwear at the Fashion for the Forties show (photo by Ann Marie Leshkowich).

attire, sportswear, and eveningwear (figures 5.1 and 5.2). In keeping with fashion show practices in Vietnam, the women also modeled *áo dài*, the outfit to which the prime minister's wife had explicitly referred. Often touted as Vietnam's traditional or national costume, the *áo dài* consists of a long tunic with mandarin collar, raglan sleeves, and high side slits worn over wide-legged pants. The models moved gracefully, but most betrayed a hint of embarrassment. That these otherwise self-confident and successful professional women appeared uncomfortable as they paraded across the catwalk seemed only to enhance the event's charm. As one reporter wrote, "But tonight, on the fashion stage, every power, every sharp-witted skill of everyday life disappeared, and they were simply gentle women, deep, and rather shy" (Thúy Thúy 1997).

In addition to the personal pleasure many felt on seeing the women in their lives transformed into demure models for the night, audience and participants alike seemed to embrace Minh Hạnh's pedagogical project of showing women in their forties how to dress appropriately. One participant, a professional singer, said that the event taught her that women in their forties had value, and that they had to choose styles and colors appropriate for themselves (Thúy Thúy 1997). Another woman, a housewife, gushed, "In the eyes of my husband, I'm so much more beautiful now than ever before. From now on, I will be more careful when I buy clothes" (ibid.). The journalist recounting their words echoed their sentiments: "Although they're in their forties, women are still as beautiful as twenty-year-olds and will be even more attractive if they know how to choose for themselves outfits that fit their individual figures, jobs, and positions" (ibid.).

The outfits themselves showcased new looks that were nonetheless viewed as appropriate for wear in the real world (Thúy Hà 1997). Observers positively compared the event's pragmatic approach to the frivolity of most fashion shows. A male journalist told the *Women's Newspaper*, "This is the most practical fashion show, from liberation [1975] until now. For so long, young people have paid attention to fashion shows primarily for . . . fun! But here, these ladies have a genuine need, a real benefit" (ibid.). Another man told a television reporter that his only criticism was that men, too, needed such an evening of instruction. The appearance of the prime minister's wife and her later remarks to the press gave the event the seal of official approval. Indeed, in commenting on the importance of women's appearance on the eve of Vietnam's global integration, First Lady Phan Lương Cẩm also praised "the Women's Newspaper's initiative in organizing this event with the idea of directing fashion for women in their forties like this" (ibid.).

The Field of Modern Vietnamese Femininity

Fashion for the Forties ended with a spectacular finale. The designer Minh Hạnh received a standing ovation, further securing her position as an expert crafting contemporary Vietnamese femininity and individuality. Through her care and stewardship that night, she had projected her vision of how Vietnamese women of achievement and serious purpose could express their unique identities and inner beauty, particularly their shy grace, outward in ways that would be both appropriate and attractive. In doing so, she positioned herself as an arbiter of how women could indeed be fashioned as fitting symbols of Vietnam's careful integration with worldly modernity. But what exactly did Vietnamese in the 1990s envision modernity (*hiện đại*) to be? And why had "the behavior and comportment" of women, especially the goal of "appropriateness," become so central to attaining it?

The concept of modernity is simultaneously self-evident and elusive. It is self-evident because people generally claim to know modernity when they see it and typically envision it as a kind of prosperous, technologically advanced global community through which people, things, and ideas circulate.[3] Modernity is nonetheless elusive because the precise nature of those circulating people, things, and ideas seems constantly to shift as technology, modes of doing business, and people's ideas change. What constitutes modernity and who embodies it must therefore continually be assessed, revised, and negotiated. These processes permit the emergence of "multiple," even "alternative" modernities, but they are also crosscut by hierarchies.[4] Certain groups or regions possess disproportionate authority to discern and differentiate which people are modern or traditional, which ideas are new and noteworthy, or which items of clothing are fashionable or passé; in short, which forms of modernity count as authentic, significant, and powerful. The result is that other groups may consistently find themselves approaching the finish line in the race to become modern, only to lag behind again as the parameters of modernity shift and the line moves into the distance.

It is this dynamic of an elusive modernity that seems within reach and yet always slips beyond the grasp, rather than modernity as some objective condition of being, that has shaped Vietnamese discussions over the past century and a half. The French colonial civilizing mission adeptly entrenched the worldview among Vietnamese intelligentsia that human history had been a steady march of progress based on struggle and competition (Tai 1992; P. Taylor 2001). Vietnamese came to desire the colonizers' science, technology, and commerce. Almost as soon as members of the Vietnamese intelligentsia adopted this vision of modernity, however, European conceptions of what constituted it shifted. This produced a dynamic, central to Bhabha's (1997) formulation of mimicry, in which Vietnam was perpetually "not quite" modern; in Philip Taylor's words, "Tradition is forever renewing itself, while 'modernity' is always just arriving in Vietnam" (2001, 9). But this dilemma offered a potential resolution: The racialized native Otherness that European rule both needed and derided could serve as the basis for crafting a uniquely modern nationalist identity rooted in a tradition superior to more corrupt Western values (see, e.g., Chatterjee 1993; Chakrabarty 1997; Tarlo 1996). Preserving this inner core became an explicitly gendered project, a point to which I return below.

With the embrace of a market economy and talk of global integration in the 1990s, the anxieties and possibilities of Vietnamese modernity reemerged with particular force. Trying to replicate models from Singapore, South Korea, or Japan, which in turn had been adapted from Europe and North America, Vietnam's national development project could be described as a form of mimicry.[5] Here, again, the danger was that in developing a modern exterior, Vietnam might lose its unique core: sleek new skyscrapers, hotels, office spaces, and supermarkets without cultural distinctiveness. As in the colonial era, an expedient solution to the contemporary problem of mimicry was to celebrate an essentialized racial, ethnic, or cultural core that remained unique and valuable. The neo-Confucian "Asian Values" rhetoric popularized in the 1980s and 1990s by Singapore's Prime Minister Lee Kuan Yew held enormous appeal among the Vietnamese intellectuals and policymakers I encountered, for it offered a way to borrow from the West without reducing Vietnam to an inferior copy of a superior original. If Vietnamese could remember who they are by holding on to the distinctiveness bequeathed to them by tradition and defended through revolutionary struggle, they could determine what external borrowing and adaptation would be "appropriate" (*phù hợp*).

With fashion being key to the material and ideological crafting of Vietnamese modernity, the term "appropriate" surfaced often in my conversations with Ho Chi Minh City market sellers, boutique owners, designers, and consumers. Widespread excitement about the new fashions made available by economic reforms—the fashion craze mentioned above—was tempered by assertions that international styles had to be carefully mediated so that consumers would learn how to select styles appropriate for their personal attributes, cultural setting, and socioeconomic position. The required modifications involved notions of modesty, but my interlocutors also repeatedly noted that changes to cut and color were necessary to make European and North American fashions suitable for Vietnamese women's racialized bodies. Accustomed to seeing fashion as a realm of personal expression, I was surprised by the hunger of many fashion retailers and customers for expert guidance. Minh Hạnh catered to and further entrenched this desire with pedagogically motivated collections, shows, and media statements, Fashion for the Forties being just one example.

These conversations provide glimpses into how, in Vietnam as in many other countries, debates about cultural appropriateness often hinge on claims about gender. Some observers hold colonial regimes responsible for creating a gendered distinction between Western modernity and local tradition so that men, particularly those in the burgeoning ranks of the middle class, enjoyed greater latitude to pursue modernity through Western education, employment, and dress, while women, as keepers of domestic order and socializers of children, bore greater responsibility for maintaining an appearance, behavior, and morality consistent with prevailing views of tradition.[6] Women's savvy appreciation of tradition could admit some aspects of modernity, such as domestic science (Hancock 1999), so long as they also recognized its flaws—materialism, lack of spirituality, moral decay, domestic discord, etc. Elite nationalist men expected women to wear "traditional" clothes, although some of these outfits were "reformed" in dialogue with European clothing aesthetics.[7] This dynamic gave birth to the Vietnamese áo dài (Leshkowich 2003). Women who directly adopted Western dress, cosmetics, or styles of comportment were condemned as gross or shocking "new women" akin to hussies (Chakrabarty 1997; Tai 1992, 96). While most scholars see these debates as largely symbolic, Ikeya argues in her study of Burmese nationalist condemnation of women's "sheer blouses" that critiques of women's inappropriate mimicry reflected the actual material transformations wrought by colonial labor, education, and migration policies that had appeared to lower the status of Burmese men and to raise that of women (Ikeya 2008).

Market economic growth reignited both this gender symbolism and concerns about how changing relations of production and consumption might differentially affect men's and women's status. Initial waves of foreign investment and rising domestic affluence generated feminized jobs in light industry, retail, and administrative support (Earl 2014), while perceptions of lessened commitment to the state sector threatened male jobs in the bureaucracy or military. Defining who Vietnamese women were or should be thus became key to securing Vietnam's national identity. This is why the prime minister's wife identified women's behavior and appearance, particularly continued wearing of the *áo dài*, as crucially important during Vietnam's global integration.[8] At the same time, women were depicted in cautionary tales in the media and popular fiction as liminal and untrustworthy. They therefore needed to be scrutinized and held accountable to strict standards for appropriate behavior.

The field of opinion about Vietnamese modernity thus involved disciplining women's expressions of identity with dimensions that were both material—the limitation or monitoring of women's access to foreign cultural elements—and ideological—the assertion that femininity rested on the passive expression of a preexisting core, rather than any conscious process of imitation or performance. These came together in the fashion show, with Minh Hạnh pedagogically enacting her ideological claims to expertise about appropriate Vietnamese femininity through the concrete contours of the clothes that she had crafted. Like the creators of the *áo dài* decades earlier, she was asserting her role as gatekeeper who could borrow cultural features from powerful outsiders such as China, France, or the United States—a role also asserted by other intellectuals, political leaders, revolutionary veterans, and credentialed experts eager to shape Vietnam's future.[9]

The 40 or so women in the fashion show, in turn, enacted an appropriately modern and status-enhancing Vietnamese femininity, in three distinct ways. First, the styles they wore and their movements during the event epitomized respectability, modesty, and simple elegance. Second, the circumstances that brought them to the stage—their willing submission to Minh Hạnh's expertise in fashioning them—reinforced social expectations that women's encounters with modernity needed to be superintended and assessed by someone else, in this case a high-status, state-employed designer. Third, the women's positions as wives and mothers and the fact that they were old enough to remember the struggles of what the Vietnamese government refers to as the American War allowed them to occupy stable, respectable subject positions. While their gender made them liminal subjects in need of surveillance, these were women of accomplishment and substance who had internalized the standards of appropriate Vietnamese femininity, who understood the stakes involved in maintaining them, and who had made an investment in conforming to them as part of their movement toward the middle class.

When Fieldwork(er) Becomes Field

The discussion thus far has focused on how Fashion for the Forties revealed the centrality of dress to a gendered pedagogy of appropriateness: an ideological and material assertion of authority to shape Vietnam's future by determining how Vietnamese women should act and appear. I would soon learn, however, that I was no mere observer of this Bourdieu-esque "field." Indeed, the very fact that I, as a foreign researcher, showed an interest in Vietnamese fashion at all quickly became deployed as a didactic lesson about the desirability of the path that Minh Hạnh was forging.

I had first met Minh Hạnh in February 1997, when she judged a youth fashion contest. During that event, she had taken the young women contestants to task for an excessive form of mimicry that strove too hard to embody a vision of Western high fashion that she deemed inappropriate for their age and daily activities (Leshkowich 2009). Surprised by her diatribe, I requested an interview. During our lengthy conversation the next day, Minh Hạnh articulated her desire to create a unique Vietnamese style that would serve as a foundation for the country's fashion industry. Such an endeavor required structure and hierarchical expertise to guide Vietnam away from its current global market position as merely a source of cheap labor to manufacture foreign designs. It also required actively inculcating an appreciation for local and traditional styles, such as silk jacquard (tơ tằm) or the woven textiles (thổ cẩm) associated with different ethnic minority groups. She continued by ascribing fashion faux pas committed by newly affluent Vietnamese women to a lack of discerning knowledge needed to cultivate compelling personal style. Nearly forty at the time, Minh Hạnh described how her "adventurous" next step would be to lead a fashion "revolution" for women whose survival of the war and postwar periods and current pursuit of success had perhaps come at the cost of their beauty and, consequently, family happiness.[10] She promised to get me a ticket to her upcoming show, which I received shortly before the event.

Figure 5.3. The author, wearing a suit designed by Minh Hạnh, being interviewed at Fashion for the Forties for the Vietnamese television show, "Fashion and Life."

In the intervening month between our interview and the show, buzz in the press began to build, thanks in part to sponsorship of the event by the *Women's Newspaper* (*Báo Phụ Nữ*). Meanwhile, on a trip to Hanoi at the end of February, I had occasion to meet Vũ Thanh Hường, a reporter for the television show, "Fashion and Life" (Thời Trang và Cuộc Sống), that had just begun airing as part of the popular lifestyle offerings on Vietnam Television 3 (VTV3). Thanh Hường told me that she would be covering Fashion for the Forties and suggested that she might interview me there. I agreed.

On the night of the show, I arrived at the packed theater wearing an ensemble that I hoped would be attractive, yet businesslike: a maroon cotton pantsuit made-to-order from Minh Hạnh's own FADIN line (figure 5.3). Conspicuous for my foreignness, I was easily located by Thanh Hường for an on-camera interview focusing on my impressions of the event and of Vietnamese women's dress more generally. Thanh Hường then told me that she wanted to do a feature segment on my research based on a longer interview and some footage of me working in my apartment. We arranged to meet at my rented room two days later. I dressed for that occasion more casually, with plain black pants paired with a t-shirt and what I recall as another of Minh Hạnh's designs, a striped, fitted vest made from ethnic minority textiles (figure 5.4).

Figure 5.4. The fieldworker typing up notes in her apartment: "Traveling from Hanoi to Ho Chi Minh City, this future PhD already clearly understands our country's customs and culture."

The episode featuring Fashion for the Forties and my interview aired on national television later that month. Thanh Hường opens the show by declaring that every woman wants to be beautiful, but that fashion is skewed toward the young. A marketplace filled with jeans and short skirts has little to offer women in their forties that is attractive and appropriate for their family and life circumstances. Amidst footage of the career, special occasion, and casual wear segments from Minh Hạnh's show, Thanh Hường's voice-overs echo other press coverage about the event: the difficulty that women in this age range have choosing appropriate clothing and the notable fact that the models were regular women who wished to dress in ways that would reflect and advance the country's modern development. Snippets of interviews with audience members praise the event for showing women what to wear and include the suggestion mentioned above about the need for a similar program for men. The program then turns to a segment from CNN Style featuring Trish McEvoy makeup with dubbed Vietnamese translation. Fashion coverage in Vietnam frequently included this kind of interlude that served to introduce the audience to international trends and compensated for the lack of domestic footage.

After coverage of the dress rehearsal for Fashion in the Forties, the show turns to my interview, all of it in Vietnamese. Thanh Hường introduces me as an American graduate student conducting research about fashion in Vietnam. When asked why I chose to conduct this research in Vietnam, I answer by noting the importance for Americans of learning about Vietnam not just as a war, but as a country and people with "a rich civilization and history." Explaining that I have conducted research "from Hanoi to Ho Chi Minh City," Thanh Hường asks what had by then become a familiar question, "What do you think about the way that Vietnamese women in general dress?" Deciding to err on the side of diplomacy rather than analytical depth, I earnestly declare that Vietnamese women dress in a manner that is very polite, very beautiful, and very fashionable. I note that this may be a new trend, perhaps something that has become possible only in the past five years or even more recently.

From here, the scene shifts to footage of the fieldworker at home—a contemporary video equivalent to the "researcher in a tent" photos in classic ethnographies that imparted the authority of having been there. After an establishment shot of my desk, armoire, and modest cooking area, the camera zooms in to show me typing notes on my computer, my spiral notebook propped up at my side. In accordance with my wishes, the camera angle and movement make it impossible to decipher my notes, but it is evident that they are written in Vietnamese. The camera then closes in on the Vietnamese dictionaries piled on my desk and newspaper clippings adorning my walls. Thanh Hường's voice-over describes my research:

> It's not just me, but also the traders at Bến Thành market who are very surprised when they meet this young American woman with her fairly fluent Vietnamese conducting research about Vietnamese fashion. Yes, foreigners like Ann Marie who are researching Vietnamese fashion don't just look at fashion, but also consider culture, because fashion is one part of our ethnic culture. [Camera shows me holding a picture that I've taken in Bến Thành market.] Traveling from Hanoi to Ho Chi Minh City, this future PhD already clearly understands our country's customs and culture.

The scene concludes with a shot of me underlining and annotating my notebook, as Thanh Hường declares, "Ann Marie in particular, plus a lot of other foreign entities, are turning toward the Vietnamese fashion market to understand more about a particular perspective, a culture collected together." The camera zooms in on a framed snapshot of my husband and me that, as our attire clearly suggests, was taken at our wedding.

Returning to the interview at the fashion show, Thanh Hường asks me to compare how women in the United States and Vietnam dress. Ever ready with bland generalizations, I note the tendency to dress for comfort in the United States, in spite of comparative wealth and fashion options, versus the focus on dressing elegantly and decorously in the relatively new Vietnamese fashion scene. I predict that "convergence between these two tendencies will make both sides more beautiful." Gathering momentum, I invoke Vietnam's national costume: "In the past in Vietnam, there was the *áo dài* that served as a symbol for the entire Vietnamese nation. And when women wore the *áo dài*, they made an unforgettable impression." As edited for broadcast, this part of the interview serves as a voice-over for a quick scene from the *áo dài* portion of Minh Hạnh's show. Lest my statement imply that embracing Western-style clothing might make a less favorable impact, the camera returns to me as I conclude, "As Vietnamese women today pay so much attention to fashion and have such a decorous, beautiful way of dressing, they will direct the development of Vietnamese fashion so that it can be more beautiful every day."

I found the whole exercise—then and now—cringe-worthy. My goal was to repay a reporter for the access and information that she had provided in a manner that would sacrifice neither my dignity nor research prospects. So nervous was I about the possibility of causing offense that I pandered to my audience by praising Vietnamese women, Vietnamese culture, and Vietnamese fashion in a manner that no doubt seemed well-intentioned, but perhaps gave the audience cause to question my credentials as a "future PhD." As my always-frank landlady put it when we watched the segment, "You look better on tv, but you sound better in person."

Reflections on Fashion Fieldwork in Vietnam

Happy to have my three minutes of fame on Vietnamese television behind me, I completed my dissertation fieldwork on clothing and market traders. I began to present my research on Vietnamese fashion, including an unpublished paper on Fashion for the Forties that featured much the same analysis as I offer above, but omitted my moment in the media spotlight. Other, published pieces explored the high stakes surrounding women's appearance and behavior to argue that these illuminated how market socialism was ideologically and materially constructed in class- and gender-specific ways (Leshkowich 2003, 2008, 2009, 2012). I commented on the overblown rhetoric surrounding women's dress choices within Vietnam and the ways that international celebration of the *áo dài* or of Indo-chic—moments with rhetoric that I and a co-author critiqued as Orientalist and self-Orientalizing (Leshkowich and Jones 2003)—were met with acclaim by the Vietnamese designers and merchants I knew. The cultural and economic dimensions of these moves were fraught. On the one hand, identifying particular styles as quintessentially Vietnamese, and hence unique for that fact, could provide a point of entry for Vietnamese designers and entrepreneurs into global fashion or local tourist markets. On the other hand, this label risked reproducing Orientalist stereotypes of Vietnamese fashion as somehow essentially Vietnamese and hence consigning its styles to ethnic chic or other "exotic" niche markets. Designers might sell clothes, but they would consequently become known not as individual auteurs and innovators, but as repositories of cultural heritage or, perhaps slightly better, as skilled translators and intermediaries between the local and global, the traditional and modern. Stereotypical or not, such praise at least signaled to the clothing entrepreneurs that I met in the 1990s that Vietnam might capture a spot on the international runway.

Similar dilemmas have plagued designers elsewhere in Asia and diasporically. Dorinne Kondo (1997) offers an astute analysis of the opportunities and pitfalls of the fraught intersections between race, ethnicity, and global fashion. When Issey Miyake, Rei Kawakubo, and Yohji Yamamoto gained international prominence in the 1980s, the international fashion press took to touting their emergence as a "Japanese invasion." As Kondo points out, this drew attention to their lines, but the racialized and martialized metaphor raised the specter of a contemporary "Yellow Peril." It also lumped three designers' diverse style innovations into a single category, as if intricate pleating techniques (Miyake) or avant-garde deconstructionism (Kawakubo) were expressions of an immutable Japanese essence (Kondo 1997; see also Tu 2011). Lise Skov has chronicled how Hong Kong designers viewed self-exoticization as a way to gain a "competitive edge" in global markets, but "doing something Chinese" risked confining them to the marginalized ranks of ethnic chic—an especially ironic outcome because such traditional motifs were alien to the designers' own modernist fashion sensibilities (Skov 2003, 215–216). Chinese, Indian, and Asian American designers have likewise navigated the pitfalls and opportunities of, to borrow Thuy Linh Nguyen Tu's phrase, "how Asianness has become a resource in this creative economy" (Tu 2011, 5; see also Lindgren 2015; Radclyffe-Thomas and Radclyffe-Thomas 2015; Tarlo 1996; Zhao 2013). As Minh-Ha T. Pham observes, however, "wearing one's ethnicity on one's sleeve" plays into essentialist, racialized logics that marginalize Asians as other and consequently devalue their fashion labor, ideologically and materially (Pham 2015).

Although I still cringe when I view the footage of my appearance on "Fashion and Life," the passage of two decades affords critical distance to consider how my verbal and visual performance might have been implicated in these dynamics. Watching the clip now, I see that what mattered was not that I praised Vietnamese fashion (although that certainly was preferable to insulting it), but the very fact that I had decided to study it and could speak about it in Vietnamese. As Thanh Hường's voice-over suggests, that a foreigner saw Vietnamese dress as a window on a rich culture amounted to a seal of approval that both Vietnamese fashion and culture had value. Through my own implication in global hierarchies of race, nation, and class, my interview marked Vietnamese fashion as worthy of notice and suggested that the television reporter, Minh Hạnh, and even Vietnam's First Lady were right in seeing this as an issue of the "utmost importance" to be approached with far more care and intentionality than my own blithely uttered platitudes.

That I was featured in the national broadcast of Minh Hạnh's self-described "adventurous" and "revolutionary" fashion show also suggests that my presence served as a seal of approval of the soundness and necessity of her endeavor in particular. My expertise—the fact of which I never asserted and which my trite, bumbling comments most likely called into doubt—played into Orientalist dynamics in which a Westerner authoritatively defines that which is valuable about Asian cultural heritage. Only here, it was a Vietnamese reporter and a Vietnamese designer positioning me as a foreign expert in order to shore up the importance of their own projects of cultural production: Fashion matters because this American graduate student says it does. Minh Hạnh's direction is sound because this future PhD is paying attention. What's more, our visions coincide: Modernize through adopting and adapting Western clothing but be sure to preserve that distinctive Vietnamese beauty embodied by the *áo dài*.

My authority as a foreign researcher thus mattered a great deal to the success of this project, at least for that moment. Once I decided to participate and to say nothing that might offend, however, the agency to assert and delineate my authority shifted to the reporter and her crew. As a result, a large part of my authority as "expert" rested on how Thanh Hường chose to portray my own femininity visually. I was certainly complicit in this, as I deliberately chose to wear clothing designed by Minh Hạnh as a gesture of appreciation for her talents and because it was the most businesslike outfit in my otherwise lackluster graduate student wardrobe. At the same time, my portrayal on the television segment exceeded my own intentionality. While the audience would likely not have realized who had designed my outfit, the similarity between my own clothes and those on the runway, made evident through interspersing shots of the interview with those of the models on stage, certainly could have conveyed the message that Minh Hạnh's vision of the Vietnamese woman converged with global tastes. Similarly, my "at-home" outfit of "ethnic" vest over plain shirt and pants mirrored what the reporter herself had worn at the fashion show. I had not been aware of this fact then, but in retrospect it again suggests comparable tastes, as foreign authority and local experts encountered each other on a common playing field of style. Finally, the shot of me and my husband in our wedding finery established me as having achieved the pinnacle of heteronormative femininity and fashion: the bride with her updo in a white gown, tuxedo-clad groom at her side.

To the extent that I had allowed myself to be portrayed as a foreign expert, I had assumed that my authority would lie in my ideas and analysis. That is why I had been disappointed by my failure to be more articulate and was happy to put the episode behind me. Two decades on, as I review the grainy VHS tape and reflect on the debates then taking place about the national and global position of both Vietnamese women and fashion, I realize that while my academic credentials and the content of my speech mattered, my embodied, clothed, and gendered form was perhaps even more important. It was my appearance, both in real time and in the past as a bride, and my ability to speak and comport myself in a way that might seem both foreign and familiar, that the reporter highlighted. This lent me an aura of authority and of comprehensibility as mediator between the local and the global that Thanh Hường could then invoke to bolster her own claims about the significance of the Vietnamese fashion scene of which she was a part. In my graduate student, in-the-moment myopic despair that my landlady was right that I had not sounded as good as I normally did, I missed what upon more distanced reflection would occur to me to have perhaps been the point of the exercise: in fashioning me to look better than I did in real life, the segment presented me as part of an idealized vision of fashion and femininity that underscored the need to attend to both in precisely the manner that Thanh Hường and Minh Hạnh had identified. My racialized, embodied femininity represented a "global modernity" that buttressed their approach to fashion as a gendered pedagogy of appropriateness.

Postscript: Resisting the Field

To be sure, there was something particular about Vietnam in the 1990s that shaped this episode. Anxiety about the market economy and fears that global integration would mean cultural homogenization lent urgency to declarations of Vietnamese distinctiveness. The novelty of foreign, especially American, researchers was taken as a sign that Vietnam mattered, even as our presence aroused suspicion about our motives. The result was that the fieldworker was often asked to opine about the subjects of his or her study, with select quotes enlisted in service of particular agendas, thus feeding back into those very same cultural dynamics. Given my own personal, political investment in postmodern critiques of anthropology's implication in Orientalist and colonialist knowledge production, I recognized that my anticipated publications in English-language academic venues would always need to be answerable to a legacy of speaking for "the natives." It therefore seemed only fitting to have the tables turned so that my less than eloquent words might shore up Vietnamese projects of self-representation. Who, indeed, was the expert here?

Intersectionality, however, complicates this already fraught and politicized field of cultural production. Two dimensions of this strike me as particularly worth underscoring. First, the segment highlights how the relationship between race, class, and gender shaped how I appeared and what claims about my significance might be made. While it might seem apt comeuppance for the words of a white American expert to be turned to different purposes in different venues—all the more so given the history of US involvement in Vietnam—the fact that the clothed, hetero, cisgendered femininity of this particular "expert" was central to the representation would seem to reproduce a crude, tenacious sexism that reduces women to their embodied appearance. As a woman, should I really be surprised that my words, even if far from spellbinding, might matter less than what I looked like?

Second, "the natives" whose voices anthropologists have rightly been critiqued for usurping are not a singular, univocal entity. The politics of who gets to speak about and for whom are no less fraught in Vietnam than they are transnationally. With the 1990s expansion of a market economy intensifying class, regional, and ethnic differences in Vietnam, and these differences often mapping in complex ways onto issues of gender, the use of my words to make disciplining claims about the significance of women's "appropriate" appearance worked to bolster the cultural and hence economic capital of particular experts. State functionaries who have inherited a revolutionary socialist tradition are not often viewed as fashion tastemakers. Deploying me as one of many mediators between the globally fashionable and the locally meaningful aided the state's broader pivot from engineer of socialist economic planning to promoter of cultural capitalism and consumer citizenship that would foster market economic growth. It also worked to make fashion seem a matter of individual taste and discernment, rather than a reflection of an individual's socioeconomic position. This naturalizing sleight of hand worked directly counter to my own intellectual project by obscuring the fact that the field of 1990s Vietnam, in Bourdieu's sense, was shaped by, and contributed to, the increasing inequality generated through a market economy.

Twenty years later, the prospects and challenges of global economic integration are no longer novel in Vietnam. Yet foreign fieldworkers continue to be called upon to lend legitimacy to particular interests in the field of cultural production. In my current research on social work, I chronicle a situation akin to fashion in the 1990s, only now those eager to adapt foreign knowledge are Vietnamese social workers seeking to advance particular material and ideological visions of Vietnam's future and to consolidate their own status as experts employing scientific methods to assess and address "social problems." Once again, my interest is interpreted as a sign of approval, my attention to their efforts a resource to validate their projects.

In November 2011, I made a whirlwind trip in the middle of the semester to attend World Social Work Day, an event hosted that year by the department that sponsors my fieldwork. One faculty member repeatedly pressed me to be interviewed by Ho Chi Minh City television. "You have to talk to the reporter," he insisted. "You're a foreign professor who has studied about social work in Vietnam, and you speak Vietnamese." Claiming jetlag and the onset of a nasty cold, both of which were true, I politely but adamantly resisted his multiple requests. Anthropological knowledge production is dialogic and ideally entails reciprocity, but prior experience made me wary of how, projected through a television screen, my appearance and comportment might convey messages about race, gender, and status that could lend authority to my casual statements beyond what I might intend and in ways that could easily be enlisted in service of other agendas. Fieldwork as an intersubjective, embodied process of knowing becomes fodder for the field, the terrain in which social, cultural, and economic capital are asserted and contested. Having learned firsthand that all knowledge is situated, that all scholarship is inherently political, and that observer and observed inevitably shape each other and readily switch places, I realize that fieldwork and fieldworker cannot be separated from field. But in the ongoing, high-stakes environment of claims-making about Vietnamese culture, I've decided, for now at least, that this relationship need not be televised.

NOTES

1 Traders had ambivalent visions of the United States. Many expressed admiration for its professed values of democracy or entrepreneurial freedom, yet were critical

of aspects of US military intervention in Vietnam and blamed the Ford administration for not rescuing the Republic of Vietnam ("South Vietnam") in April 1975. Meanwhile, from relatives and friends who had immigrated to the United States, traders had a sense that the economic prosperity that many enjoyed (although their visions here often seemed inflated) carried the price of racial discrimination, lack of time for anything but work, and weakened family and community relationships.

2 The gendered subjectivities that traders constructed through their daily performances in the marketplace did play a crucial role in shaping market socialism, but this point was not readily apparent to traders or other observers in the 1990s (Leshkowich 2014).

3 Narratives of modernity have usually mythically and Eurocentrically attributed its origins to seventeenth-century Europe, from which it spread around the globe over the course of the ensuing centuries (see, e.g., Giddens 1990). Scholarship on colonialism over the last two decades provocatively reverses this causal relationship by suggesting that the dynamics of colonial rule enabled the emergence of modernity in Europe (Barlow 1997; Burton 1999b; Stoler 2002).

4 Brenner 1998; Ferguson 1999; Gaonkar 2001; Knauft 2002; Ong and Nonini 1997; Piot 1999; Rofel 1999; Walley 2003.

5 China might seem to provide an even more immediate model of grafting market economics onto a socialist political system, but the lengthy history of animosity between the two countries has made Vietnamese policymakers reluctant to acknowledge this resemblance.

6 Burton 1999a; Chakrabarty 1997; Chatterjee 1993; Clancy-Smith and Gouda 1998; Djajadiningrat-Nieuwenhuis 1987; Gouda 1999; Marr 1981; Stoler 1989; Tai 1992; Tarlo 1996; Taussig 1993: 177–185; Tiwon 1996; Wieringa 1988; Yuval-Davis 1997: 23. In this way, the native woman could also serve as a mute rebuke to the European woman, whose presence in the colonies was supposed to symbolize the nurturing, maternal purity of European colonization, but who in her actual behavior was prone to inappropriate commingling with the natives or ignorant and unseemly expressions of racism (see, e.g., Stoler 1989; Edwards 1998).

7 Chakrabarty 1997; Chatterjee 1993; Niessen 2003; Ruhlen 2003; Tarlo 1996; Taussig 1993; J. Taylor 1997; Wilson 1985.

8 Durham similarly notes that throughout southern Africa at this time, women were pressured to wear traditional dress in such settings as political meetings so that they could literally embody national identity (Durham 1999, 395).

9 As a woman then approaching 40 and daughter of a former captain in the South Vietnamese army who spent nine years in a re-education camp, Minh Hạnh might not seem part of a revolutionary elite. As a designer heading a state-run company whose status depended on popular acceptance of her fashion knowledge, however, she was deeply invested in maintaining a hierarchy based on expertise. She was thus aligned with other political, cultural, and economic leaders in attempting to steward Vietnamese women's engagements with modernity.

10 Here, Minh Hạnh references the widely held anxiety, one reinforced by the beauty and fitness industries, that the husbands of successful middle-aged women would have affairs with younger, presumably more attractive women (see Leshkowich 2008; Nguyen 2015).

REFERENCES

Barlow, Tani E. 1997. "Introduction: On 'Colonial Modernity.'" In *Formations of Colonial Modernity in East Asia*, edited by Tani E. Barlow, 1–20. Durham, NC: Duke University Press.

Bhabha, Homi. 1997. "Of Mimicry and Man: The Ambivalence of Colonial Discourse." In *Tensions of Empire: Colonial Cultures in a Bourgeois World*, edited by Frederick Cooper and Ann Laura Stoler, 152–160. Berkeley: University of California Press.

Bourdieu, Pierre. 1977. *Outline of a Theory of Practice*, translated by R. Nice. Cambridge: Cambridge University Press.

Brenner, Suzanne. 1998. *The Domestication of Desire: Women, Wealth, and Modernity in Java*. Princeton, NJ: Princeton University Press.

B. T. 1997. "Đêm 'Thời Trang Tuổi 40' Nhân Ngày Quốc Tế Phụ Nữ" [The Night of 'Fashion for the Forties' on the Occasion of International Women's Day]. *Sài Gòn Giải Phóng (Saigon Liberation Daily)* (January 31): 3.

Burton, Antoinette, ed. 1999a. *Gender, Sexuality, and Colonial Modernities*. London: Routledge.

———. 1999b. "Introduction: The Unfinished Business of Colonial Modernities." In *Gender, Sexuality, and Colonial Modernities*, edited by Antoinette Burton, 1–16. London: Routledge.

Chakrabarty, Dipesh. 1997. "The Difference-Deferral of a Colonial Modernity: Public Debates on Domesticity in British Bengal." In *Tensions of Empire: Colonial Cultures in a Bourgeois World*, edited by Frederick Cooper and Ann Laura Stoler, 373–405. Berkeley: University of California Press.

Chatterjee, Partha. 1993. *Nationalist Thought and the Colonial World: A Derivative Discourse*. London: United Nations University and Zed.

Clancy-Smith, Julia and Gouda, Frances, eds. 1998. *Domesticating the Empire: Race, Gender, and Family Life in French and Dutch Colonialism*. Charlottesville: University Press of Virginia.

Djajadiningrat-Nieuwenhuis, Madelon. 1987. "Ibuism and Priyayization: Path to Power?" In *Indonesian Women in Focus: Past and Present Notions*, edited by Elsbeth Locher-Scholten and Anke Niehof, 43–51. Dordrecht: Foris.

Durham, Deborah. 1999. "The Predicament of Dress: Polyvalency and the Ironies of Cultural Identity." *American Ethnologist* 26(2): 389–411.

Earl, Catherine. 2014. *Vietnam's New Middle Classes: Gender, Career, City*. Copenhagen: NIAS Press.

Edwards, Penny. 1998. "Womanizing Indochina: Fiction, Nation, and Cohabitation in Colonial Cambodia, 1890–1930." In *Domesticating the Empire: Race, Gender, and*

Family Life in French and Dutch Colonialism, edited by Julia Clancy-Smith and Frances Gouda, 108–130. Charlottesville: University Press of Virginia.

Ferguson, James G. 1999. *Expectations of Modernity: Myths and Meanings of Urban Life on the Zambian Copper Belt*. Berkeley: University of California Press.

Gaonkar, Dilip Parameshwar, ed. 2001. *Alternative Modernities*. Durham, NC: Duke University Press.

Giddens, Anthony. 1990. *The Consequences of Modernity*. Stanford, CA: Stanford University Press.

Gouda, Frances. 1999. "Gender and 'Hyper-Masculinity' as Post-Colonial Modernity during Indonesia's Struggle for Independence, 1945 to 1949." In *Gender, Sexuality, and Colonial Modernities*, edited by Antoinette Burton, 163–176. London: Routledge.

Hancock, Mary. 1999. "Gendering the Modern: Women and Home Science in British India." In *Gender, Sexuality, and Colonial Modernities*, edited by Antoinette Burton, 149–161. London: Routledge.

Ikeya, Chie. 2008. "The Modern Burmese Woman and the Politics of Fashion in Colonial Burma." *Journal of Asian Studies* 67(4): 1277–1308.

Knauft, Bruce, ed. 2002. *Critically Modern: Alternatives, Alterities, Anthropologies*. Bloomington: Indiana University Press.

Kondo, Dorinne. 1997. *About Face: Performing Race in Fashion and Theater*. London: Routledge.

Leshkowich, Ann Marie. 2003. "The *Ao Dai* Goes Global: How International Influences and Female Entrepreneurs Have Shaped Vietnam's 'National Costume.'" In *Re-Orienting Fashion: The Globalization of Asian Dress*, edited by Sandra Niessen, Ann Marie Leshkowich, and Carla Jones, 79–115. Oxford: Berg.

_____. 2008. "Working Out Culture: Gender, Body, and Commodification in a Ho Chi Minh City Health Club." *Urban Anthropology and Studies of Cultural Systems and World Economic Development* 37(1): 49–87.

_____. 2009. "Fashioning Appropriate Youth in 1990s Vietnam." In *The Fabric of Cultures: Fashion, Identity, and Globalization*, edited by Eugenia Paulicelli and Hazel Clark, 92–111. London and New York: Routledge.

_____. 2012. "Finances, Family, Fashion, Fitness, and . . . Freedom? The Changing Lives of Urban Middle-Class Vietnamese Women." In *The Reinvention of Distinction: Modernity and the Middle Class in Urban Vietnam*, edited by Van Nguyen-Marshall, Lisa B. Welch Drummond, and Danièle Bélanger, 95–113. ARI-Springer.

_____. 2014. *Essential Trade: Vietnamese Women in a Changing Marketplace*. Honolulu: University of Hawai'i Press.

Leshkowich, Ann Marie and Jones, Carla. 2003. "What Happens When Asian Chic Becomes Chic in Asia?" *Fashion Theory* 7 (3/4): 281–300.

Lindgren, Tim. 2015. "How Do Chinese Fashion Designers Become Global Fashion Leaders? A New Perspective on Legitimization in China's Fashion System." *International Journal of Fashion Studies* 2(1): 63–75.

Marr, David G. 1981. *Vietnamese Tradition on Trial: 1920–1945*. Berkeley: University of California Press.

Nguyen, Minh T. N. 2015. *Vietnam's Socialist Servants: Domesticity, Class, Gender, and Identity*. London: Routledge.

Niessen, Sandra. 2003. "Three Scenarios from Batak Clothing History: Designing Participation in the Global Fashion Trajectory." In *Re-Orienting Fashion: The Globalization of Asian Dress*, edited by Sandra Niessen, Ann Marie Leshkowich, and Carla Jones, 49–78. Oxford: Berg.

Ong, Aihwa and Nonini, Donald M., eds. 1997. *Ungrounded Empires: The Cultural Politics of Modern Chinese Transnationalism*. New York: Routledge.

Pham, Minh-Ha T. 2015. *Asians Wear Clothes on the Internet: Race, Gender, and the Work of Personal Style Blogging*. Durham, NC: Duke University Press.

Piot, Charles. 1999. *Remotely Global: Village Modernity in West Africa*. Chicago: University of Chicago Press.

Rabinow, Paul. 1977. *Reflections on Fieldwork in Morocco*. Berkeley: University of California Press.

Radclyffe-Thomas, Natascha and Babette Radclyffe-Thomas. 2015. "The New Shanghai Xiaojie: Chinese Fashion Identities." *International Journal of Fashion Studies* 2(1): 43–62.

Rofel, Lisa. 1999. *Other Modernities: Gendered Yearnings in China after Socialism*. Berkeley: University of California Press.

Ruhlen, Rebecca N. 2003. "Korean Alterations: Nationalism, Social Consciousness, and 'Traditional' Clothing." In *Re-Orienting Fashion: The Globalization of Asian Dress*, edited by Sandra Niessen, Ann Marie Leshkowich, and Carla Jones, 117–137. Oxford: Berg.

Skov, Lise. 2003. "Fashion–Nation: A Japanese Globalization Experience and a Hong Kong Dilemma." In *Re-Orienting Fashion: The Globalization of Asian Dress*, edited by Sandra Niessen, Ann Marie Leshkowich, and Carla Jones, 215–242. Oxford: Berg.

Stoler, Ann Laura. 1989. "Making Empire Respectable: The Politics of Race and Sexual Morality in Twentieth-Century Colonial Cultures." *American Ethnologist* 16(4): 634–660.

———. 2002. *Carnal Knowledge and Imperial Power: Race and the Intimate in Colonial Rule*. Berkeley: University of California Press.

Tai, Hue-Tam Ho. 1992. *Radicalism and the Origins of the Vietnamese Revolution*. Cambridge, MA: Harvard University Press.

Tarlo, Emma. 1996. *Clothing Matters: Dress and Identity in India*. Chicago: University of Chicago Press.

Taussig, Michael. 1993. *Mimesis and Alterity: A Particular History of the Senses*. New York: Routledge.

Taylor, Jean Gelman. 1997. "Costume and Gender in Colonial Java, 1800–1940." In *Outward Appearances: Dressing State and Society in Indonesia*, edited by Henk Schulte Norholdt, 85–116. Leiden: KITLV Press.

Taylor, Philip. 2001. *Fragments of the Present: Searching for Modernity in Vietnam's South.* Crows Nest, Australia: Allen & Unwin.

Thúy Hà. 1997. "Chương Trình 'Thời Trang Tuổi 40' Tối 8/3/97: Đầy Ấn Tượng" [The Show 'Fashion for the 40s' on the night of March 8, 1997: Full of Impressions]. *Phụ Nữ* (March 12): 1, 9.

Thúy Thúy. 1997. "'Thời Trang Tuổi 40': Như một cuộc dạo chơi" ['Fashion for the Forties': Like a Stroll]. *Sài Gòn Giải Phóng (Saigon Liberation Daily)* (March 16).

Tiwon, Sylvia. 1996. "Models and Maniacs: Articulating the Female in Indonesia." In *Fantasizing the Feminine in Indonesia,* edited by Laurie J. Sears, 47–70. Durham, NC: Duke University Press.

Tu, Thuy Linh Nguyen. 2011. *The Beautiful Generation: Asian Americans and the Cultural Economy of Fashion.* Durham, NC: Duke University Press.

Walley, Christine J. 2003. "Our Ancestors Used to Bury their 'Development' in the Ground: Modernity and the Meanings of Development within a Tanzanian Marine Park." *Anthropological Quarterly* 76(1): 33–54.

Wieringa, Saskia. 1988. "Aborted Feminism in Indonesia: A History of Indonesian Socialist Feminism." In *Women's Struggles and Strategies,* edited by Saskia Wieringa, 69–90. Aldershot: Gower.

Wilson, Elizabeth. 1985. *Adorned in Dreams: Fashion and Modernity.* London: Virago.

Yuval-Davis, Nira. 1997. *Gender and Nation.* London: Sage.

Zhao, Jianhua. 2013. *The Chinese Fashion Industry: An Ethnographic Approach.* London: Bloomsbury.

6

Splitting the Seams

Transnational Feminism and the Manila-Toronto Production of Filipino Couture

DENISE CRUZ

A few years ago, Caroline Mangosing—who was at the time the director of Kapisanan Philippine Centre for Arts and Culture—began fielding some unusual phone calls. Based in the heart of Toronto's bustling Kensington Market, the center, which has since relocated, offers arts-based programming for the Filipino Canadian community and its allies.[1] But Mangosing noticed that a good number of people calling Kapisanan were picking up the phone not to learn more about cultural, arts, or educational initiatives, but rather to ask about clothes. "Do you sell *barongs* and *ternos*?," they would ask, referring to the traditional forms of clothing often worn for weddings and other social events (the barong is usually worn by men; the terno by women). As the calls started coming in more frequently, she recognized that there was a market for Filipino formal wear in Toronto, and that there were limited options available in the city. Moreover, she knew that the barongs and ternos most readily available in Toronto are made for tourist export, quickly stitched together out of synthetic materials meant to mimic the real thing, which is ideally custom-designed, hand-embroidered, and fashioned from a translucent, delicate material woven from natural fibers like *piña* (pineapple) or *jusi* (banana leaf).

Mangosing grew up in the Philippines. She watched her mother manufacture children's clothes, attended fashion school, and dabbled in design. She quickly saw an opportunity. Inspired, she began to sketch out the outlines of a social enterprise that would combine the goal of fundraising for Kapisanan with her background in fashion to answer the need for Filipino formal wear in Toronto. After several years of development, in 2013, Mangosing began creating a small run of barongs and ternos under the name VINTA (a Tagalog word that translates to boat). In the early days of this transnational operation, the clothing was custom-fit for Canadian and US consumers; produced by Lita Lagman, a master sewer in Manila; and then, under the coordination of Mangosing's partner, Ria Limjap, shipped back to Toronto for distribution.[2] While Mangosing was directing Kapisanan, the proceeds from VINTA supported the center.[3] Although the cost of textiles, embroidery, and labor influenced her decision to manufacture in the Philippines, she explained that transnational production was also necessary because Lagman's skills were required to create the garment. The terno's trademark large, stiff "butterfly sleeves," for example, must be carefully pleated so that they extend up and above the woman's shoulder in a process that, until relatively recently, has become a lesser known art form (figure 6.1).

As someone with a long-standing commitment to cultural education and social justice, Mangosing was well aware of the political implications of outsourcing and its conflict with her objectives. "VINTA," proclaims the line's 2014 lookbook, "aims to bring Filipino cultural clothing into the North American fashion consciousness, while promoting and raising awareness around ethical labor practices in the garment industry globally, and stimulating entrepreneurship among Filipino-Canadian young people and women."[4] Though initially she could only remunerate Lagman by the piece (a set price for each item of clothing completed), Mangosing nevertheless paid her significantly more than the usual rate for garment labor in Manila. She asked Lagman to name her price per piece and even worked to exceed the initial offer. But this arrangement became increasingly unsatisfactory to Mangosing, and she became committed to the goal of giving Lagman a salary, a space to work, and the opportunity to teach others her skills.

Since our first conversation in June 2014, when I originally began interviewing Mangosing for this chapter, VINTA has developed substantially. She has expanded her clientele to include mostly customers from the United States. In 2016, Mangosing secured an investor, and in addition to the couture option, VINTA now has an e-commerce site, vintato.com, with a limited run of women's and men's clothing in ready-to-wear, pre-set sizes (figure 6.2; the 2017 season included 12 pieces). But most important, Mangosing has used the investment to fund her staff:

Figure. 6.1. VINTA Couture Ruffle Terno, 2017. Photo by Caroline Mangosing and printed with permission.

Lagman has her own work space, a monthly salary, a percentage of the company, apprentices who also earn a salaried wage, and a high-school-aged intern (figures 6.3, 6.4).[5]

Despite these achievements, the process has not been easy, for in managing VINTA, Mangosing negotiates competing demands: her desire to work toward fair remuneration; her refusal to outsource to a factory, which means that her ability to take on enough orders for profit is limited; and a consumer in the global North who is not always willing to pay the price commensurate with a laborer's living wage. In the pages that follow, I document and analyze the VINTA story and the emotional uneasiness that accompanies it. I contend that this fledgling fashion enterprise serves as an illustration of—and potential alternative to—the difficult and challenging crossings of transnational exchange, ethical fashion, and the Filipino diaspora, manifested in the affective and the material. As a business venture and fashion line, VINTA illustrates what happens when transnational fashion seeks to be ethical and attempts to resist the global North's easy consumption of labor in the global South.

While the garments Mangosing and her team create are beautiful, their production depends upon material and affective friction (what

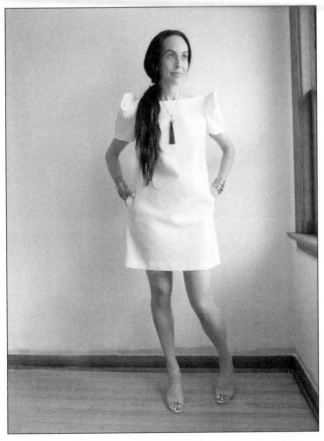

Figure 6.2. Ready-to-wear VINTA Shift Dress Terno, 2017. Photo by Caroline Mangosing and printed with permission.

Figure 6.3. Lita Lagman in the foreground, working in VINTA's new space. Photo by Caroline Mangosing and used with permission.

Anna Tsing—and, more recently, Martin Manalansan, have described as "the messy," "surprising," and "sticky engagements" of global interactions).[6] Another way of thinking about these dynamics is via what Priti Ramamurthy calls "perplexity," "a way of marking the tension between overlapping, opposing, and asymmetric forces or fields of power. Perplexity indexes the puzzlement of people as they experience both the joys and aches of the global everyday, often simultaneously."[7] Attending to these forms of friction, asymmetry, and perplexity, my analysis highlights the affective and other difficulties that Mangosing has encountered in creating VINTA. These challenges stem not only from a business but also from her own discomfort and uneasiness, especially her recognition of her privileged position as a Filipina in Canada. Such raw affective edges offer a model of critical engagement with fashion that forcefully go against first, the easy consumption of Filipino labor by global North consumers and second, a diasporic Filipino community endeavoring to influence change in the Philippines from a distance.

VINTA is ultimately an attempt to work against a system in which the most intimate of objects and relations—the very clothing that lies against your skin, the care for your child or aging grandmother—depend

Figure 6.4. Lagman's apprentice, Hilda, working with VINTA's high school intern. Photo by Ria Limjap and printed with permission.

crucially on both the necessity and the invisibility of low-paid and "deprofessionalized" Filipino laborers.[8] Toronto is an important cultural site for such inquiries, both because of the size of the Filipino community here and because of the conditions of Filipino labor and its representation. Filipinos comprise the fastest growing and largest migrant population in Canada, numbering at 837,135 in the 2016 Statistics Canada census.[9] As Roland Coloma, Robert Díaz, Philip Kelly, Bonnie McElhinny, Geraldine Pratt, Ethel Tungohan, and Eleanor Ty have argued, Filipinos in the Canadian diaspora are both prominent—because of their large numbers—yet also rendered invisible by a city that constantly devalues their labor.[10] Contemporary discourse about Filipinos in Canada can thus be organized into two categories that cast the Philippines and Filipinos as providers, in one form or another, for global North desires and needs. On one hand, public discourse centers on Filipina women's proliferation as domestic service providers and caregivers (the nanny, nurse, or the mail-order bride); they are "servants of globalization" (Rhacel Salazar Parreñas), "migrants for export" (Robyn Rodriguez), and contributors to an "empire of care" (Catherine Ceniza Choy).[11] On the other hand, the Philippines itself is tied to constructions of global labor as a threat to the local workforce, illustrated not only by products "made in the Philippines" but also by the number of corporate call centers in Manila.

Mangosing's efforts to address these dynamics, however, are riddled with perplexity and friction—especially in her desire to provide a unique experience for her clients and the political objectives of her work with Lagman. The VINTA line represents the dovetailing of two forms of fashion that have gained increased currency in the last decade or so: slow fashion and ethical fashion. In order to provide salaries for the VINTA team, Mangosing must also convince her North American consumers, for whom "made in the Philippines" often signals "inexpensive," to pay for the higher cost of a VINTA garment. A ready-to-wear VINTA shift dress costs $200; a couture terno dress, $400.[12] According to Hazel Clark, "the slow approach," which began emerging in the mid-2000s, is "more than a literal opposite to fast fashion"; rather, slow fashion is a term "used to identify sustainable fashion solutions, based on the repositioning of strategies of design, production, consumption, use, and reuse, which are emerging along side [sic] the global fashion system, and are posing a potential challenge to it."[13] Scholars, designers, corporations, and the fashion press have coined "ethical fashion" (the slow approach's more blatantly politicized cousin) to describe the industry's response to concerns about global garment labor.[14] Although, as Catrin Joergens notes, there is no "industry standard" for ethical fashion, in general, it is grounded in attempts to "source garments ethically while providing good working standards and conditions to workers and to provide a sustainable business model in the clothes' country of origin" (often with close attention to principles of biodegradability and organic agriculture).[15] Ethical fashion carries with it a politics, a desire to promote consumers' awareness of their place in the global system of transnational production and consumption.

While some scholars have recognized the capacity of ethical fashion to address globalization's ills, others have also underscored two important areas of critique. The first centers on the ways in which companies, while calling attention to the plight of global workers abroad, also often tend to reify their image in ways that rely on stereotypes of gender, race, and place. Building upon foundational work by Diane Elson and Ruth Pearson, feminist scholars such as Ramamurthy have long been suspicious of the absence of attention to gender in debates about globalized labor, which often coalesce around the iconic figure of the garment worker as a Third World woman in need of saving.[16] These critics underscore that female garment workers in the global South are doubly exploited by fashion that is marketed as "ethical": first, by an industry in need of women who are supposedly "nimble" and "docile," and second, by companies who rely upon the portrayal of these workers as in need of rescue in order to ultimately sell their products.[17] For Naila Kabeer, activism stemming from the global North on behalf of women in the global South can often "both feed on, and feed into, widespread preconceptions about poor Third World women as helpless victims of the global free-trade economy."[18]

The second critical problem lies in whether or not ethical fashion has actually led to changes in the lived social realities of two different constituencies: garment workers and consumers. For example, even though corporations might have adopted codes governing ethical conduct, in a comparative study of companies in India, the Philippines, Sri Lanka, Bangladesh, Pakistan, and Indonesia, Angela Hale and Linda M. Shaw

found that corporations frequently did not directly consult with workers when instituting these guidelines. Moreover, workers were often unaware of their rights and also refrained from asking about them because
they feared reprisal.[19] This is certainly the case for the Philippines. Rosalinda Pineda Ofreneo, R. del Rosario, Bernadita L. Catalla, and Jane
Hutchison have documented the extensive practice of outworking, the
multiple levels of subcontracting in the Philippines, and its effects on
labor practices and organizing. Many sewers take their work home;
companies and corporations hire subcontractors to complete job orders;
these subcontractors often further hire out their work to others. As a
result, garment laborers in the Philippines and other areas of the global
South often do not have recourse to unionize.[20] Thus, while ethical conduct regulations might be adopted by a corporation, the effect of these
practices does not always trickle down to the workers.

At the other end of the spectrum, scholars have found that the purchase of "ethical" or "fair trade" goods does not always lead to an ethically minded consumer. Shoppers often consider multiple factors when
choosing clothing, and fair or ethical labor practices are just one aspect of the decision-making process. Initial studies of ethical fashion
enterprises reveal that while a company's designation as "fair trade" or
"ethical" might help influence a buyer, a consumer also weighs such
characterizations against other qualities (such as whether they deem the
item of clothing fashionable or a good value). Moreover, consumers who
select an item of clothing that is ostensibly ethically produced may tem-
porarily feel satisfied (or perhaps absolved of their potential guilt) with
the swipe of a credit card or the click of the checkout button; these single
transactions don't necessarily correspond to other "ethical" behaviors.[21]
And, as Minh-Ha T. Pham observes, well-publicized critiques of fast
fashion (as the antithesis to "ethical fashion") also vilify working-class
and racialized consumers and producers, while failing to acknowledge
continued labor problems in high fashion: "Today, more expensive fashions are still associated with higher-status consumers whose tastes are
not just 'better' but also morally superior, ethically discriminating, and
knowledgeable about the 'high costs of cheap fashion.'"[22]

The critical trends encapsulated above provide the conceptual backdrop for my reading of VINTA. Of course, Mangosing's venture works on
a far smaller scale. Nevertheless, she is constantly aware of the problems

affecting wage labor in the Philippines. As I recount below, a repeated difficulty encountered by the VINTA team stems from managing the desire for fair compensation alongside their struggle to find and market the line to consumers. For Mangosing and her partner, Limjap, attempting to pay Lagman more than the usual piecework wage was in part feasible only because both Mangosing and Limjap had other sources of income. The discussion that follows unravels the material and affective perplexities of VINTA. The first section examines the terno, and especially its trademark butterfly sleeves, as material object and metaphor riddled with diasporic perplexity. I contend that Mangosing's version of the terno responds to patterns of representation that affect Filipinas in the diaspora, allowing these women to connect to their Filipina heritage and to, in the words of one VINTA customer, "stand out" in ways other than how Filipinas are primarily depicted in Canada (as nurses or caregivers). I then focus on the terno's sleeves as symbolic of the shifting dynamics of global Filipino labor and their material traces on the fashion industry. The last section examines the perplexity stitched into the creation of a VINTA terno, via interviews with Mangosing and her coordinator in Manila. Mangosing's own uneasiness about transnational production and her desire to do something about it—however fraught and uneven in their results—nevertheless still revise the terms of how both fashion producers and consumers often engage with Asian labor in the world of fashion: as facilitating quick, easy, and unthinking forms of material and affective exchange.

Fashioning the Terno for the Diaspora

The terno, observes Lucy Mae San Pablo Burns, is an "overprivileged icon—of ideal womanhood and of the mother nation."[23] Burns, with historian Mina Roces, Genevieve Clutario, and others, contends that the terno is a symbol of the intersection of the construction and performance of gender and sexuality, fashion and dress, and their display.[24] Extending this work, here I consider the terno as an object of representational and material perplexity. The terno is a dress with important representative power at home and abroad, but it is also a garment that requires specific methods of construction. A vexed signifier, the terno has multiple valences and meanings within the Filipino North American context. The terno is not usually worn by diasporic Filipinas in their twenties or thirties (who are today Mangosing's primary customer base): Mangosing and her customers describe the stereotype of the terno as a dress that their mother or tita (aunt) might wear. Thus, while the Filipino community in Toronto who sought out ternos and barongs may have inspired VINTA, this audience is not the target of Mangosing's marketing.

For those who are not familiar with the terno, the sleeves of Mangosing's VINTA dresses will nevertheless still be recognizable to anyone who has seen a photo of Imelda Marcos, the terno's most famous wearer. As Burns and Roces have noted, Marcos transformed the dress by wearing it frequently for state and international appearances. Mangosing herself has observed that Marcos had a "monopoly on the terno."[25] In wearing the terno to national events, Marcos merely capitalized on a practice that had already been regularized in Philippine culture in the early twentieth century. In the mid-twentieth century, designers such as Ramon Valera, Salvacion Lim Higgins, Pitoy Moreno, and Ben Farrales reformulated the terno, tailoring its lines so that it resembled other global fashion trends.[26] Although the terno had already made appearances in the United States (the dress was worn by other diplomatic figures, socialites, or students for public events), Imelda Marcos took its public exhibition to new heights. As the terno's global cover girl, she reconfigured this fashion item such that it became allied not only with special events—charity balls, debuts of young socialites, or weddings—but also with the Philippine nation-state on display abroad. Marcos's dual function as a fashion icon and as first lady, however, was also part of the Marcoses' violent, oppressive regime. Indeed, Marcos's fashion choices—such as her thousands of pairs of shoes—have been read as symbolic of her hypocrisy, an example of the Marcoses' comparative wealth amid the economic depression of the nation.

In the past Mangosing has underscored her desire to wrest the terno from Marcos's iconic figure. In this project she is not alone. In the last decade, even though the terno has, in the words of *Philippine Star* writer Millet M. Mananquil, "died a thousand deaths," the gown has been the cultural site of reclamation and renewed inquiry.[27] On one hand, designers have begun to refashion the terno in competitions dedicated to its renewal; reconceptualized versions have reappeared on the red carpet, especially for events like the State of the Nation Address (SONA).²⁸ On the other hand, the terno, argues Burns, has also been satirized by performance artist groups like MOB (Mother of the Bride) who playfully critique the garment as symbolic of the Filipina's oppression.²⁹ These contemporary refashionings of the terno are meant for extraordinary wearers: the celebrity, movie star, or politician in the Philippines, or the performance artist who deliberately dons the garment in order to satirize it.

In contrast, Mangosing underscores the terno's possibility for a diasporic clientele. She markets her version of the couture terno as an opportunity for the consumer to participate in a unique experience, explicitly tailored to members of the Filipino diaspora. Rather than the generically produced garment more popularly circulated for tourist export, Mangosing sells the prospect of working with her, to consult with her on what length might work best or whether you might look better in an A-line or pencil skirt. Though Mangosing initially thought of designing ready-to-wear (and began including this model in 2016), VINTA began as bespoke. After running the numbers, she realized that the initial capital required for ready-to-wear would be prohibitive. But when discussing VINTA more recently, she also described the nagging importance of another factor: what to her was integral not only to the look of the dress but also how a VINTA might look on the potential consumer. "The further we went along," she recalled, "the more I realized that these dresses have to be bespoke. They have to be bespoke . . . Because the [size of the] sleeves are so out of control, they're so big that you don't want an ill-fitting body that's holding up those sleeves, you know what I mean? You need the body to fit properly and to look like it's made-to-measure so that the sleeves look regal." She sought to divest the dress from its affiliation with the national costume, to promote instead a version that fit a woman's body perfectly. She alters the lines of the dress, uses fabrics like silk rather than piña because of North America's drier and colder climate, and has recently redesigned the sleeves so that they are smaller and can collapse in order to fit underneath a woman's coat (figure 6.2).³⁰ But she underscores that for her, the garment is still "very traditional. [. . .] People keep saying it's 'modern take, modern take,' but really I'm not deviating from the traditional sleeves. [. . .] At all. What I'm doing is I'm making it fit better."³¹

Mangosing also offers her diasporic customers an aspirational experience: a chance to participate in a practice that has long been central to elite forms of dress in the Philippines. As a made-to-measure line, the emergence of VINTA parallels renewed interest in bespoke tailors in Toronto and other global cities. This trend, most popular in the last decade or so for men's suiting, has also led to similar ventures for women.[32] Rather than clothing quickly and cheaply made in factories in the global South, clients of bespoke tailors are interested in garments that are supposedly distinctive and individualized, made in-house by a "master." Mangosing's VINTA, however, has a context that, while connected to these developments in Toronto, is also distinct from them: the long-standing Filipino tradition of what Tagalog-speakers call "*pagawa*," the custom-making of clothes. Although there are tailors and dressmakers in Manila, many Filipina and Filipino designers and their clients readily use the term *couture* to refer to custom-made clothing. This is not *haute couture* as it has been traditionally defined in Parisian fashion, where the term denotes a house that is recognized by the *Chambre Syndicale de la Haute Couture* (clothing designed by a single figure, made-to-measure for a client, and constructed in-house and by hand, often at an extremely high cost). Rather, couture as a term and practice in the Philippines occupies a space in between ready-to-wear and haute couture. Having a made-to-measure gown is a common practice for weddings and special events in Manila, but it is also much more affordable than it would be in the United States or Canada (for comparison, a gown made by a Filipino designer might cost in the low thousands of US dollars).

VINTA's version of pagawa thus combines the material (the construction of a garment) with the affective (the creation of a highly individualized, participatory experience that makes a client feel unique, special and, Mangosing notes, connected to the Philippines). In our conversations, Mangosing recalled the context of pagawa in her narration of the VINTA story, and more specifically, what pagawa meant for her as a Filipina returning home for visits. She was born in the Philippines, but her family eventually moved to Canada. When her parents returned to live in the Philippines, she would visit every year and, on each trip, would "pagawa" a dress or an outfit. Eventually, Mangosing decided that she would offer Filipina and Filipino clients in Toronto (and elsewhere in Canada and the United States) a version of the pagawa experience.

In its current form, VINTA is based on this hybrid format. Mangosing designs the dresses without an initial consultation process with the client. Clients then can view the current VINTA line through Mangosing's lookbook, or more often by finding it on Instagram or other forms of social media. Once they contact her and place the order, these garments are then custom-tailored and shipped to the client.

In creating bespoke or made-to-measure ternos for a North American clientele, Mangosing offers her clients in Canada a model of diasporic fashion that they might only otherwise encounter in the Philippines. Mangosing works against the terno's associations in a diasporic context as garments associated with an older (and for some, more conservative) generation. When I ask her to encapsulate the VINTA terno, she describes the dress as "something that a normal Filipino girl [in Canada or North America] who has no touchstone of anything cultural would pick it off a rack and go, 'Oh yeah, I'd wear this to my friend's wedding.'"[33] When I asked her to describe VINTA customers, Mangosing's "normal" Filipina is also someone who might not have any connection or "touchstone" other than perhaps Filipino food, a penchant for karaoke, and knowledge of Manny Pacquiao. This potential client would, despite a more tenuous link to Filipino culture, nevertheless see the dress and feel compelled by it.

Mangosing's customers do represent this profile. When anonymously surveyed about the reasons for their decision to purchase a VINTA, one woman in her twenties observed that even though "it is very much out of my comfort zone to wear something that would attract attention to myself," she "knew I had to wear it because it would be a reflection of showing how much it mattered to me that I was connected to my heritage." She was proud to be seen in her VINTA, and especially for an event that was not directly connected to the display of Filipino culture and identity: "As a kid growing up in Canada I never felt fully connected to being Filipino, other than visiting the Philippines once in 2010. This was an opportunity to lean into my culture, but through a medium that I knew well and knew how to express: Fashion. Overall I'm proud that I own one, and not because I needed to wear one at a pageant, but because it was a choice."[34]

Another customer describes herself as "half Filipino"; her father was "100% Filipino" while her mother was "100% Caucasian." She, too, grew up feeling somewhat disconnected from her heritage in part because her Filipino father died when she was only nine years old. In a response worth quoting at length, she recalls how she experienced a form of perplexity, an emotional friction resulting from her in-between status as biracial:

> We never learned Tagalog or any other dialect. Growing up, we kept in touch with my father's side of the family, though they live more than a few states away. We would visit at least once a year, which I loved. Being around my Filipino family made me feel closer to my father, and also made me feel less culturally-starved. I love my mother dearly, but just the fact that my sister and I looked different than her always warranted an explanation to people we met for the first time. After explaining to them that "no, we are not adopted," they would ask me questions about Filipino culture, and I would be embarrassed to say that I knew very little, if anything, specific to their question. I felt (and still feel) like the worst Filipino in the world because I lost that consistent influence in losing my father. I guess it's that traditional conundrum of bi-racial kids: you KIND OF fit in one side, you KIND OF fit in on the other side, but you don't LOOK like either side, so you feel you have to justify your existence on BOTH. Maybe it's not entirely that bad, but as a kid it was the biggest thing on my mind. Thank God I outgrew that. At least for the most part.[35]

For these women, wearing a VINTA was influenced by their perceptions of their Filipina identity within the diaspora (a different customer explicitly defined herself as a "global Filipina"). Highlighting various forms of perplexity, they underscore their awareness of the spectrum of visibility and invisibility affecting Filipinos in Canada and the United States, and they connect their decision to buy a terno to a fraught experience as mixed-race Filipina in Canada, or as Filipina American. Both report having a somewhat tumultuous relationship to this cultural heritage, feeling "culturally starved," or experiencing anxiety in their relationship to their Filipina-ness. One wonders (though she later questions why she did so) whether she will be judged by Mangosing as being "Filipina enough" to wear a terno. The other uses the dress as a stand-in for personal memories and attachments to her lost father and culture. Both remark that by wearing this garment, they would be calling attention to themselves and to their Filipina-ness. The customer in her twenties, for example, wrote that those seeing her dress noticed and told her how unusual it was (she wore it to a wedding). Standing out for her was in part because of the unique qualities of the dress, but it was also because the gown emphasized her Filipina identity.

Mangosing's VINTA ternos repoliticize the dress's relationship to diasporic Filipino fashion. The promise of a VINTA centers on how the dress prompts its wearer to reclaim her visibility, her unusualness within the diaspora. The customers' comments relate how the VINTA ternos disrupt patterns of cultural invisibility in several ways. First, the act of wearing a VINTA, as the customers and Mangosing note, makes the wearer conspicuous because the dress itself is unusual. Second, the VINTA terno is not like other ternos in its cut (form-fitting), color (black), or material (from lightweight floral canvas to satin). Third, the making of the terno itself differs from the types of ternos usually available in the diaspora, for it is custom-created.

The question of who does and does not (or perhaps also can and cannot) afford a VINTA must be read amid the class divide that separates a population of upwardly mobile second-generation Filipinas and immigrant Filipina newcomers. VINTA customers have enough disposable income to afford an expensive piece of clothing. Feeling a desire to reconnect to the Philippines, they choose to wear a VINTA terno. The customer clientele for VINTA, then, also subtly indexes the friction within the diasporic Filipino community in North America, the economic divide that separates these second-generation women from Filipinos who have arrived more recently in Canada to work.

Mangosing's customers feel that their VINTA garments make them visually conspicuous, and this is undoubtedly because of the terno's sleeves. The terno's upright, pleated, and rigid butterfly sleeves can be read as symbolic of the shifting dynamics of fashion labor in the Philippines. Creating these sleeves is not an easy process. The architecture of the sleeve is itself complex, involving a number of pleats that must be positioned accurately so that the sleeve is flat and sharply edged on the sides yet rounded at the top. The sleeves themselves are meant to be freestanding (they were designed so that they could, in theory, be taken on or off a dress for washing and ironing). Mangosing's ternos come with a card that identifies the importance of proper storage; VINTA ternos should not be hung on a hanger but rather folded carefully in a box with the sleeves flat to preserve their unique butterfly shape.

The construction of the terno sleeves, once easily replicated in the Philippines, has become somewhat of a lost art form. Recognizing this diminishing skill set, Slim's School of Fashion and Arts in Manila now devotes a section of dress design to the creation and construction of the sleeves. The Philippines was part of the global shift to garment manufacture to the global South in the 1980s and 1990s, when the creation of special export processing zones made outsourcing financially lucrative for many retail fashion outlets, who contracted with garment production companies to manufacture their clothing.[36] In contrast, the made-to-order industry in the Philippines operates on a smaller scale that is based much more locally. Designers have long relied on a "back room" of local pattern-makers, sewers, embroiderers, beaders, and finishers.

While many high-fashion designers still operate within this system, today fashion-related labor in the Philippines has begun to feel the ripple effects of the global contracting of Filipino workers around the world. As many have noted, the Philippine economy depends heavily on remittances sent home from Filipinos working abroad.[37] In the late twentieth century these laborers were deemed a national asset, a boon to the nation for their willingness to live far from home in places that range from North America and Europe to the Middle East and other parts of Asia. Although Filipinos overseas have now become a dominant version of the intersection of transnational dynamics and labor, corporations from abroad also hire Filipinos to staff call centers based in the Philippines. For a class of young and upwardly mobile Filipinas and Filipinos, these call centers are viewed as promising financial opportunities.

Though the fashion industry may seem initially to have little in common with the call center, the rise of business outsourcing in the Philippines (emblematized by the call center) as a lucrative alternative to working abroad has had lasting effects on the local fashion industry, which now must contend with these competing forms of employment. In contrast to companies like H&M or Zara, the majority of designers who work in Manila still have their garments produced in small, limited runs. Many of them employ sewers (who often work with them for years at a time), and employees with experience in pattern-making and piecework are in high demand. Since the structure of wages for paid fashion work in the Philippines has historically centered on piecework and not on salaried labor, designers I spoke with have noticed that skilled and talented sewers are much more difficult to find.[38] Fashion school programs in Manila, for example, have seen increased enrollment, but the students who graduate from these programs are not necessarily interested in the back room. Instead, they dream of owning their own businesses, having their own clients, or working abroad. For a younger generation of workers, compensation by the piece cannot compare with the financial benefits of regular salaried work. As a result, designers report the difficulty of finding sewers with specialized skills such as embroidery, beadwork, or the ability to construct the trademark butterfly sleeves of the terno.

The terno and its sleeves thus serve as both material object and metaphor of the changing conditions of the global marketplace in the Philippines and how they have affected labor. Now identified by many as the closest garment the Philippines might have to a national costume for women, the terno's sleeves, with their careful pleats that fewer and fewer people know how to reconstruct, also call attention to a trajectory that threatens artisanal craft and practice. This decline in an industry that depends upon specialists with the skills to engineer a designer's creative vision means that the terno is once again a garment that is in danger of disappearing, this time not because there is a lack of women who might wear it, but rather because there is a dwindling number of people who can make it.

A Manila-Toronto Production

Moving from the symbolic visibility of the terno and the materiality of its creation, in this section, I unravel the emotional perplexities that are attached to Mangosing's project of transnational and ethical fashion, especially in its relationship to labor. The threads that hold this transnational venture together are importantly warped and frayed, twisted and entangled. The discussion that follows examines these forms of affective perplexity, especially as they emerge in the friction that lies beneath Mangosing's envisioning of VINTA as an ethical form of fashion, and the emotional registers of discomfort between a designer in the diaspora and the labor of fashion. This perplexity, I emphasize, is not a failure but rather a potentially resistant model that works against the usual trajectory of fashion and its easy consumption of labor from the global South.

In the early days of VINTA's production, Mangosing worked with a pared down staff of just two other women: her cousin, Ria Limjap, who coordinates the operation in Manila; and their master sewer Lita Lagman. Mangosing juggled designing, fitting, sales and marketing, working with customers, and product delivery in North America. Limjap managed the garment's physical production, acquiring materials, ensuring prompt delivery, and shipping. Lagman, a woman in her sixties who once worked for an established designer in Manila, created every single VINTA terno. VINTA was therefore limited by Lagman's schedule (since she is also subcontracting or sewing as a freelance artist for others). This meant that in 2015, Mangosing was only able to complete roughly 20 orders. She laughs when she recalls this number, for she recognizes that achieving her goals for the business are impossible to attain at their current rate. As her plan to develop VINTA progressed, Mangosing soon encountered multiple challenges. How could she generate enough revenue to keep the business going while still maintaining her commitment to pay Lagman more than the usual sewer's wages? How could she also price the garments competitively for a North American consumer? When I asked her if it might have been possible to construct the VINTA ternos elsewhere (somewhere in Toronto or in Canada) she said that she did consider it. But when I asked her again whether she would consider moving the production to another place abroad in Asia, she says without hesitation, no. Because, she underscores, the point was always to help the Philippines, Kapisanan, or the Filipino Canadian community.

Despite the difficulties of supply and demand, Manila-based coordinator and production manager Limjap firmly believes that VINTA wouldn't be possible without transnational exchange. For her, VINTA is "really a Manila-Toronto production. It is. It wouldn't work without [Mangosing] and it wouldn't work without me," she observes.[39] Prompted to elaborate, Limjap began by explaining that VINTA depends upon Mangosing's design sensibility, because she can reformulate the terno with the flair of someone who has been educated in fashion and worked in the retail industry abroad. Mangosing also had the initial funding, which is virtually nonexistent in a federal form in the Philippines. But on the Manila end, Limjap has access to the materials and fabrics, and a local fashion network, including the third actor in this scheme, Lita Lagman, who they call Manang Lita. Limjap had a previous connection to Lagman, a master sewer and cutter who once worked for a designer in the Philippines but then left to go into business on her own because, as she told Mangosing, she had worked for many years yet was still poor.

With Lagman's personal history in mind, Mangosing soon began to become more and more committed to using VINTA as a platform to address the conditions of garment labor in the Philippines. In order to accomplish these goals, however, VINTA will eventually need to reach a much higher level of production. It is here that Mangosing is running into difficulty. "The Philippine side of this enterprise actually needs more attention," she observed at a 2014 talk for Next Day Better Toronto (a series that highlights artists and entrepreneurs in the Filipino diaspora). She continued, "it requires more from the consumer. It requires more understanding from the consumer to actually effect change."[40] She needed to keep the price point at a certain level—what Limjap describes as pricing for a North American audience—in order to one day be able to offer Lagman a salary with benefits, the opportunity to train other sewers, and a living and fair wage in the Philippines. In the first two years of VINTA's execution, after exhausting her initial funding, Mangosing did her part by forgoing profit for herself, such that proceeds went first to pay Limjap, Lagman, and for materials and shipping, before funneling the remainder into Kapisanan.

But what Mangosing now finds most difficult is how to negotiate the demands of marketability for her customers and her desire to pay Lagman, and now, her staff, salaries instead of by the piece. While currently her investor's funding allows her to do so, once these funds are exhausted she will face a chicken-and-egg dilemma: How can she generate enough money, ensure a quality product, pay workers enough, and promote a customer base who will be willing to pay this amount? The current price point for a VINTA made-to-measure dress (figure 6.1) is in US currency and hovers at about $400, depending on the length of the dress, the type of fabric, and the complexity of the design. Customers often, she said, initially hesitate when she tells them how much their garment will cost (despite the fact, she observes somewhat ruefully, that they might be willing to spend hundreds of dollars on a pair of shoes or a purse or for a special-occasion dress from another label). She constantly runs up against these difficulties when promoting VINTA, and she meets these challenges not just by personalizing the fit of the dress, but also by telling her customers about the woman who is making them. She tells them about Lagman's life and the very meager amount that sewers are usually paid. She emphasizes Lagman's skill, how long she works, the beauty of the garment she produces, her position as an artisan.

If the North American consumer would rather forget the work of people like Lagman, Mangosing does not allow them to. Her Next Day Better presentation was an example of how she communicates these urgent objectives. Speaking to a hushed and attentive crowd, she closed her description of VINTA with the sobering assessment of the usual relationship between the North American consumer and garments produced in the Philippines: "I have to challenge our consumer to wrap their heads around the idea of investing in a garment that is not disposable. A garment that is not necessarily cheaper because it's coming from the Third World, the Philippines." Asking her audience to do the opposite, she compelled them to "Think about investing in a garment that's made in the Philippines." She paused, drawing out the last few moments for emphasis: "I want to challenge all of you to think about what you're wearing and why and maybe who made them. Whose hands touched them. Because when you wear a VINTA, you can answer all of those questions very clearly and hopefully change the way you see fashion, the way you wear fashion, and the way that you represent your cultural pride."[41]

Once customers learn about these specifics, she says, some of her clients, especially those who are millennial and second-generation Filipinas, understand and are able to rationalize their purchases (or at least justify them to themselves). In the end, though, she admitted that most potential customers have other objectives in mind. One woman, after hearing Mangosing's eloquent explanation, responded by agreeing in principle. She later followed up by telling Mangosing that because of the sewer's schedule, she was excited by the fact that she would be the only one to have the item she was purchasing.[42]

In discussing Lagman with her clients, Mangosing treads carefully. Going too far would exploit Lagman's image, rendering her into mere object for display, the Third World woman doubly exploited as described by Ramamurthy. The smaller scale of VINTA's production gives Mangosing an important advantage, one that, along with her own political imperatives, also prevents her from falling into the trap of setting up Lagman as an iconic figure, a woman from the global South desperately in need of salvation. Mangosing differs from the ventures criticized by scholars such as Ramamurthy and Kabeer because of her strong commitment to Lagman, and her desire to—even on a smaller scale—effect a critical change in Lagman's life. Mangosing also maintains a crucial level of self-reflexivity, an awareness of the hierarchical relationship that structures her encounter with Lagman. This form of self-critique stemmed from her continued work with Lagman through VINTA. To consider an example of this self-awareness, I turn now to an interview with Mangosing in which she related the story of her experience visiting Lagman in her home. This account and Mangosing's complicated emotional response are critical, for they illustrate how a Filipina woman in the global North finds herself confronted by her relationship to labor in the Philippines as uneven and discomforting.

Mangosing herself had to recognize the realities of Lagman's life and her role in it when she visited the sewer's house. This more personal story is not part of the VINTA sales pitch, but the experience clearly fuels Mangosing's drive to attempt to alter Lagman's living and work conditions. As we sat in her office in Kapisanan, she recalled the visit with difficulty. At times she was animated, her voice trembling with outrage as she spoke. At others she sank in her chair, her voice dropping as she looked away. The visit to Lagman's house, she remembered, was not easy to arrange. Lagman had been avoiding their invitations to come by with a variety of excuses ("*Ay ma'am kasi, may bisita kami*" [Oh no ma'am, we have visitors], or "*Oh, sige, next week na lang*" [okay next week then], or "*yung bahay naming dalawang kwarto lang*" [in our house we only have two rooms]). These excuses come again and again but Mangosing insisted, telling her, "*Okay lang 'yan*" (that's okay).

"And then of course," she recalled, "I was slapped in the face when I got there." Lagman lived in quarters comprised of only two rooms. She had about a ten-foot-square space that was her primary living area, with a kitchen off to the side. There was a mattress on the floor, and two sewing machines, and a dusty laptop. "After we went to her house,"

Mangosing confessed, "I was like, 'Oh God.' I was getting choked up. [So I said], '*Okay Manang, pausapan na lang nating ang production*' [Okay, Manang, let's just talk about production]." She swore angrily first before continuing, "Where am I? I didn't want to sit down. I wanted . . . my whole plan was I wanted to take photos so that we can have it. This is where it's made [referring to the garments]. And I was like—wow this isn't very photogenic—and I'm just going to take a picture anyway because at some point something's gotta give, right?" After leaving Lagman's house, Mangosing and Limjap process the experience in disbelief: "And we just sat in the car going, 'Oh my god, honestly.' And Ria is like a little bit more desensitized than me . . . So she's like, 'To be honest, *hindi ko alam ha. Hindo ko alam ganoon pala ang bahay ni Manang*' [I didn't know, okay? I didn't know that was what Manang's house was like]."[43]

Mangosing underscored for me, again and again, her disbelief, the fact that she was not aware of these conditions and her dismay at her failure to recognize the signs and read the clues. But she was also struck by the incongruence, the material traces of the difference between her position and Lagman's. She highlighted the sight of dust on the laptop, oil on the sewing machine, scraps of fabric stashed on a table. The question that lingers on the tip of her tongue was not just, how do you live here?, but also, how do you make these "beautiful things" and keep them, somehow, amazingly "immaculate," such that there is no trace of the life that accompanies their production?[44] Her initial reaction to the dirt, dust, oil, and cramped living space was perplexity: a mixture of horror, guilt, and shame. Later, during our conversation, she connected this moment to an earlier memory of Lagman telling Mangosing's mother about how she never was able to see her children and had to work all the time. In hindsight, Mangosing recoiled as she comprehended—perhaps for the first time—that all of Lagman's efforts must have been concentrated on the creation of the clothing. While she pointed out Lagman's embarrassment in this moment, what was also readily apparent is hers and Limjap's shame, registered here by the repeated use of expressions about honesty. Limjap's confession, "To be honest, *hindi ko alam ha. Hindo ko alam ganoon pala ang bahay ni manang*," uses a Tagalog word, "*pala*" that, while difficult to translate exactly into English, registers a speaker's shock and surprise.

Mangosing's emotional response was shaped by her own experience as a member of the Filipino diaspora, marked by concepts of *utang na loob* (translated variably as a "debt of goodwill," gratitude, or literally, of the "inside") and *hiya* (shame). Filipino scholars have explored how these concepts relate to a network of social relations that are critical to the making of the Filipino self.[45] But *utang na loob* and *hiya* also have important class constraints. For Mangosing as an employer to recognize her debt to Lagman, or to feel shame when confronted by their class difference, would be remarkable within the context of the Philippines. Thus, when she tells other Filipinos about Lagman's situation, some of them attempt to rationalize it (She has wifi, right? a well-meaning family member asks), but Mangosing is frustrated both with them and the argument that she shouldn't "impose" North American standards on Lagman. She also knows that this response is fueled by the entrenched class system in the Philippines and her position as someone who lives comfortably in North America. "So to even open up that conversation," she recalls bitterly, "that's me being North American and idealistic."[46]

Mangosing's perplexity counters the usual dynamics that structure the relationship between North American consumers of fashion and the relationship to labor in the global South. In recent years, the rise of what might be called feel-good fashion has been the industry's response to concerted attention to the political stakes of fashion and labor. These are emotional appeals to the shopper, meant to satisfy a consumer's desire to support sustainable environmental and "fair" practices, while at the same time they are also meant to assuage potential guilt and discomfort about participating in these forms of consumption.

But does the woman who purchases a VINTA remember these transfers and their origin when she slips into the dress, zips it up, looks in the mirror, and stands perfectly poised for photos that she'll eventually share with her followers in a swipe or tap? Will this recall become more than a fleeting recognition and lead to material difference? Mangosing's first desire was to document Lagman's life with photographs, but she also recognized that the documentation isn't "very photogenic." This is perhaps why when she gave her VINTA lecture at Next Day Better, she showed a close-up photo of Lagman's face and then a photo of the neighborhood where Lagman lived but refrained from showing the audience documentation of the living quarters themselves. Her labeling of these photos as "not photogenic" indicated her awareness of the disjunction between what a North American consumer would want to see, and what she wanted to show them. She understood that a North American shopper might find this visual evidence of Lagman's life too disorienting and disturbing. And she was right. Of the customers who responded to my 2015 survey, not one mentioned the dressmaker's life or labor as important to her decision.

In contrast, Mangosing's interaction with Lagman was punctuated by perplexing emotions that were uncontained, unavoidable, and for her, unforgettable. These emotional responses, however, also led to action: Mangosing's sustained commitment to reckon with these forms of perplexity and to respond. Lagman and her staff now create VINTA only in a work space rather than at their homes; Mangosing rented a brightly lit and air-conditioned house for the staff. She instituted more regularized work hours and, although Mangosing has been advised otherwise by people in the Philippines, the staff only works five days a week. Lagman, Limjap, and Mangosing collaborate together, and Mangosing offers Lagman's apprentices a small amount of funding while they are in school so that they might continue formal education while still learning the techniques of dress production and construction.[47]

Mangosing and VINTA offer a useful model of how perplexity might lead to critical self-reflexivity, political engagement, and more careful methods of addressing labor disparities that connect the global North and South, even though such responses might lead to material and emotional links to diaspora that are raw, untidy, and unfinished. Mangosing's concrete forms of action are crucially important, because they call attention to the fraying seams of transnational relations and ethical fashion that are potentially obscured by the beautiful fit of the VINTA garment. This enterprise bridges the oceans that separate the hands that make a VINTA dress from the hands that eventually put the dress on, the socioeconomic distance between the very different homes that these women live in, and the layers of difference that too easily are forgotten as a garment transfers from designer to sewer, distributor, retailer, and consumer. This affective interfacing—webbing together garment, designer, sewer, and consumer—is the true revision of VINTA, which presents us with a politics that is necessarily difficult and frayed, an uneasiness that puckers the immaculate fit of a beautiful dress.

NOTES

1 Like other Filipino studies scholars, I use "Filipino" as a general term for Philippine-based and diasporic cultural forms, identity expressions, and communities, but I acknowledge and align with the contemporary usage of terms such as Filipino or Filipnx, which seek to imagine nongendered and nonbinary expressions and collectivities. See for example the introduction to *Diasporic Intimacies: Queer Filipinos and Canadian Imaginaries*, ed. Robert Diaz, Marissa Largo, and Fritz Pino (Evanston, IL: Northwestern University Press, 2018), xx–xxi.

2 The process to create VINTA took several years. Mangosing began developing a business plan and received several grants from social and urban innovation funding programs. Although she was advised to model VINTA as a for-profit business, she decided to launch as a nonprofit. The line debuted in 2013 as part of Canada Philippine Fashion Week, and Mangosing had her first clients in August of that year. Caroline Mangosing, interviews with author, June 2014, Toronto, Ontario.

3 Kristina Rodulfo, "VINTA's Caroline Mangosing: Reimagining Filipiniana," *Rappler*, June 25, 2014, www.rappler.com.

4 See also Casandra Debartolo, "Canadian Designer Vinta Re-Invents Philippine Fashion," *Faze*, n.d., www.faze.ca.

5 Caroline Mangosing, email message to author, December 4, 2015; Mangosing, interview with author, June 16, 2017, Toronto, Ontario.

6 Anna Lowenhaupt Tsing, *Friction: An Ethnography of Global Connection* (Princeton, NJ: Princeton University Press, 2005), 3, 6. See also Martin F. Manalansan IV, "Queer Worldings: The Messy Art of Being Global in Manila and New York," *Antipode* 47, no. 3 (2015): 566–79, and my earlier elaboration of these forms of messy global couture in "Global Mess and Glamour: Behind the Spectacle of Transnational Fashion," *Journal of Asian American Studies* 19, no. 2 (2016): 143–67.

7 Priti Ramamurthy, "Material Consumers, Fabricating Subjects: Perplexity, Global Connectivity Discourses, and Transnational Feminist Research," *Cultural Anthropology* 18, no. 4 (2003): 524–50, 525.

8 Philip F. Kelly, Mila Astorga-Garcia, Enrico F. Esguerra, and the Community Alliance for Social Justice, Toronto, "Filipino Immigrants in the Toronto Labour Market: Towards an Understanding of Deprofessionalization," in *Filipinos in Canada: Disturbing Invisibility*, ed. Roland Sintos Coloma et al. (Toronto: University of Toronto Press, 2012), 68–88.

9 Statistics Canada, Ethnic Origin (279), Single and Multiple Ethnic Origin Responses (3), Generation Status (4), Age (12), and Sex (3) for the Population in Private Households of Canada, Provinces and Territories, Census Metropolitan Areas and Census Agglomerations, 2016 Census—25% Sample Data, Last Updated February 14, 2018, http://www12.statcan.gc.ca/.

10 This chapter builds upon a foundation of research in the humanities and social sciences that has analyzed the social disparities of Filipinos in Canada and examined how Filipinos are working to respond in venues that range from artistic

and cultural production to collaborative, community-based activism. See Philip
F. Kelly, "Understanding Intergenerational Social Mobility: Filipino Youth in
Canada," IRPP Study 45 (Montreal: Institute for Research on Public Policy, 2014);
and essays published in Coloma et al., *Filipinos in Canada*, including Valerie G.
Damasco, "The Recruitment of Filipino Healthcare Professionals to Canada in the
1960s," 97–122; Josephine Eric, "The Rites of Passage of Filipinas in Canada: Two
Migration Cohorts," 123–41; Lisa M. Davidson, "(Res)sentiment and Practices of
Hope: The Labours of Filipina Live-In Caregivers in Filipino Canadian Families,"
142–60; and Ethel Tungohan, "Debunking Notions of Migrant 'Victimhood':
A Critical Assessment of Temporary Labour Migration Programs and Filipina
Migrant Activism in Canada," 161–80. For work analyzing forms of Filipino
cultural production that contest these trends, see Christine Balmes, "Kapisanan:
Resignifying Diasporic Post/colonial Art and Artists," in Coloma et al., *Filipinos
in Canada*, 341–59; Kale Bantigue Fajardo, "Queering and Transing the Great
Lakes: Filipino/a Tomboy Masculinities and Manhoods Across Waters," *GLQ: A
Journal of Lesbian and Gay Studies* 20, nos. 1–2 (2014): 115–40; Geraldine Pratt and
Caleb Johnston, "Translating Research into Theatre: Nanay: A Testimonial Play,"
BC Studies 163 (2009): 123–32; Eleanor Ty, "Filipino Canadians in the Twenty-First
Century: The Politics of Recognition in a Transnational Affect Economy," in Co-
loma et al., *Filipinos in Canada*, 46–67; and Eleanor Ty, *Unfastened: Globality and
Asian North American Narratives* (Minneapolis: University of Minnesota Press,
2010).

11 Rhacel Salazar Parreñas, *Servants of Globalization: Women, Migration, and
Domestic Work* (Stanford, CA: Stanford University Press, 2001); Robyn Magalit
Rodriguez, *Migrants for Export: How the Philippine State Brokers Labor to the
World* (Minneapolis: University of Minnesota Press, 2010); and Catherine Ceniza
Choy, *Empire of Care: Nursing and Migration in Filipino American History* (Dur-
ham, NC: Duke University Press, 2003).

12 Pricing reflects summer 2017 costs as listed on "Dresses," VINTA Gallery,
accessed October 2, 2017, www.vintato.com/dresses/.

13 Hazel Clark, "Slow + Fashion—an Oxymoron—or a Promise for the Future . . . ?,"
Fashion Theory: The Journal of Dress, Body & Culture 12, no. 4 (2008): 427–46,
428.

14 Ellen Groves, "Ethical Fashion Goes Mainstream," *WWD: Women's Wear Daily*,
October 31, 2006, 12, ProQuest. Initial studies found that consumers prioritized
their own interests before being swayed by a brand's "ethical" practices (in other
words, when faced with the decision of purchasing clothing, a consumer would
not purchase a garment that she or he found to be unfashionable just because it
was ethical). See for example Catrin Joergens, "Ethical Fashion: Myth or Future
Trend?," *Journal of Fashion Marketing and Management* 10, no. 3 (2006): 360–71;
and Nathaniel Dafydd Beard, "The Branding of Ethical Fashion and the Consumer: A Luxury Niche or Mass-Market Reality?," *Fashion Theory: The Journal of
Dress, Body & Culture* 12, no. 4 (2008): 447–67. A more recent study recognizes

the high growth potential for "ethical fashion," but found that while designers might use the term "ethical" or sustainable fashion, its eventual success will depend upon consumers' abilities to recognize these differences and, more importantly, to see them as valuable. Lisa McNeill and Rebecca Moore, "Sustainable Fashion Consumption and the Fast Fashion Conundrum: Fashionable Consumers and Attitudes to Sustainability in Clothing Choice," *International Journal of Consumer Studies* 39, no. 3 (2015): 212–22.

15 Joergens, "Ethical Fashion: Myth or Future Trend?," 361.

16 Diane Elson and Ruth Pearson, "'Nimble Fingers Make Cheap Workers': An Analysis of Women's Employment in Third World Export Manufacturing," *Feminist Review*, no. 7 (Spring 1981): 87–107. For examples of this scholarship, see Deepita Chakravarty, "'Docile Oriental Women' and Organised Labour: A Case Study of the Indian Garment Manufacturing Industry," *Indian Journal of Gender Studies* 14, no. 3 (2007): 439–60; Jane L. Collins, "Mapping a Global Labor Market: Gender and Skill in the Globalizing Garment Industry," *Gender & Society* 16, no. 6 (2002): 921–40; Saniye Dedeoğlu, "Visible Hands—Invisible Women: Garment Production in Turkey," *Feminist Economics* 16, no. 4 (2010): 1–32; Angela McRobbie, "Reflections on Feminism, Immaterial Labour, and the Post-Fordist Regime," *New Formations*, no. 70 (Winter 2011): 60–76; and Priti Ramamurthy, "Material Consumers, Fabricating Subjects."

17 Elson and Pearson, "'Nimble Fingers Make Cheap Workers,'" 93. See also Ramamurthy, "Material Consumers, Fabricating Subjects," and Priti Ramamurthy, "Why Is Buying a 'Madras' Cotton Shirt a Political Act? A Feminist Commodity Chain Analysis," *Feminist Studies* 30, no. 3 (2004): 734–69.

18 Naila Kabeer, "Globalization, Labour Standards, and Women's Rights: Dilemmas of Collective (In)Action in an Interdependent World," *Feminist Economics* 10, no. 1 (2004): 3–35, 10.

19 Angela Hale and Linda M. Shaw, "Women Workers and the Promise of Ethical Trade in the Globalised Garment Industry: A Serious Beginning?," *Antipode* 33, no. 3 (2001): 510–30.

20 Bernadita L. Catalla, "Global Roots of Exploitation in the Garment Industry," *Philippine Labor Review* 9, no. 2 (1985): 47–60; Jane Hutchison, "Women in the Philippines Garments Export Industry," *Journal of Contemporary Asia* 22, no. 4 (1992): 471–89; Rosalinda Pineda Ofreneo and R. del Rosario, "Industrial Homeworking in the Philippines," *Philippine Labor Review* 12, no. 1 (1988): 32–45; and Rosalinda Pineda Ofreneo, "The Philippine Garment Industry," in *Global Production: The Apparel Industry in the Pacific Rim*, ed. Edna Bonacich, Lucie Cheng, Norma Chinchilla, Nora Hamilton, and Paul Ong (Philadelphia: Temple University Press, 1994), 162–79. For parallel concerns in other sites, see Kabeer, "Globalization, Labour Standards, and Women's Rights."

21 For examples of the scholarly debate regarding ethical consumption, see Clive Barnett, Paul Cloke, Nick Clarke, and Alice Malpass, "Consuming Ethics: Articulating the Subjects and Spaces of Ethical Consumption," *Antipode* 37, no. 1 (2005):

23–45; McNeill and Moore, "Sustainable Fashion Consumption and the Fast Fashion Conundrum"; Belinda T. Orzada and Kelly Cobb, "Ethical Fashion Project: Partnering with Industry," *International Journal of Fashion Design, Technology and Education* 4, no. 3 (2011): 173–85; and Kanchana N. Ruwanpura, "Women Workers in the Apparel Sector: A Three Decade (R)-Evolution of Feminist Contributions?," *Progress in Development Studies* 11, no. 3 (2011): 197–209.

22 Minh-Ha T. Pham, "The High Cost of High Fashion," *Jacobin*, June 13, 2017, www .jacobinmag.com. See also Minh-Ha T. Pham, "Feeling Appropriately: On Fashion Copyright Talk and Copynorms," *Social Text* 34, no. 3 (128) (2016): 51–74.

23 Lucy Mae San Pablo Burns, "'Your *Terno*'s Draggin': Fashioning Filipino American Performance," *Women & Performance: A Journal of Feminist Theory* 21, no. 2 (2011): 199–217, 201. For a historical study of links between dress and nationalism for the Filipino diaspora, see Sarah Steinbock-Pratt, "'It Gave Us Our Nationality': US Education, the Politics of Dress and Transnational Filipino Student Networks, 1901–45," *Gender & History* 26, no. 3 (2014): 565–88.

24 Genevieve Clutario, "The Appearance of Filipina Nationalism: Body, Nation, Empire" (PhD diss., University of Illinois at Urbana-Champaign, 2014), ProQuest (diss. no. 3646472); and Mina Roces, "Gender, Nation and the Politics of Dress in Twentieth-Century Philippines," *Gender & History* 17, no. 2 (2005): 354–77.

25 Caroline Mangosing, "Reimagining Filipiniana" (talk, NextDayBetter + TOR, Next Day Better, Toronto, Ontario, June 19, 2014).

26 See Salvador Bernal and Georgina R. Encanto, *Patterns for the Filipino Dress: From the Traje de Mestiza to the Terno, 1890s–1960s* (Manila: Cultural Center of the Philippines, 1992); and Gino Gonzales and Mark Lewis Higgins, *Fashionable Filipinas: An Evolution of the Philippine National Dress in Photographs 1860–1960* (Manila: Slim's Legacy Project and Suyen Corporation, 2015).

27 Millet M. Mananquil, "Making the Terno Cool and Hip and Relevant," *Philippine Star*, October 29, 2003, www.philstar.com.

28 In 2003, the Metropolitan Museum of Manila organized a design competition, "The Terno for Twenty-One Competition," a national showcase of emerging designers. Mananquil, "Making the Terno Cool and Hip."

29 For an excellent reading of this ironic reformulation, see Burns, "'Your *Terno*'s Draggin.'"

30 Mangosing, interview, June 16.

31 All quotes from Mangosing, interview with author, June 26, 2014, Toronto, Ontario.

32 For a detailed study of Toronto's fashion history, see Alexandra Palmer, *Couture and Commerce: The Transatlantic Fashion Trade in the 1950s* (Vancouver: University of British Columbia Press, 2001). An example of a successful bespoke (men's) tailor is Michael Nguyen's Garrison Bespoke in Toronto. See Ashante Infantry, "His Bespoke Suits Reflect Michael Nguyen's Love of Fashion," *Toronto Star*, June 26, 2015, www.thestar.com; and Rita Zekas, "Garrison Bespoke Sports Upscale Gatsby-Like Vibe for Men: Stealth Shopper," *Toronto Star*, August 13, 2013, www

.thestar.com. For women's made-to-measure, see Gillian Reagan, "Stitch by Stitch and Block by Block," *New York Times*, February 16, 2011, www.nytimes.com; and Camille Ricketts, "The $3,000 (Non-Designer) Suit," *Wall Street Journal*, August 12, 2006, www.wsj.com.

33 Mangosing, interview, June 26.

34 Anonymous customer survey, June 8, 2015.

35 Anonymous customer survey, June 5, 2015.

36 Catalla, "Global Roots of Exploitation."

37 See for example Parreñas, *Servants of Globalization*, and Rodriguez, *Migrants for Export*.

38 The observations in these pages are based on fieldwork conducted in Manila in the summers of 2014 and 2015.

39 Ria Limjap, interview with author, July 24, 2014, Manila, Philippines.

40 Mangosing, "Reimagining Filipiniana."

41 Ibid.

42 Mangosing, interview, June 26.

43 Ibid.

44 See Manalansan's "Queer Worldings" for an important critique of this normative reaction.

45 For key examples of scholarship on these concepts, see Vicente L. Rafael, *Contracting Colonialism: Translation and Christian Conversion in Tagalog Society Under Early Spanish Rule* (Ithaca, NY: Cornell University Press, 1988), 121–35; Martin F. Manalansan IV, *Global Divas: Filipino Gay Men in the Diaspora* (Durham, NC: Duke University Press, 2003), 40–44; and especially Francis Dancel, "Utang Na Loob [Debt of Goodwill]: A Philosophical Analysis," in *Filipino Cultural Traits: Claro R. Ceniza Lectures*, ed. Rolando M. Gripaldo (Washington, DC: Council for Research in Values and Philosophy, 2005), 109–28, and Emil V. Tabbada, "A Phenomenology of the Tagalog Notions of *Hiya* [Shame] and *Dangal* [Dignity]," in Gripaldo, *Filipino Cultural Traits*, 21–56.

46 Mangosing, interview, June 26.

47 Mangosing, interview, June 16.

7

Manicures as Transnational Body Labor

MILIANN KANG

In the summer of 2015, the *New York Times* (*Times*) published an explosive front-page series by Sara Maslin Nir on the "The Price of Nice Nails" and "Perfect Nails, Poisoned Workers."[1] This series shined much-needed light on labor rights violations, toxic chemical exposures, and occupational health risk in New York City nail salons. Nir's language and arguments, however, particularly her focus on a "rigid racial and ethnic caste system,"[2] placed most of the blame on Korean immigrant small business owners for labor conditions they alone did not create and by themselves cannot fix. This framing of the story not only oversimplified a sense of Korean owners as villains, but it presented Latina and other Asian workers as victims, ignoring their active participation in efforts to reform the industry. Substandard working conditions in nail salons are widespread, and nail salon owners must be held responsible for unfair and discriminatory labor practices and labor rights violations. But by focusing on ethnic relations within the salons, this coverage neglected to give sufficient attention to the systemic economic, social, and political forces outside of the salons. Specifically, the *Times* coverage and the responses to it serve as an instructive case to examine the invisibility or misinterpretation of transnational processes and the necessity of clarifying these processes for the broader public.

Expanding on my previous concept of "body labor,"[3] this chapter updates that research empirically and reframes it as *transnational body labor* to theorize commercialized, embodied service work that is performed at the local level but is shaped by cross-border economic, political, cultural, and historical processes. This transnational framework draws attention to the full range of factors shaping labor practices in these salons and challenges the popular discourse of inter-ethnic conflict which has been invoked in inflammatory ways to explain these practices.

As Nina Glick Schiller asserts in her call for transnational analysis to counter the over-reliance on an "ethnic lens," "whether or when transnational social fields and diasporic histories produce communal ethnic identities or make such identification primary is a question for empirical research."[4] Applying this to the nail salon case, rather than a given, whether co-ethnic workers receive preferential treatment—particularly with regard to wages—varies based on a host of factors, ranging from occupational sector, location, time period, human capital, migration history, immigration status, and labor rights and enforcement. All of these factors are shaped by the interplay of local and global forces, between sending and receiving countries but also regionally and globally, that transnational analyses illuminate.

By focusing on New York City nail salons, and more narrowly on media representation of the labor issues within them, this case study contributes to this volume's examination of the "intersections between 'fashion and beauty' and 'Asia,'—as a place, a narrative, a market, and a set of ambitions and imaginaries that is geographically and historically specific but also globally connected."[5] In conversation with these themes, this chapter explores how the performance of a fashion and beauty service such as the manicure is shaped by processes that transcend nationally or geographically defined spaces. Transnational body labor addresses how working bodies are shaped by current and historical processes that traverse state, geographic, and interpersonal borders, whether or not the actual services or service providers travel frequently across these borders. The earlier framework of body labor implicitly situated nail salon work in a transnational context, showing how the provision of intimate, embodied services has become marketized through cross-border processes, including labor migration, capital flows, consumer culture, and regulatory mechanisms. The invitation to contribute to this volume provides an opportunity to make this context more explicit. The studies herein have shown that transnational circuits between the United States and Asia are especially important in charting the beauty and fashion industry.[6] This chapter contributes to understanding the specific transnational forces shaping labor processes in body-related services. Specifically, the concept of transnational body labor challenges the premise of inherent co-ethnic preferences and advantages, and directs attention to the geopolitical, economic, and historical factors that create or undermine ethnic solidarity in any given industry and location. Transnational body labor can illuminate beauty services themselves as transnational products, as well as the meanings that are given to them in popular and political discourse.

Following, I give an overview of the recent coverage of nail salon labor issues as an example of popular discourse that oversimplifies transnational processes. Next, I offer a fuller context for these concerns, drawing on my own ethnographic research in these salons and on the organizing efforts of workers and advocates who have been mobilizing to address these issues for many years. I focus here on two significant factors that have shifted in New York City nail salons that are driven by transnational forces. The first is the increasing number of workers from different national, racial, and ethnic groups. The second is the number of undocumented workers in the salons. These two issues are intricately connected. Both of them connect to transnational circuits of labor in the beauty service industry and contest the assertion that ethnocentrism is the main force driving unequal labor practices. While focusing on media coverage, I also critique the tendency of some transnational scholarship to emphasize co-ethnic advantages in immigrant entrepreneurship. This focus can inadvertently support one-dimensional arguments, such as the *Times*'s coverage, which overstates the benefits and power of a single ethnic group, in this case Koreans, while neglecting the global forces that create entrenched labor inequalities in any given employment niche. Finally, the discussion and conclusion build on this analysis of transnational body labor, understand the deeply embedded structural inequalities in the nail industry, and strategize multi-pronged approaches to addressing them.

Theorizing Transnational Body Labor

The circuits of the transnational are increasingly tangible with regard to material objects, such as clothes, cosmetics, and even images, as they are often designed in one locale, produced in others, and consumed in yet others. But it may be much harder to grasp the transnational dimensions of fashion and beauty *services*, as they appear to be performed in very local sites, on very delineated bodies, by very specific providers. How can a personal, embodied service such as a manicure be a transnational exchange if it occurs in the very local space of a neighborhood nail salon? How can the concept of transnational body labor help to understand the emergence of nail salons as an immigrant-dominated niche, the labor rights problems in this industry, and possible ways to address these problems?

In addressing these questions, I build on recent work that seeks to expand the meaning of transnationalism, particularly with regard to labor and entrepreneurship, beyond the density of ties or frequency of movement back and forth across national borders between two countries. As Susan Bagwell writes, "(T)here is a need for a broader understanding of transnationalism that does not rely solely on the physical locations of the business and the extent of travel between them, but also considers the degree to which entrepreneurs access different forms of transnational support from the overseas diaspora."[7] The concept of transnational body labor builds on this literature on transnational entrepreneurship, but in addition to addressing self-employment and business operations, it draws attention to the ways that the labor itself within these establishments is shaped by transnational processes. In addition, it focuses on the ways that transnationalism not only supports ethnic enterprises by providing resources upon which these businesses can draw, but also creates challenges to their operation. Specifically, a transnational analysis can more fully illuminate how labor inequalities are the result of conditions spanning multiple countries, rather than being produced by a single ethnic group and its advantages.

In 2010, I published a book, *The Managed Hand: Race, Gender and the Body in Beauty Service Work*, which examined Korean-owned nail salons in New York City and the complex interactions that occur in them among owners, workers, and customers. The book situated the working conditions in the salons within the growth of the nail care sector into a multibillion-dollar industry dominated by Asian immigrant women workers. Building on Arlie Hochschild's influential work on "emotional labor," it developed the concept of body labor to explore the commercialization of services performed by and on bodies, as follows:

> I introduce the concept of *body labor* to designate the provision of body-related services and the management of both feelings and bodies that accompanies it. Despite the many dimensions of emotional labor that

have been addressed by feminist scholars, more work is needed on the body-related contours of low-wage service work dominated by immigrant women of color, particularly in the beauty industry. Thus, Asian-owned nail salons serve as a rich empirical site to develop the concept of body labor as a new theoretical lens through which to study gender, migration, race relations and the emotional and embodied dimensions of service work.[8]

I argued that while manicures and other beauty regimens were once performed in the privacy of one's own bathroom, they are increasingly being purchased in newly created commercial spaces, such as the immigrant-owned nail salon. The unwritten rules and expectations of these intimate exchanges between virtual strangers set up fraught encounters between customers, providers, and owners, across barriers of language, culture, race, class, and citizenship status. Building on scholarship on emotional labor, the purchase of intimacy, gender, and migration and racialized labor markets, I discussed how these exchanges renegotiate the boundaries between public and private, individual and social, market and nonmarket. While this earlier research did examine connections between the local and global in the development and daily operations of the industry, this chapter more fully addresses how transnational processes shape working conditions within the salons, as well as the public perceptions and political discourse surrounding them.

Part of the difficulty of grasping the transnational has to do with the nature of these inherently complex, far-ranging social forces, but this difficulty is further complicated by conflicting usages of the term itself.[9] Some sources uses the term "transnational" very loosely to reference anything related to the "global" or "globalization." In popular parlance, "transnational" too often is used simply as shorthand for "outside the United States," which has the unfortunate effect of reinforcing the very US-centric perspective that it seeks to transcend. Other scholarship has designated very specific requirements for its usage, such as sustained, back-and-forth movement across binational borders of people, products, or practices such as telecommunications or remittances. The influential definition by Basch, Glick Schiller, and Szanton-Blanc conceptualizes transnationalism as "the process by which immigrants forge and sustain multi-stranded social relations that link together their societies of origin and settlement, and through which they create transnational social fields that cross national borders."[10] More specifically, with regard to transnational entrepreneurship, definitions have similarly prioritized business transactions between countries of origin and settlement and frequent back and forth cross-national movement.[11]

Attentive to these debates, transnational feminist critiques have argued for theorizing that accounts for the interplay of multiple, asymmetrical, contingent, historical, territorial, state, and nonstate forces.[12] Chandra Mohanty writes that the transnational "must be attentive to the micropolitics of context, subjectivity, and struggle, as well as to the macropolitics of global economic and political systems and processes."[13] Dingo, Riedner, and Wingard provide a succinct description of the "spirit and intentions of transnational studies: namely a cogent analysis of globalized power."[14] I draw on these arguments to theorize transnational body labor, emphasizing the power dynamics embedded in and shaped by historical and contemporary transnational processes and situating them more explicitly in conversation with transnational feminist scholarship and debates.[15]

Attention to the body as a site that is shaped by transnational processes has generated new scholarship that illuminates how embodied service work is simultaneously intimate and globalized.[16] The locus on the body highlights the materiality of work performed on bodies, by bodies, for the purpose of enhancing the appearance, function, or health of bodies.[17] In my own work, I have employed the term "body labor," as opposed to the broader term "body work," to emphasize that these services are performed and exchanged for a wage. These commercial transactions are governed by laws and regulations but also by informal social norms that reference a web of cultural circuits—not just bilateral—that are constantly being written, rewritten, and challenged by transnational migration flows.[18] Building on important themes in this scholarship on transnationalism, a full treatment of nail salon work as transnational body labor would explore: the migration and labor recruitment circuits of the service providers from multiple sending countries; the ways that the labor of workers from different countries is differently valued based on legacies of colonial, imperial, neoliberal, and racial regimes; global inequalities in wealth and status that allow certain people, particularly women in the urban centers of industrialized nations, to purchase these services; the increasing demand for these services generated by global media and consumer culture; and the global production and marketing of cosmetic products that are utilized in these services. All of these issues call for more in-depth research. My own fieldwork in New York Korean-owned nail salons only scratched the surface of many of these concerns, and I encourage other researchers to pursue them. Instead, this chapter has a narrower focus, which is to apply the lens of transnational body labor to show how transnational processes are often hidden from view and overridden by a circumscribed and essentialist ethnocentric lens, and how this distorts understandings of the labor issues within the salons. Thus, utilizing the *Times* analysis of nail salon labor issues as an ethnic caste system and how the strong public response to this framing serves as an instructive case, this chapter explores how a transnational analysis is crucial to grasp the complex inequalities that shape body labor in beauty service exchanges.

New York Times Nail Coverage and Responses

By characterizing nail salons as a "hidden world" that is "governed by their own rituals and mores,"[19] the *Times* series failed to recognize that the problems in these salons are not ethnic-specific but are embedded in widespread global economic forces. By not giving full attention to the transnational context shaping the working conditions in the salons, the *Times* attributed the exploitative working conditions in the salons mainly to the labor practices of the Korean owners, emphasizing the "stark ethnic hierarchy imposed by nail salon owners."[20] However, the two story lines of what happens inside the salons and the social conditions outside the salons are not separate, but intricately connected. The framework of transnational body labor can help to untangle the complex web of factors that determine how much, or little, workers get paid, and why these wages are not attributable to a single cause such as an ethnic caste system within any given salon.

Nir conducted extensive interviews with nail salon workers—more than a hundred. This is formidable and committed reporting. But in writing a journalistic exposé, she highlighted those with the most horrific stories to tell. This does not invalidate their stories, but it calls into question how representative they are. Many of her respondents could be considered outliers, people on the extreme side of an industry with a great deal of variation. Their experiences must be taken seriously and addressed forthrightly, but they should not be generalized to all salons.

Nir's reporting erroneously assumed ethnic solidarity, lumping Korean salon owners together with Korean workers, neglecting occupational and class differences, and emphasizing the privilege of these Korean workers over other ethnic workers. These arguments were not fully supported or explained, and unfortunately fed into inflammatory and divisive tropes of Koreans exploiting other ethnic groups. As Alison Roh Park writes, "Nir relies on every anti-Asian trope in the book—Nepalese workers are crying, enduring victims of exploitation; Koreans are greedy, decadent, shrewd, and conniving; Chinese workers are crammed into tenement-style apartments with strangers or extended family members."[21] The idea of an ethnic caste system thus draws on stereotypical images of "good" and "bad" immigrants, rather than bringing attention to the mechanisms of the global economy that make workers from certain countries and ethnic groups more vulnerable to exploitation.

Furthermore, Nir's assertion that shared ethnicity is the reason certain workers are treated better than others flies in the face of a large body of research that shows both costs and benefits of co-ethnic employment and how these are shaped by transnational processes.[22] For example, Morales demonstrates that a number of factors, including immigration status, gender, and skin color can be more significant than shared ethnicity in determining wages and other treatment of workers by co-ethnic employers.[23] Chin has shown that even within a single industry, there is great variation, as Chinese garment factory owners are more likely to hire Chinese workers who are unionized, documented, and female, whereas Korean garment factory owners largely hire Mexican and Ecuadoran undocumented workers of both genders.[24] Thus, in order to understand how co-ethnicity shapes any given industry, or even a single shop, it is necessary to understand the multiple intersecting forces of gender, class, national origin, unionization, and undocumented status that influence hiring, wages, and labor conditions within a transnational context.

By not doing this, the *Times* argument that a de facto ethnocentric bias of Korean owners results in overpayment of Korean workers and underpayment of all other ethnic groups runs into both empirical and theoretical problems. First, not all Korean owners pay Korean workers more than other workers, and second, if they do, there can be multiple reasons for this other than the simple fact that they are Korean. In my own research, I found instances in which Korean workers were paid more than other workers, but shared ethnicity was not necessarily the sole or primary reason for this. Some Korean workers get paid more because they are more experienced and take on additional duties such as managing other workers, ordering supplies, bookkeeping, and negotiating customer complaints. Others may earn more because they have specific relationships with the owners, such as family, church congregations, or they are former classmates or residents of the same hometown.

These factors are related to co-ethnicity, but are not synonymous with them, as they are forged through specific migration trajectories that in turn reflect transnational linkages between specific regions or institutions. These linkages are important, as a Korean worker with close personal ties to the owner may receive very different treatment from one who does not have such connections. For example, the way a salon owner assigns customers to manicurists is an important factor impacting earnings, as a regular clientele translates into higher tips. In one salon, I listened to Korean workers complaining about another Korean worker, a former classmate of the owner, who they perceived as doing subpar work yet receiving more than her share of these favored, high-tipping clients. But in another salon, I observed the Korean owner bypassing Korean workers and directing these expensive "big job" customers to a Chinese manicurist who was considered most skilled in doing the nail art designs desired by the mostly African American clientele at this particular salon. These examples show the different ways that shared ethnicity may or may not shape favorable treatment by the owner, as the first case shows how one specific Korean worker received favoritism over others based on a close personal relationship, but in the second case, specific skills that attracted customers outweighed co-ethnic preferences.

It is also important to note that even if Korean ethnicity in and of itself confers privileges, Korean nail salon owners would hardly be the only group to give preferential treatment to its own members. In addition, any within-group favoritism is counterbalanced by the racial hierarchy that is dominant in the broader society. For example, findings by Smith et al.

suggest that with regard to evaluations of promotability and skill level, "Asians and Blacks are more severe toward each other than either is toward Whites."[25] In short, shared ethnicity does not automatically confer advantages, and even when it does, these advantages derive from multiple factors, including the racial discrimination in the broader society, rather than simply the ethnic biases of group members themselves.

Even where it exists, co-ethnic advantage may not be a huge boon, as being the highest paid workers in a low-wage industry does not alter the fact that the entire wage structure in that industry is suppressed. In nail salons, as in many other workplaces, these low wages emerge through a mix of forces, the lens of transnational body labor highlights. These transnational forces include: globalized labor migration flows that recruit the lowest paid workers to meet consumer demand for cheap products and services; lack of regulation and lax enforcement of existing laws; obstacles and penalties for organizing; and ultimately, the bottom line of profit-driven, winner-take-all markets and mentalities. A transnational analysis of micro-macro linkages shows how salon practices reflect the social inequalities of both the local context in which they are embedded and larger global disparities.

In some places, the *Times* coverage recognized these multivalent forces. But in others, it veered into ethnocentric stories of Mercedes- and Cadillac-driving Korean salon owners with undocumented Chinese workers crammed into their basements. Such stories exist, but they do not represent the dominant model of immigrant small business owners in this niche. In fact, the vast majority of nail salons are not chains, but rather, single mom-and-pop operations, where the owners often work alongside their employees completing manicures.

Nir's article itself cites a Labor Department report that of 37 cases being investigated in 2014, "almost one-third of them involved shops from a single chain." This is a significant finding but is mostly buried. Not only did the *Times* fail to follow up on who this one main violator was, the nature of the complaints against them, and how the chain-ownership model contributed to these violations, but it instead blamed Korean immigrant owners based on ethnic group affiliation. By not investigating further why chain salons account for the large number of complaints under investigation, and how this business model is far different from that of the majority of single-owned salons, Nir missed opportunities to investigate the specific characteristics and practices of actual labor rights violators and how they can be linked to transnational processes. Increasingly, these large-scale chain salon enterprises mobilize investments from transnational capital and financial networks. Yet, even though she recognized them as the main labor violators, Nir failed to investigate the specific business model of these chain salons, and instead collapsed all Korean nail salons together with them based on shared ethnicity. Instead, the concept of transnational body labor highlights the multivalent forces that shape the establishment, operation, and labor practices within salons.

Heterogeneity of Nail Salon Businesses and Labor Practices

Interviews and participant observation with nail salon owners, workers, and customers provide a very different view of these operations from those presented in the *Times* series. Specifically, they reveal that the boundaries dividing the labor of nail salon owners versus workers can be much more fluid, as well as the differential in their earnings. As noted earlier, many owners are also manicurists—they do nails while ordering supplies, paying rent, and trying to meet payroll. Michelle Ko, a current manicurist and former owner, explains, "Well, I was an owner of a nail salon before and I don't like it as much as just being a regular worker. Owners have to invest much more of their money into paying rent and salaries and workers really don't have much worries. If it is a slow day at the job, workers will get a smaller amount of tips but owners will suffer a greater loss." Similarly, manicurist Esther Park commented on why she does not wish to start her own salon:

> I want to mention that not all Korean women who open nail salons are successful. Many nail salons that are opened are maintained and nothing more. A person like me has a lot of experience but nowadays, a lot of women who have only a few years of experience open up stores because they don't want to work for someone else. They want to be seen as "the boss." The inside story is that they open up stores without generating any profit. They are satisfied if they are able to take home their salary.

Given the relatively negligible differential in earnings between ownership and employment in many small salons, this desire to be "the boss" is increasingly outweighed by the precariousness of nail salon entrepreneurship.

In short, Korean nail salon owners are not a homogenous group, but demonstrate a wide range of business and labor practices. While labor violations are widespread, many nail salon owners want to do the right thing, but their limited English makes it difficult to understand and comply with complex and changing laws. Susan Lee, a nail salon owner in Brooklyn, shared, "[The hardest thing about the job is] American law—having to meet standards of the health department. The customers complain about it being dirty or take your license number if they think you did something wrong and they call the health department. They came once and I got a fine because they said the carpet was dirty! Everything else was clean—they just wanted to find something because someone had complained." Understaffed and underfunded city and state departments often focus on issuing fines rather than educating business to bring them into compliance, which fuels suspicion and hostility. These comments from nail salon owners attest to a pervasive sense of fear and frustration:

"We want to follow the law, but it is very confusing."

"Instead of helping us, officials just fine us or try to close our salons."

"I want to pay my workers more, but the business is barely staying open and sometimes I earn less than them."

"When customers are so impatient, we have to rush."

Jean Hwang, a long-time salon owner, describes the challenges of keeping her salon profitable in a market where prices are continually falling, "There are too many nail salons today. When I first started there weren't as many. However, the number of people getting their nails done have increased tremendously. Everyone, from little children to grandmothers, are getting their nails done. But the prices have gone down and my income remained pretty much the same. The only way it could go is down."

Even those owners who strive to support their workers find that the pressures to stay competitive influence them to enact practices that they themselves criticize. Charlie Choi, a nail salon owner in Brooklyn, sighs when she thinks of the personal toll of long hours on her workers. Many of her customers come to the salon after work so she must stay open late into the evening. "The time when I feel sorry the most is when workers who have babies cannot go home until late in the night. Even an hour is precious for a mother and a baby, but it does not work as well as I wish." She remembers when her son was young and she too was a nail salon worker and often could not see him at night. "So I thought, if I become an owner, I will be loose about children issues, which are hard to talk about to the owner." Charlie realized her dream to open her own salon, but soon found out that in order to keep her business profitable, she needed to arrive early and stay late. Since she gives her workers rides to the salon, they arrive early and stay late with her. The various external pressures that keep her salon operating at a narrow profit margin influence how she runs the salon. While she had started a second salon with a loan from her sister, it was not earning enough to stay open and she closed it with a huge loss. She had hoped to attract investors but was unable to compete with the deep pockets of those who could tap into transnational financial networks and join the ranks of the profitable nail chains discussed earlier. Voices of nail salon owners like Jean and Charlie must be taken into account in efforts to reform the industry. Many owners strive to be in compliance but struggle with the complexity of the laws, language barriers, and the realities of trying to keep businesses solvent in a very competitive market where customer demand for cheap manicures drives down prices and wages.

Likewise, nail salon workers are a very diverse group, not only across ethnic groups but within any single group. Some are working under very exploitative and precarious conditions, but many others regard this work as decent, even pleasurable, and as the best of the options available to them. In conducting fieldwork in more than a dozen salons throughout more than a decade, I have seen a vast range of working conditions, some egregious, some tolerable, some desirable. While labor rights violations occur daily, there are also thousands of mundane, daily interactions in which workers perform manicures for relatively decent wages in mostly decent working conditions, although potentially toxic exposures are always looming in the air. I have observed many changes in the industry, and even significant changes in a single salon, as owners, workers, and customers turn over rapidly in response to many influences.

One salon closed when a large construction project blocked its entrance, another when the owner moved to Seoul, another when a new, less competent manager took over.

Despite these precarious and demanding conditions, in the interviews I conducted, many workers saw this as the best alternative available to them:

"What else could I do with my limited English?"

"I worked as a nurse in Korea but I would have to go to school again here and I can't afford the time or money, so this is the only other thing for me to do."

Jinny Kim, a salon manager, states, "I get paid three times more money (in the nail salon) than in the bank so I just decided to work here. . . . The first reason is that I already knew how to do nails. . . . and I thought, 'What other work is there?'" The fact that Jinny has such a high salary has to do not simply with the fact that she shares Korean ethnicity with the owner, but that she manages the salon and is the most sought after "nail artist," known for her elaborate and original designs. This fuller range of stories regarding employment in nail salons needs to be publicized.[26]

Although the attention drawn to these issues from the *Times* coverage helped add momentum to various reform efforts, Nir's reporting was strongly criticized by several journalistic sources, including the *Times*'s own public editor, who stated that the series "went too far" and would have benefited from "giving more acknowledgment to the salons that do it right, emphasizing the ways that these low-paid jobs can help new immigrants get a toehold in their new country and dialing back some of the wording of the employment ads."[27] Korean community groups also organized several protests around the city, asserting that the *Times* reporting was biased and that Governor Cuomo's action requiring wage bonds, a form of insurance to protect against wage theft, was discriminatory in its targeting solely of nail salon owners.[28]

Unfortunately, even the more thoughtful comments in response to the *Times* series seemed to ultimately beg for simple answers to a superficial question, "Can I get a manicure and still feel good about myself?" In the deluge of comments to the *Times* piece, one interesting thread described better conditions in Vietnamese-owned nail salons. While at first glance this seems to support Nir's ethnic caste system argument, the key explanatory factor here is not Vietnamese versus Korean ethnicity, but the different migration histories of these two groups and the different contexts of cities in which they settled and operate businesses. In particular, the differences between Los Angeles and New York are significant, with the latter based on more traditional service-based enclave economies.[29] The competition in New York is fierce, as there is a nail salon on virtually every other corner. Customers in other cities expect to pay three times as much as most pay for a manicure in NYC, where prices have remained flat for more than 20 years.[30] There isn't an endless supply line of immigrant laborers who have little choice but to work for rock-bottom wages. And, perhaps most significantly, there has been sustained organizing, lobbying, and legislative change to address nail salon issues, particularly in California.[31] In order to improve the labor conditions in the salons in New York, these types of long-term campaigns, which are simultaneously grassroots and transnationally oriented, will be most effective and need greater support.

Ironically, a decade earlier, most of the publicity around nail salons hailed them as an American success story. *Crain's New York Business* wrote, "The old American dream with a special Korean polish . . . an American classic with a rich New York overlay. For it's about immigrants, with few English language skills, no great capital, but lots of hard work and widespread success. It's also the old-fashioned dream, for there are no SBA loans, no setasides, no subsidies."[32] Such story lines also are problematic, as they reproduce model minority narratives of hard-working Asian immigrants who do not rely on government support and compare other racial and ethnic groups unfavorably. At the same time, while attributing the nail salon success story to the hard work of Koreans, this article also acknowledges that multiple factors, such as government loans and other supports, are often significant factors in shaping small business ownership. In short, whether or not they take advantage of these supports, entrepreneurial efforts such as nail salons occur within a broader context of government regulation and the opportunities shaped by them. Similarly, employment in nail salons is neither uniformly desirable nor exploitative and needs to be situated and understood within the transnational context in which it emerges, especially with regard to the government policies that have contributed to the growth and vulnerability of undocumented workers.

Undocumented Status and Transnational Body Labor

Another problem with Nir's analysis is that she misattributes the increasing reliance on undocumented workers from multiple sending countries—a widespread development throughout the global economy—to a circumscribed ethnic caste system created within the salons. Rather than recognizing the transnational forces outside the salon that have created an exploitable, undocumented workforce, her ethnic caste system argument suggests that the vulnerability of undocumented workers is somehow created by the Korean immigrant owners themselves. Thus, she again overlooks the transnational processes that have simultaneously attracted more low-wage immigrant workers to the United States while increasingly limiting the options for them to find legal employment. It is this transnational context that has fostered the growth of an exploitable undocumented workforce from multiple sending countries, such as the Nepali and Chinese workers she profiles, rather than an ethnic preference system created solely by Korean owners.

At the time of my fieldwork during 1997–2009, the majority of nail salon owners and workers were Koreans. While I did interview some Chinese, Latina, and African workers for my research, these workers were far less prevalent before 2010, whereas today, they are a visible presence in almost any salon. Adhikaar for Human Rights and Social Justice, an organization that has been working with Nepalese workers in the nail industry, issued a report, "Beyond the Polish," which states, "Nepali-speaking immigrant women are the newest and fastest growing group of workers entering the nail salon industry in New York."[33] The reason for the decline in co-ethnic employment in Korean-owned salons is linked to the decline in wages, which in turn is linked to the decrease in prices for the services and increasing competition. This downward pressure on wages results in the most attractive workers being those who will work for the lowest wages, which often means undocumented workers.

It is very difficult to produce precise statistics on the number of undocumented workers in the nail industry, and from which countries they come. This population lives in the shadows, and by definition lacks documentation. Nonetheless, various indicators support the claims that the employment of undocumented workers is increasing, and that this trend draws from multiple sending countries. A 2015 study by the Pew Research Center found that while the overall number of unauthorized immigrant workers in the three largest sectors—construction, production, and service—increased from 1995 to 2007, after the 2008 recession, "the total either leveled off or declined."[34] Nonetheless, the number of undocumented in services industries remains high. The same study reported, "Service occupations are the top job category for unauthorized immigrants in most states. In 39 states and the District of Columbia, service occupations have the largest number of unauthorized immigrants (and share of the unauthorized immigrant workforce in those jobs). Overall, service occupations make up 19 percent of the total US workforce and 33 percent of the unauthorized immigrant workforce nationwide."[35] Low-wage, low-skilled service sector jobs thus are more likely to have greater numbers of unauthorized workers. Furthermore, these sectors are harder to regulate, as they function in the informal, shadow economy and often fly under the radar of regulation.

With the rapid expansion of the nail salon industry, the number of undocumented workers is most likely to grow as well. The Bureau of Labor Statistics projects, "Employment of manicurists and pedicurists is projected to grow 10 percent from 2014 to 2024, faster than the average for all occupations. New nail services being offered, such as minisessions and mobile manicures and pedicures, will drive employment growth. High turnover and a growing number of nail salons will result in very good job opportunities."[36] Nail industry trade publications estimate a nearly fourfold increase in the overall number of nail salon workers in the last decade. As the nail industry continues to expand, the growth in undocumented workers could be proportionally as high. This is not, however, a unique situation. By employing undocumented workers, Korean salon owners are guilty of the very same practices that have driven down wages in multiple industries throughout the United States. These industries, which include domestic and care work, construction, agriculture, and food services, to name a few, often underpay undocumented workers in order to meet customer demand for low prices. Employers undeniably collude in these practices. But they can get away with hiring undocumented workers and paying them extremely low wages because of a broken immigration system that refuses to acknowledge our reliance on low-wage immigrant labor and to allow sufficient pathways for legal entry and long-term stay. Instead, the high demand for immigrant workers to fill these supposedly "unskilled" jobs is met with anti-immigrant sentiment and a lack of political will to provide legal status and protections for these workers. And this situation is only worsening with the inflammatory anti-immigrant rhetoric of the Trump administration. A deeper understanding of transnational forces could shift the current anti-immigrant political and cultural discourse and allow undocumented immigrants to come out of the shadows, not just in the nail industry but in many low-wage service occupations.

Discussion

What can the concept of transnational body labor contribute to the study of beauty, bodies, and labor, and the growing industries in which these intersect? More narrowly, how could the concept of transnational body labor have informed the *Times*'s reporting and influenced the nature of the barrage of indignant, guilty, and confused comments that appeared after the story? The *Times* characterization of an ethnic caste system unfortunately distorts certain trends in transnational studies that emphasize co-ethnic advantages. Countering this argument requires emphasizing broader approaches to transnationalism that do not just focus on the cross-border movement of actors and products, and how these mobilize resources to a particular group's advantage. Racial and ethnic hierarchies do exist within some salons, but what explains them, and are they the main force dictating how workers are paid and how they are treated? Sociologists call this the problem of determining salience, that is, figuring out how much weight different factors exert in explaining a given problem or outcome. What emerges at the shop level is a by-product of a host of factors that need to be evaluated systemically and synergistically. Greater sensitivity to the immigration histories that have shaped entrepreneurship and labor in the nail salon industry could have anticipated the uproar the focus on an ethnic caste system would cause in the Korean community, unfortunately sparking defensiveness more than efforts toward compliance. Rather than positioning a single cause such as a supposed ethnic caste system as the most salient factor, the framework of transnational body labor can highlight the full range of issues that shape labor conditions in the nail salon industry. But in our current soundbite-driven world, this is a much harder story line to sell.

In this chapter, I have raised a number of questions regarding the driving forces behind nail salon labor conditions and have offered ways of thinking about them through the lens of transnational body labor that can inform more sustained, informed, and effective responses. These approaches include educational, rather than punitive, approaches to regulation; partnerships, rather than antagonistic relations, among labor, community, media, and policy groups; and legal and social recognition of the full value of work that is too often denigrated as unskilled and unnecessary. I would not go as far to say that a manicure is a necessity, but these services support a $6 billion industry for a reason. They provide a bit of respite, care, connection, and whimsy into packed days that are too often lacking any of these. While many people may dismiss the beauty culture of hair, nails, and fashion as superficial and exploitative—and these critiques are valid—it is also possible to argue that the longing for beauty is part of the human condition and fulfills deep-seated needs that fuel consumption of these services around the globe.

Even if they could be dismissed as completely frivolous, these industries are not likely to disappear, and in fact are expanding globally at a rapid pace. Customers should not be vilified for wanting a service that brings them pleasure, and in many cases, relief, and many want to support good business practices. As one woman asked me, "Now that summer sandal weather is upon us, what is the socially conscious thing to do?" In order to improve wages in the salons, customers will have to pay a little more for manicures, with the understanding that a $10 manicure carries heavy social costs. Customers are sadly misinformed if they think that simply boycotting these businesses en masse, or singling out Asian, specifically Korean-owned ones, will wipe their hands clean. The solution to the problem of exploitation of immigrant workers is not to boycott the salons (unless there is an active call to boycott a particular salon as part of an organized campaign). Instead, customers can pay a fair price, tip well, support salons that have good labor practices, and join local and national efforts to support salon workers and demand nontoxic, green products. Consumers can treat workers with respect and appreciation for their hard and skillful work. Nail salons need better, more informed customers who are aware of the transnational elements of this practice and how it perpetuates global inequalities, especially among women.

While transnational body labor fulfills both the emotional and physical needs of customers to access a former luxury service, the performance of this work can translate into debilitating, long-term conditions for manicurists. While customers express sensitivity to their own health risks, they are much less concerned about the health of their manicurists. Pressures to work quickly undermine manicurists' ability to follow safety and health procedures not only for their customers' protections but for their own. Customers can provide crucial support to help upgrade working conditions and raise wages.

Likewise, nail salon owners must be held responsible for violating labor laws, but immigrant small business owners should not be blamed for problems that they singlehandedly did not create and that many others, particularly customers and cosmetics manufacturers, contribute to, and benefit from. Various concrete measures can improve working conditions in the salons, but they require cooperative, sustained, and multi-pronged approaches to reforming the nail industry. Owners, workers, and customers can work together with journalists, policymakers, advocates, academics, and community leaders for industry-wide changes, without vilifying immigrants or making them more vulnerable.

Active organizing campaigns, such as that of the NY Healthy Nail Salons Coalition, Workers United, Adhikaar, and New York Committee for Occupational Safety & Health are providing the necessary work on the ground.[37] These advocates have informed discussions with state officials to make recommendations about enforcement, legislation, outreach and alternative pathways to licensure.[38] An understanding of the complex dimensions of transnational body labor can lend support to this work by reframing issues away from ethnic to transnational explanations to inform journalists, social media, policymakers, community organizations, and individuals who are directly impacted by the research findings.

Conclusion

What makes a manicure a transnational product and exchange? Wages and labor conditions in New York City nail salons appear at first glance to be confined to intimate, personal interactions and spaces. In fact, they are part of global circuits that connect Asian workers to immigrant niches in the United States, and forge material and aesthetic ties back to Asia. In this chapter, I argue that the professional manicure has become a transnational product through multiple, overlapping processes. The concept of transnational body labor can illuminate how body-related services link consumers, workers, owners, and regulators into a complex web of relations, which no individual or group fully controls, but in which all are implicated with varying levels of accountability.

I have focused on the *Times* coverage of nail salon labor issues as arising from an ethnic caste system as an example of popular understandings, or misunderstandings, of transnational processes. Transnational scholarship has demonstrated that, far from being a given, the degree to which co-ethnics receive preferential treatment and non-co-ethnics are disadvantaged, varies based on a host of factors. These factors are best understood through a transnational framework that takes into account occupational sector, location, time period, skill level, and immigration status.

With regard to reforming the nail salon industry, the framework of transnational body labor could support policymakers to better evaluate and implement enforcement of labor rights and regulation of chemical exposures, without singling out a group by ethnicity to cease practices that are widespread throughout the US service sector, and globally. Immigrant workers across the United States and around the world, in sectors from domestic service, to restaurants, to nail salons, are now standing up to demand their rights, and they need widespread support. But nail salon owners, and immigrant entrepreneurs broadly, also need support and education to run good businesses, rather than punitive approaches to shut them down. Long-term solutions to problems in the nail industry need to address transnational issues, such as the global manufacturing of cosmetic products with potentially toxic chemicals (which Nir did address but again focused mainly on the problems at the shop level, as opposed to the production process), a global economy that pays the least amount for labor, goods, and services, and a broken immigration system that relies on the migration of workers from countries with destabilized economies to do this work at low wages, but does not give them secure protections.

It may seem like a tall order, but if we can do this for a manicure, then perhaps we can bring this understanding to other areas of our lives that are similarly bound up with the lives of others in the complex web of transnational body labor.

NOTES

Many thanks to Sonny Nordmarken for research assistance and to Donald Tomaskovic-Devey, Moon-Kie Jung, C. N. Le, Erin Khue Ninh, Eiko Strader, and Leslie Wang for helpful feedback. Any errors are those of the author alone.

1 Sarah Maslin Nir, "The Price of Nice Nails," *New York Times*, May 7, 2015, http://www.nytimes.com/.

2 Ibid.

3 Miliann Kang, *The Managed Hand: Race, Gender, and the Body in Beauty Service Work* (Berkeley: University of California Press, 2010).

4 Nina Glick Schiller, "The Transnational Migration Paradigm: Global Perspectives on Migrant Research," in *Migration and Organized Civil Society: Rethinking National Policy*, edited by Dirk Halm and Zeynep Sezgin (London: Routledge, 2015).

5 See the introduction to this book.

6 Thuy Linh Nguyen Tu, *The Beautiful Generation: Asian Americans and the Cultural Economy of Fashion* (Durham, NC: Duke University Press, 2010).

7 Susan Bagwell, "Transnational Entrepreneurship amongst Vietnamese Businesses in London," *Journal of Ethnic and Migration Studies* 41, no. 2 (April 17, 2014): 329–49 (330).

8 Ibid., 3.

9 Jose Itzigsohn, Carlos Dore Cabral, Esther Hernandez Medina, and Obed Vazquez, "Mapping Dominican Transnationalism: Narrow and Broad Transnational Practices," *Ethnic and Racial Studies* 22, no. 2 (January 1, 1999): 316–39.

10 Linda Basch, Nina Glick Schiller, and Christina Szanton Blanc, *Nations Unbound: Transnational Projects, Postcolonial Predicaments, and Deterritorialized Nation-States* (Amsterdam: Gordon and Breach, 1994), 6.

11 Israel Drori, Benson Honig, and Mike Wright. "Transnational Entrepreneurship: An Emergent Field of Study," *Entrepreneurship Theory and Practice* 33.5 (2009): 1001–22; Patricia Landolt, "Salvadoran Economic Transnationalism: Embedded Strategies for Household Maintenance, Immigrant Incorporation, and Entrepreneurial Expansion," *Global Networks* 1.3 (2001): 217–42; Andreas Wimmer and Nina Glick Schiller, "Methodological Nationalism and Beyond: Nation-State Building, Migration and the Social Sciences," *Global Networks* 2.4 (2002): 301–34; Patricia Landolt, Lilian Autler, and Sonia Baires, "From Hermano Lejano to Hermano Mayor: The Dialectics of Salvadoran Transnationalism," *Ethnic and Racial Studies* 22.2 (1999): 290–315; Katja Rusinovi, "Transnational Embeddedness: Transnational Activities and Networks among First- and Second-Generation Immigrant Entrepreneurs in the Netherlands," *Journal of Ethnic and Migration*

Studies 34.3 (2008): 431–51. Other sources have broadened these definitions to examine business transactions and travel across multiple borders, rather than just between sending and receiving countries (Anna Amelina and Thomas Faist, "De-Naturalizing the National in Research Methodologies: Key Concepts of Transnational Studies in Migration," *Ethnic and Racial Studies* 35.10 (2012): 1707–24; Peggy Levitt and Nadya Jaworsky, "Transnational Migration Studies: Past Developments and Future Trends," *Annual Review of Sociology* 33.1 (2007): 129–56; Glenn Morgan, "Transnational Communities and Business Systems," *Global Networks* 1.2 (2001): 113–30; Aihwa Ong and Donald Nonini (eds.), *Ungrounded Empires: The Cultural Politics of Modern Chinese Transnationalism* (New York: Routledge, 1996).

12 Inderpal Grewal and Caren Kaplan, "Introduction: Transnational Feminist Practices and Questions of Postmodernity," in *Scattered Hegemonies: Postmodernity and Transnational Feminist Practices,* edited by Inderpal Grewal and Caren Kaplan, 1st ed. (Minneapolis: University of Minnesota Press, 1994); Liisa Malkki, "Citizens of Humanity: Internationalism and the Imagined Community of Nations," *Diaspora: A Journal of Transnational Studies* 3.1 (1994): 41–68; Chandra Talpade Mohanty, Ann Russo, and Lourdes Torres, *Third World Women and the Politics of Feminism* (Bloomington: Indiana University Press, 1991); Chandra Talpade Mohanty, *Feminism Without Borders: Decolonizing Theory, Practicing Solidarity* (Durham, NC: Duke University Press, 2003); Ella Shohat, *Talking Visions: Multicultural Feminism in a Transnational Age* (Cambridge, MA: MIT Press, 1999); Ella Shohat, *Taboo Memories, Diasporic Voices* (Durham, NC: Duke University Press Books, 2006); Gayatri Chakravorty Spivak, *Outside in the Teaching Machine* (New York: Routledge, 2008).

13 Chandra Talpade Mohanty, "Transnational Feminist Crossings: On Neoliberalism and Radical Critique," *Signs: Journal of Women in Culture & Society* 38.4 (2013): 967–91 (p. 967).

14 Rebecca Dingo, Rachel Riedner, and Jennifer Wingard, "Toward a Cogent Analysis of Power: Transnational Rhetorical Studies," *JAC* 33.3/4 (2013): 517–28 (p. 518).

15 Inderpal Grewal and Caren Kaplan, "Global Identities: Theorizing Transnational Studies of Sexuality," *GLQ: A Journal of Lesbian and Gay Studies* 7.4 (2001): 663–79 (pp. 663–79); Hijin Park, "Migrants, Minorities and Economies: Transnational Feminism and the Asian/Canadian Woman Subject," *Asian Journal of Women's Studies* 17.4 (2011): 7–38; Ella Shohat, "Area Studies, Transnationalism, and the Feminist Production of Knowledge," *Signs: Journal of Women in Culture and Society* 26.4 (2001): 1269–72.

16 Kang, *The Managed Hand*; McDowell, *Working Bodies*; Sirijit Sunata, *Thailand and the Global Intimate: Transnational Marriages, Health Tourism and Retirement Migration* (Göttingen: Max Planck Institute for the Study of Religious and Ethnic Diversity, 2014); Julia Twigg and others, "Conceptualising Body Work in Health and Social Care," *Sociology of Health & Illness* 33.2 (2011): 171–88.

17 Gimlin, *Body Work*; McDowell, *Working Bodies*; Carol Wolkowitz, *Bodies at Work* (London: Sage Publications, 2006).

18 Rhacel Parrenas and Eileen Boris, Introduction," in *Intimate Labors: Cultures, Technologies, and the Politics of Care*, edited by Rhacel Parreñas and Eileen Boris (Stanford, CA: Stanford Social Sciences, 2010); Arlie Hochschild, *The Managed Heart: The Commercialization of Human Feeling* (Berkeley: University of California Press, 1983); Jennifer L. Pierce, *Gender Trials: Emotional Lives in Contemporary Law Firms* (Berkeley: University of California Press, 1995); Viviana A. Zelizer, *The Purchase of Intimacy* (Princeton, NJ: Princeton University Press, 2005).

19 Nir, "The Price of Nice Nails."

20 Ibid.

21 Alison Roh Park, "The Neoliberal Mani-Pedi: Wage Theft Is Not an Interethnic Issue," Race Files, 2015.

22 Lisa Catanzarite and Michael Bernabé Aguilera, "Working with Co-Ethnics: Earnings Penalties for Latino Immigrants at Latino Jobsites," *Social Problems* 49.1 (2002): 101–27; Tarry Hum, "The Promises and Dilemmas of Immigrant Ethnic Economies," in *Asian and Latino Immigrants in a Restructuring Economy: The Metamorphosis of Southern California*, edited by Marta Lopez-Garza and David R. Diaz (Palo Alto, CA: Stanford University Press, 2002); Dae Young Kim, "Beyond Co-Ethnic Solidarity: Mexican and Ecuadorean Employment in Korean-Owned Businesses in New York City," *Ethnic and Racial Studies* 22.3 (1999): 581–605; Alejandro Portes and Robert D. Manning, "The Immigrant Enclave: Theory and Empirical Examples" (Boston: Allyn and Bacon, 1986); Alejandro Portes and Min Zhou, "Self-Employment and the Earnings of Immigrants," *American Sociological Review* 61 (1996): 219–30; Jimy M. Sanders and Victor Nee, "The Limits of Ethnic Solidarity in the Enclave Economy," *American Sociological Review* 52 (1987): 745–73; Kenneth Wilson and Alejandro Portes, "Immigrant Enclaves: An Analysis of the Labor Market Experiences of Cubans in Miami," *American Journal of Sociology* 85 (1980): 295–319; Yu Xie and Margaret Gough, "Ethnic Enclaves and the Earnings of Immigrants," *Demography* 48.4 (2011): 1293–1315; Min Zhou and John Logan, "Returns on Human Capital in Ethnic Enclaves: New York City's Chinatown," *American Sociological Review* 54 (1989): 809–20.

23 Maria Cristina Morales, "Ethnic-Controlled Economy or Segregation? Exploring Inequality in Latina/o Co-Ethnic Jobsites," *Sociological Forum* 24.3 (2009): 589–610.

24 Margaret Chin, *Sewing Women: Immigrants and the New York City Garment Industry* (New York: Columbia University Press, 2005).

25 D. Randall Smith and others, "Favoritism, Bias, and Error in Performance Ratings of Scientists and Engineers: The Effects of Power, Status, and Numbers," *Sex Roles* 45.5–6, 337–58.

26 I was interviewed by Nir early in her research and shared background and contacts, as well as concerns about the racial and ethnic caste system argument, but was not cited. In the weeks following the coverage, I submitted multiple letters

to the editor and op-eds, two of them co-authored with other sociologists and advocates to the *Times* and other media outlets. These pieces supported the labor rights organizing, enforcement efforts, and media coverage, but also cautioned against measures such as sweeps or boycotts (which unless they are part of coordinated campaigns have little positive impact).

27 Benjamin Mullin, "NYT Public Editor: Nail Salon Probe 'Went Too Far' in Generalizing About Industry," *Poynter*, 2015; Jim Epstein, "The New York Times' Nail Salons Series Was Filled with Misquotes and Factual Errors. Here's Why That Matters. (Part 1)," *Reason.Com*, 2015; Richard Bernstein, "What the 'Times' Got Wrong About Nail Salons," *New York Review of Books*, 2015.

28 Elizabeth A. Harris, "Some Nail Salon Owners in New York Push Back Against Increased Regulation," *New York Times*, September 3, 2015; Andrew J. Hawkins, "Nail Salons Say They Will Sue Cuomo Over Wage Bond, Claiming Discrimination," *Crain's New York Business*, 2015.

29 C. N. Le, "New Dimensions of Asian American Self-Employment in Los Angeles and New York," *Asian American & Pacific Islander Nexus* 10.2 (2012): 55–76.

30 James Surowiecki, "The Economics of New York's Low Nail-Salon Prices," *New Yorker*, May 13, 2015.

31 Renée C. Byer, "Curb Nail Salon Worker Abuse," *Sacramento Bee*, May 16, 2015.

32 Alair A. Townsend, "The Old American Dream with a Special Korean Polish," *Crain's New York Business*, April 17, 1989 (17).

33 Adhikaar for Human Rights and Social Justice, "Behind the Polish: Experiences of Nepali-Speaking Women in Nail Salons in New York City," 2015, http://www.adhikaar.org/.

34 Jeffrey S. Passel and D'Vera Cohn, "Chapter 2: Industries of Unauthorized Immigrant Workers," *Pew Research Center's Hispanic Trends Project*, 2015.

35 Ibid.

36 US Department of Labor Bureau of Labor Statistics, "Manicurists and Pedicurists: Occupational Outlook Handbook," Occupational Outlook Handbook, 2016–17 Edition, https://www.bls.gov/.

37 NY Healthy Nail Salons Coalition, http://www.nyhealthynailsalons.org; Workers United of New York and New Jersey, http://www.workersunitednynj.org; Adhikkar, http://www.adhikaar.org/news; Healthy Nail Salons, New York Committee for Occupational Safety & Health, http://www.nycosh.org; Mónica Novoa, "Nail Salon Advocates and Workers Celebrate Historic Win in New York Legislature," *New York Committee for Occupational Safety & Health*, 2015.

38 Novoa, "Nail Salon Advocates and Workers Celebrate Historic Win."

8

"Little Freedoms"

Immigrant Labor and the Politics of "Fast Fashion" after Rana Plaza

JESSAMYN HATCHER

It's early in the morning when Sita heads from the B train up a quaint cobblestone street in lower Manhattan to the nail salon where she's worked for five years, 10–12 hours a day, six days a week, for $6 an hour and what she can garner in tips.[1] Like her co-workers, Sita lives in one of the neighborhoods in Queens that's home to a small but growing Nepali community. She is 25, from Kathmandu, and more than a little resembles the Bollywood movie stars whose films she enjoys. Like her colleagues, she came from Nepal to the United States on a student visa and then stayed, and now is undocumented. She pushes through the front door. It's painted the same shade of yellow as a nail polish called "Soft Daisy," one of the hundreds of varnishes from which clients can choose, although mostly they always seem to pick the same few. A burgundy so inky it's nearly black; a "classic" red, as she puts it; and for some reason this year a gray color.

Miliann Kang argues in her groundbreaking study of nail salon workers that New York City's salons can be grouped into three distinct categories. One is characterized by "high-service body labor involving physical pampering and emotional attentiveness serving mostly middle- and upper-class white female customers."[2] The salon where Sita works fits this description to a T. As clients arrive she'll offer them a choice of drink, a glossy magazine, the scent of the aromatherapy for their pedicure baths (Lavender? Tea tree oil? Grapefruit?). She'll pare and shape their finger- and toenails; push back cuticles and cut hangnails. She'll massage other people's feet and hands and slough off their dead skin. She'll apply a clear coat of polish, and then a colored coat, and then yet another, with a few careful, deft strokes of the tiny brush. All the while making conversation, or not, as the client talks on the phone, flips through a magazine, checks her email, or texts, according to the client's wishes.

Sita makes a beeline through the small front room where the reception desk and manicures stations are. She walks past the tiny enclosed space reserved for waxing, through the back room with its four pedicure stations, and through the door into what counts as the staff room, but is really just a stairwell. The parts of the salon the clients see are bright and chic; amenities of any kind for the staff are non-existent. Sita stows her belongings on the steps—her purse, the lunch she's brought from home. Like other women she works with, she prefers a hot lunch, but the salon's owner won't allow the workers to have a microwave. Food smells bother clients. (The nail technicians have developed a workaround: They put their lunches on top of the machines that heat the towels and the hot rocks for the $55 hot rock pedicure.) The pervasive smell is the astringent odor of nail varnish and remover. Citrus and powder are the top notes, scents that barely mask DBP, toluene, formaldehyde, formaldehyde resin, camphor, ethyl tosylamide, xylene, and the other chemicals found in nail products.[3]

Most of the things about the salon, and Sita's work in it, are being repeated across the city seven days a week. Over the last several decades, the New York metropolitan area has experienced more than a 45 percent rise in the number of nail salons, as Kang has detailed. The boom in the nail salon industry is at the intersection of developments characteristic of global capitalism: an expanding service economy; the commercialization of regimes of hygiene and adornment that used to be performed privately; new forms of feminized, racialized labor; and massive waves of migration by the Asian women who mostly occupy these jobs.[4]

One of the only ways in which the salon is atypical is in the workers' dress. The norm in most salons is for workers to wear either actual uniforms, supplied by the salon, or unified dress, usually black pants and a black or white shirt, not necessarily supplied by the salon, for labor that is, among other things, toxic, messy, and rough on clothes. But today, like every day, Sita is wearing her own clothes.

The long days at the nail salon are largely structured by the rhythms of work and the preferences of the clients. For this, Sita dresses practically. She wants to wear something that will be modest when she has to bend down, and she'll be bending down all day long. Lifting up and putting down heavy baths for pedicures; applying oil to her clients' finished toenails to help them dry more quickly and last longer; helping clients wrap their feet in saran wrap so they don't mar their nails; helping them into their shoes. She also dresses for style. Because at this particular salon, the workers' days are also shaped by fashion, and in particular fast fashion—the industry name for the likes of H&M, Forever 21, and Zara. Wearing fast fashion, being drawn into chat about it, deriving meaning from it, and even shopping for it.

In the summer of 2011, I began interviewing the eight Nepali women who work in this salon about their fast-fashion practices. The project didn't start out being about fast fashion, or about immigrant laborers' use of it. At the time, I had begun a study about clothing storage and discard practices in New York City, and it was research for this project that brought me to the salon. Eventually, as I got to know the women better, we met outside of their workplace, and exchanged messages over Facebook. My first conversations with the workers, though, took place in the salon during regular business hours. The women gamely answered my questions about how they stored and discarded their clothing. But my attention was quickly drawn away from these inquiries to other, more charged and urgent exchanges taking place in the salon.

I began, for instance, to register more closely the constant conversations about fashion I overheard between the clients and workers.

These conversations were almost always initiated by the clients, and they were most often struck up by clients in a very particular way: by complimenting the workers' clothing. I began to notice the bags from H&M and Forever 21 the workers routinely seemed to have with them. And I began to take in more fully the stylish ensembles the workers wore to labor at the salon: Manju in a sharply cut v-neck t-shirt with an abstract black-and-white graphic over shiny copper leggings. Sita sporting a loose, sheer georgette blouse printed with flowers over a black camisole and skinny black jeans. Jaya, in one of the bright, colorful, "happy" dresses (as she called them) that she favored, with a special preference for royal blue. These outfits, I came to learn, were all assembled from fast-fashion purchases.

I was compelled by this group of workers' use of fast fashion for a number of reasons. During the period of my research between 2011 and

2016, the urgency surrounding fast fashion in the salon was matched by a different kind of urgency outside of it. In April 2013, Rana Plaza, a factory in Bangladesh in which thousands of workers manufactured fast fashion, collapsed. One thousand one hundred and thirty-eight workers were killed and twenty-five hundred were injured, making it the deadliest accident in the history of the garment industry.[5] The horrific, preventable event brought fast fashion to the front page. In the process, it brought scrutiny to fast-fashion consumption and use. What this scrutiny routinely amplified, however, was a highly specific notion of fashion consumption. Fast fashion appeared as a desultory leisure activity and a psychological, environmental, as well as ethical problem. Where did this leave the subjects I had been spending time with? Undocumented immigrant women dressing for their service industry jobs?

This chapter examines two different, often conflicting understandings of the uses, meanings, and ethics of fast fashion in the era of Rana Plaza. The first is generated by my ethnographic study of the women I met in the nail salon. The second is exemplified by a pair of timely books, Elizabeth Cline's 2012 *Over-dressed: The Shockingly High Cost of Cheap Fashion* and Lucy Siegle's 2011 *To Die For: Is Fashion Wearing Out the World?*, whose authors served as the go-to pundits on the subject of "consumer ethics" in the wake of Rana Plaza's collapse, and whose work generated a particularly strong picture of the fast-fashion consumer as leisured, desultory, and problematic.[6]

In the pages that follow, I want to suggest that when the ethnographic data I've been collecting at the nail salon is set next to the data presented in books like *To Die For* and *Over-Dressed*, two very different kinds of consumer/users emerge.

First, the case of the nail salon workers fundamentally contradicts the idea that fast-fashion consumption is a desultory leisure practice. This particular group of workers is explicitly required by their boss to dress fashionably. For the nail salon workers, consuming fashionable clothing is both a mandated form of uncompensated labor, and a cost to labor. As I will explain, fast fashion is their best if not their only option to fulfill these requirements.

Part of what I want to ask here is: When we think about fast-fashion companies' massive global retail presence and the ever-growing number of fast fashion consumers, can we use a singular form of consumption as the rubric to understand fast-fashion's users or the meanings users attach to their clothing? Furthermore, does the ethnographic evidence that not all fast-fashion consumers are alike also indicate that consumers are not going to be—or maybe even that they should be—ethical in the same ways?

Second, workers recognize to a certain extent that dressing fashionably in this context is at once a form of unremunerated labor and a cost to labor enforced by their employer. Yet at the same time they insist that wearing these clothes to work at the salon holds important affective meanings to them that exceed their boss's imperative. One subject described these affective meanings as "little freedoms." My working definition of "little freedoms" is as an amelioration that can shift—to a certain, meaningful but delimited degree—the affective experience of everyday life, without being able to do much to change the larger structures that produce its conditions.

Finally, Cline and Siegle intended to offer the critical paradigm and universal program through which fast fashion's massive consumer base could recognize and then reimagine itself. But I suggest that it's the theorization on the part of the nail salon workers of little freedoms that offers the more incisive and broadly applicable tool through which to think about fast fashion and its ethics.

I suspect that little freedoms are one of the primary forms of compensation for fast-fashion consumers across the board, including the nail salon workers and the consumer imagined by Siegle and Cline. Little freedoms take multiple forms, differ in their intensity, and differ in important ways from group to group and within groups—dependent on factors Siegle and Cline seem largely blind to, including economic security and immigration standing, race, education, nationality, and culture. In fact, I want to suggest that the program of "ethical fashion" prescribed by the two authors in their books itself might be usefully understood not as a panacea for the ills of the garment trade as they intend but instead as another instance of little freedoms.

I suspect closer investigation of little freedoms may do several things: Point toward the larger structural ways all fast-fashion consumer/users are being shaped by this quintessential form of global capitalism; exemplify the delimited forms of freedom possible within it; point toward important forms of difference between consumer/users; and offer clues to fast-fashion wearers' other, longed for, and potentially more enabling futures.

Rana Plaza and the Problem of Fast Fashion

When the Rana Plaza factory complex collapsed in Dhaka, Bangladesh in April 2013, the number of hurt and dead was staggering. At the same time much of the story was familiar. Since 2005, a string of fires in nearby factories had killed hundreds of other Bangladeshi garment workers.[7] Most of the deceased were the young women who make up 80 percent of the country's 3.2 million textile laborers.[8] Many were migrants from rural areas, participants in the massive urbanization fueled by the rapid expansion of clothing manufacturing in Bangladesh.[9] An $18 billion industry, textile exports are the key economic engine for this poor country.[10] Workers' share in this relative bounty is meager: Minimum wage at the time of the collapse was a stagnant $37 per month.[11] There's little will to make substantial changes to working conditions on the part of politicians in the Bangladeshi government, many of whom are heavily involved in the textile business. In a country of 150 million people, there were just 12 collective bargaining agreements and only a handful of unions in the garment industry. Workers who try to form unions are often fired and beaten. In 2012, the labor leader and former textile worker, Aminula Islam, was tortured and killed in retaliation for his efforts to organize garment workers.[12] Despite poor pay, long hours, abuse from employers, no job security, physical danger, and an entrenched political climate hostile to organized labor, sewing is less arduous than alternative employment such as farming or domestic labor.[13]

In the rubble of Rana Plaza, and the ashes of the factory fires, there were also clues that pointed to a less well-known story of the dramatic changes to the clothing industry that have taken place over the last three decades, and that have arguably made textile workers' lives even more precarious. These clues came in the form of tags, purchase orders, design specifications, and half-made garments for, among many others, Mango, Benetton, Joe Fresh, and Inditex, the parent company of Zara— the brand names of so-called fast-fashion companies.[14]

Fast fashion is the shorthand for a particular business model called "quick response" or "QR" in industry parlance. Adopted by an increasing number of fashion apparel companies since the 1980s, QR has drastically changed the way clothing is made and distributed. Its hallmark is speeding inexpensive versions of the latest fashions to stores by greatly reducing the time it takes to design, source, produce, order, and deliver clothing. In 1970, it took on average six months for clothing peddled by big fashion retailers to go from a designer's sketch to a store rack; now it can take as little as two weeks.[15]

As Rana Plaza made clear, nowhere are the stakes of fast fashion's time pressure higher than in the factories where the clothes are manufactured. Constant orders for a huge number of styles that must be delivered in compressed periods of time mean that workers have to produce more garments in more varieties more and more quickly. If a factory doesn't deliver on time, it won't get the next order. As Richard Locke, a political scientist whose work has focused on "corporate responsibility" programs, explained to a reporter: "Often the only way that factories can make the variety and quantity of goods that brands want at the price points they're willing to pay is to squeeze the workers."[16] By "squeezing," Locke was indicating an array of common practices: squeezing the most labor out of workers for the least pay; squeezing the number of garments workers were required to manufacture in a day; wringing the maximum amount of hours a worker could labor in a day; and packing the largest possible number of workers into factory complexes—in the case of Rana Plaza, beyond the building's capacity to withstand the weight.

Speed has also become an imperative for the work of consuming fast fashion. Companies that have adopted QR have significantly altered historic patterns of consumption. By 2006, Zara was reporting that consumers were visiting its stores 17 times a year, as opposed to the historic average of three or four annual visits to clothing retailers.[17]

By the mid-2000s, US consumers were buying on average four times as many garments as they did before the advent of QR.[18] And fast fashion is in no way a phenomenon peculiar to the United States: QR companies have a huge global retail presence. As the *New York Times* reported: "Inditex now makes 840 million garments a year and has around 5,900 stores in 85 countries, though that number is always changing because Inditex has in recent years opened more than a store a day."[19]

Adopting QR has been enormously successful for fast-fashion companies. Inditex made two billion euros in profits in 2013, its founder edging out Warren Buffett as the world's third richest man.[20]

In the aftermath of Rana Plaza, QR—long a known quantity in the fashion industry—was for the first time routinely mainstream news.

Front-page reports peeled back the opacities of fast fashion's supply chain; editorials parsed responsibility for the collapse, and urged corporate, governmental, and activist pressure and change. A whole subgenre of stories and opinion pieces with titles such as "Before You Buy That T-Shirt," "Clothed in Misery," "The Shirt on Your Back," and "The Deadly Cost of Fashion" interpellated readers and viewers as consumers and asked: "What can a consumer do?"[21]

Many reports acknowledged the difficulty of giving any easy answer to this question, perhaps informed by decades of scholarship that has offered nuanced accounts of the complex and contradictory effects of export production on workers' lives, and documented the unintended consequences of the efforts of Northern labor rights and consumer groups eager to set things right.[22] Yet, in the immediate aftermath of Rana Plaza, images of familiar brand-name tags strewn among the rubble of factories and the bodies of workers offered a graphic depiction of globally connected lives and the unevenness of material conditions in which we live them. The "logic of distance" assumed to govern the relationship of the people who buy clothes to the people who make them seemed to fray.[23] Finding ways "American and European consumers might assert their power to change appalling factory conditions half a world away," as one writer put it, seemed to demand concrete answers.[24]

What Can a Consumer Do?

In response to the question "What can a consumer do?" news organizations turned repeatedly to the authors of those two timely books, published shortly before the collapse of Rana Plaza: Elizabeth Cline's *Over-Dressed: The Shockingly High Cost of Cheap Fashion*, and Lucy Siegle's *To Die For: Is Fashion Wearing Out the World?*. Both women's bonafides were as journalists; Siegle as a longtime reporter on fashion for the *Guardian*, and Cline, who claimed not to be much interested in fashion at all, as a former writer for *New York* magazine. In the days following Rana Plaza, Cline appeared, for instance, on *NBC Nightly News* and MSNBC, was the subject of a *New York Times* "TimesCast," and was quoted in that paper, was interviewed by the *Wall Street Journal* and in an hour-long segment on "Fresh Air." Siegle reported from her post as the "ethical living columnist" at the *Guardian* and on BBC television.[25]

Cline's book is marketed to US readers, and Siegle's to a British audience. But both volumes aspire to "[do] for T-shirts and leggings what *Fast Food Nation* did for burgers and fries," as Katha Pollitt put it in her review of Cline's book, which was then quoted on its dust jacket. The books share similar narrative arcs and deploy a similar narrative conceit. Each author positions herself as an "every woman" "addicted" to fast fashion who, one day, peers into her closet packed with fast-fashion purchases, feels blasé or worse about the clothes hanging there, and sets out to "unravel fashion's back story."[26]

Each sets out to document the decline of local textile manufacturing; investigates the conditions in factories where fast fashion is produced; and recounts the story of how clothing donated to charitable organizations in wealthy northern countries floods secondary markets in the global south. The authors draw the same conclusion from their investigations: their unsatisfying aesthetic choices are also bad ethical choices.

As a result, each author decides to give up fast fashion. She puts herself on a diet of "buying better and less," particularly by buying from small, local ecologically conscious fashion brands, shopping for second-hand garb, and learning to make or alter clothes. Each author presents her regimen as a way to simultaneously act on behalf of her own sartorial and psychological well-being, local economies, exploited workers, deluged secondary markets, and the environment.

In each book, the author imagines her readers to be like herself: they are "intelligent fashion consumers" who have unconsciously drifted into becoming "passive, herdlike consumers."[27] "I don't have to come around to your house and have a look to make a good guess at what you've got in your . . . fat wardrobes and hard-to-shut drawers," writes Siegle.[28] Each author explicitly offers herself and her book as a "how-to" guide for readers to follow: "to help you forge a fashion future that matches your aesthetic to your ethics."[29]

Sifting through this material, I recognized the good intentions of Cline's and Siegle's books, and was hopeful about the will to change that seemed to exist in the wake of Rana Plaza. I was also sure that when news organizations drew on these two authors as experts, I was learning as much about the demands and structures of the 24-hour news cycle as I was about these organizations' knowledge of or commitment to these two writers' views. But at the same time, I was struck by the conception of the fast-fashion consumer that emerged in these accounts.

The subject that Cline and Siegle have imagined is white, western, native-born, educated, cosmopolitan, female. This imagined consumer is privileged financially. She can afford to purchase clothes that are much more expensive than those sold at fast-fashion outlets, even if she has been choosing not to. And she can afford to buy and store clothes she doesn't actually need. This imagined consumer is also privileged socially. She identifies herself as a member of the public and professional sphere, and she understands that dressing fashionably is an important part of her participation in it. But she has lost her way—become disaffected, careless. Her fast-fashioned self is impoverished, even degraded. Her purchases, and her person clothed in those purchases, are without quality, ethics, agency, consciousness, and anything but the most fleeting and trivial experience of pleasures. As Cline writes:

> Here we are, having arrived in a so-called fashion democracy, where everyone can afford to be stylish and follow trends. How does it feel? . . . My wardrobe ultimately left me feeling slavish and passive.[30]

As for the clothes themselves? They are without beauty, meaning, or craft. They are, to quote Cline, "homogenous," "generic," and "crudely slapped together."[31] But through education, sympathy for the other—particularly for textile workers—although not for the clothes they make, and by shopping differently, this subject can change both herself and the world.

Part of what intrigued me about the description of this imagined consumer is how vastly this subject differed from the nail salon workers with whom I was spending time. These women labor in the service industry. They are women of color. They are undocumented immigrants. They make, at best, minimum wage. They have marginal disposable income. They spend a large portion of their wages on remittances to their families. They don't imagine they have the same kind of relationship to fast-fashion textile workers as do Cline and Siegle. And they *aren't* blasé about fast fashion.

How does inserting these subjects into analysis of fast fashion change it? Does a different story "in front" of fast fashion's label matter? How much do we know about who uses fast fashion and why? What can these subjects who have not been part of the imaginary of fast-fashion consumption help us to learn about fast fashion? Cline and Siegle are right that Rana Plaza horrifically demonstrated the need for a critique of fast fashion. Is the regimen of "ethical fashion" Cline and Siegle prescribe as the corrective to fast fashion one-size-fits-all? How can we move forward with a critique of fast fashion that takes into account a diversity of use and users?

A Mandated Form of Uncompensated Labor and a Cost to Labor

The differences between the two groups, then, are to begin with differences of profession, class, race, economics, citizenship status, family structure, and affective stance. At the same time, the very reasons the nail salon workers found themselves at H&M and Forever 21 purchasing cheap, chic clothes to wear to work in the first place is a story of difference.

My attention was alerted to this difference by trying to do a math problem: The small income the workers drew from their labor was difficult to reconcile with even a conservative estimate of the amount they were spending on clothes for work. Cline opens her book with a scene in which she buys seven pairs of seven-dollar canvas slip-ons.[32] For her, this purchase, like her other fast-fashion purchases, are "almost inconsequential," as she puts it.[33] For the nail salon workers, that same expenditure would require more than eight hours of wages.

When I asked Sita: "How did it happen that you guys wore your own clothes in the salon? Was that something the owner wanted you to do? Was it something that you guys asked if you could do?" she responded: "[The] dress we . . . wear there was not our wish. Our owner doesn't want us to wear any uniforms. She simply doesn't like us wearing uniforms. She always requests us to look a little fashionable, though."[34] When I inquired if the owner reimbursed workers' for these expenditures, or provided her employees with some kind of clothing allowance, or supplement to their take-home pay, Sita and the other women laughed.

At this moment I began to feel like I had some idea of what was going on. I wasn't precisely sure how having fashionably dressed workers could confer economic benefits on the salon's owner. Where the money was coming from for these expenditures was still mysterious. But certainly the clients' constant compliments of the workers' clothes seemed to be structuring or lubricating their at once intimate, commercialized, and hierarchical exchanges in some crucial way. Indeed, the nail salon workers' take on compliments from clients was that it was essentially extractive: Praise from clients was intended to wrest better service from the nail technicians. "Frankly speaking," Jaya told me, "we think the admiration is a way to get the job done very well. When it's too much, we feel like that." I began to see how the owner's economic dividends from her workers' fashionable bodies could be a central question of my inquiry. On the one hand, Sita confirmed this precisely: "In my opinion," she wrote to me on Facebook, "the owner wants us to be fashionable to attract customers."

Contrary to the idea encompassed in Cline and Siegle that consuming fast fashion is a leisure activity, part of what this group of workers makes clear is that in their case fast-fashion consumption is a mandated form of uncompensated labor and a cost to labor. Shopping for clothes, laundering them, and juggling the finances to accumulate them all required tremendous work on their part. And wearing fashionable clothing is a requirement.

As with with lunch warmed up over the towel and hot stones heater, the workers often found ingenious workarounds to fulfill or elude salon rules. These workarounds were made easier by the fact that the owner, who by that time had opened a chain of the salons, was often not on site, and generally showed up at predictable times.

Shopping for clothes for work was a case in point. The women evolved a practice they called "Stolen Kisses Are Always Sweeter," a name they told me derived from a Nepali saying. It involved dashing out of the salon in pairs during slow days and times, taking the express train up to Herald Square, doing some quick shopping at H&M or Forever 21, and then tearing back downtown to work. At the salon, someone—usually Jaya, who was the maternal figure for the bunch—was at the ready to call the shoppers if the salon was busy or the owner showed up. This left no time to actually try on the clothes. The workers depended on their sharp eye for style and standardized sizing. The trickiest part was gaming the checkout line. As one of the women wrote to me on Facebook with a few weeping emoticons affixed to the end of her message: "When Jaya calls that [the] store is getting busy then if we were in line and waiting for pay . . . Then forget about it . . . We just run . . ." [ellipses are hers]. "It's fun," another worker told me. But the pleasure derived from "stealing kisses," even as it has the mark of defiance, still worked to fulfill the salon owner's mandate that the women dress fashionably, and does nothing to make this requirement less exploitative.

Cline and Siegle dramatize their fast-fashion purchases as non-choices. Cline tells a story about how one day she took all the clothes out of her closet, drawers, and trash bags and found herself confronted with "a mountain." Cline's roommate, upon encountering the mountain, observes that "'I find owning so much clothing overwhelming.'" Cline replies: "It was such a simple statement, but she said it as if I'd done it on purpose."[35] Cline narrates the creation of this mountain of unloved clothes as if it happened mysteriously, without her will. But what the author is showcasing might be properly understood as a "melodrama of uncertain agency," to borrow a phrase from the literary critic Mark Seltzer.[36] That is to say, a dramatic performance of non-agency dependent on possessing it in abundance. In contrast, when the nail salon owner required her workers "to look a little fashionable," the nail salon workers' agency was compromised, even as they tried to steal some back through their shopping practices. As Sita put it: "The dress we wear there was not our wish."

The owner's specific reasoning remains unclear. But it's possible that requiring the workers she employed to dress fashionably was a strategy to obscure the conditions of the salon workplace to her customers. The mask of luxury that "high-service" salons traffic in and their high prices should not confuse us about the difficulty of this kind of labor or its poor pay. As Kang strongly argues, a salon with an enhanced aura of luxury does not necessarily translate into better working conditions or better wages for workers.[37] This is in large part because in "high-service" salons, workers are paid a low hourly wage in expectation that they will be well tipped. Body service workers' dependence on clients for tips intensifies an already fraught relationship in the "intimate publics" of "high service" salons.[38]

This system also does not translate into higher income. As it turns out, the well-off clients who visit these salons do not in general tip particularly generously, perhaps because they mistakenly think the high cost of the service translates into high compensation for workers.[39] The women told me they could expect to earn about $25–$35 in tips during a ten-hour weekday, and $45–50 on a weekend day.

Coupled with this, the women who work in the salon are under intense economic pressure. The women I interviewed had found themselves in the nail technician's chair because they support family members who have remained in Nepal. Two of the women I met had left their young children behind with relatives in the hopes of providing better lives for their kids with the money sent home from the United States—even if this meant that they might not see them for many years. The tremendous difference in the cost of living in Nepal and New York means that even a portion of a nail salon worker's salary can improve the daily lives of her family in Kathmandu. Remittances provide almost a quarter of Nepal's GDP and the figure is probably substantially higher, as remittances are routinely underestimated. "The rule of thumb is to add 40% to the official figures."[40] The women were also supporting themselves and often additional dependents in New York City.

But this kind of toil shows on the body, even the bodies of the young and relatively young women who worked in the salon. (The age range of the women at the salon is 21–35.) Indeed, when in 2015 the *New York Times* published a two-part, long-form, front-page exposé on working conditions for nail salon workers in the New York metropolitan area, the second piece was called "Perfect Nails, Poisoned Workers." "A growing body of medical research shows a link between the chemicals that make nail and beauty products useful—the ingredients that make them chip-resistant and pliable, quick to dry and brightly colored, for example—and serious health problems," wrote the author Sarah Maslin Nir. The health problems the women I met in the salon experienced ranged from hands peeled raw from chemicals and latex, to respiratory system and back problems, to heartbreakingly, because she wanted a child so badly, what Sita increasingly came to believe was an infertility possibly connected to her long tenure at the salon. This possibility was borne out by the research conducted by the *Times*, which linked work in nail salons with "abnormal fetal development, miscarriages and other harm to reproductive health."[41]

If the salon owner's mandate that the women dress fashionably is connected to hiding effects of work on workers' bodies, she would be in a long line of bosses who have deployed fashion and beauty to this same end. As Nan Enstad writes in her account of the fashion and beauty practices of women garment workers in New York City at the turn of the twentieth century, they "similarly recorded that many Lower East Side working women wore 'paint' on their faces, not first for love of make-up, but because 'employers did not like to have jaded-looking girls working for them.'"[42]

The Plot Thickens

Clear enough, I thought: The women bought a lot of fast fashion, even with their scant income, because they were made to do so to keep their jobs. However, this was not where the story was to end. Sita and the other women vehemently insisted—no matter how hard I pressed—that the salon owner's injunction that they wear fashionable clothing to work was only part of the story of their use of fast fashion in the nail salon. The workers were emphatic that they vastly *preferred* wearing their own clothes.

In a long exchange in a group interview in which I said that I thought it was coercive for the owner of the salon to require the women to dress fashionably, to invest in clothes that were likely to be irreparably stained, and to spend their time shopping for these clothes even if they'd found a clever if risky workaround, all for the owner's own economic benefit, the women became frustrated with me. "Is it really better even though it's expensive for you?" I asked. Jaya, valued by me and by her colleagues for the fact that she was always the most frank, responded: "Jessamyn, it is much better. Much. Much." Her answer was again echoed by the whole group. "Much. It is much better. Much."

When I followed up with Manju, she said:

We were all glad not to wear uniforms. We feel like [if we wore uniforms] we are wearing boundaries, or something. It doesn't feel comfortable. And [with uniforms] it's always like black pants and black shirt. It was much, much better to wear whatever we like to wear. To use our own clothes. Our own comfortable dresses . . . I like all these bright colors . . . Our dress is important.

On the one hand, Manju's language—of comfort, ownership, colorfulness, boundaries, import—was something worth paying close attention to. Still, the basic economics of the workers' expenditures on fast fashion remained confounding. The conversation about the uniforms was confusing, too. I knew, for instance, that Sita had proudly worn the uniform of front desk clerk at the global hotel chain for which she'd worked in Kathmandu before immigrating to the United States. What was it about the nail salon uniform that made the women universally feel "uncomfortable"? What could wearing fast fashion possibly offer the women who labor in the salon that is powerful enough to be worth the investment of their marginal or non-existent disposal income? Why fashion and not another consumer good? Was there in fact an economic benefit to the *workers* if they were fashionably dressed? Are there other, less tangible benefits to the workers?

Perhaps most strikingly, the word Sita and others routinely used to describe wearing clothing of their own choosing in the salon was "freedom." Certainly, Sita spoke of it as a highly qualified freedom, as in: "It gives us a little freedom." And: "It feels like a kind of freedom." But a "freedom" nonetheless. What notions of freedom was she deploying? What are the horizons of this freedom?

"Little Freedoms" + Kathmandu, the Fashion Capital of the World

Body service work might not be the single worst job in the world, but as should be obvious it's also not one of the best. It's highly toxic, physically and emotionally taxing, poorly paid, and the hours are long.[43] The workers' undocumented status is a source of constant anxiety; it also makes finding a better job almost impossible. In addition, there are particular hardships for the Hindu women who work in the salon. As the scholar Krishnendu Ray, whose scholarship is on immigrant laborers in New York City's food-service industry, wrote to me in an email exchange:

> [F]or Hindus the feet are the most important and visible site of assigning ritual hierarchy . . . Every time I see my elders, including my parents, I touch their feet in a gesture of pleasurable subservience by signifying that I take the dust from their feet to put it on my head so that they can bless me in exchange . . . What happens when such a symbolically charged body part as feet enters a commercial exchange? There must be immense

value contradictions here—touching other people's feet for money but not for blessings is incomprehensible (not disgusting), unbearable.[44]

But this is a job that these workers have found that they must do—to support themselves and to fulfill their family obligations. Given this, when the women insisted that they preferred wearing their own clothes to labor in the nail salon, I came to believe that what they were telling me was this: That the use of fashion in the workplace ameliorates—to a certain delimited degree—some of the daily experiences of hardship they endure there, although without changing the workplace conditions in any fundamental way. An amelioration that can shift to a certain delimited degree the affective experience of everyday life without changing the larger structures that produce its conditions might also serve as a starter definition for the concept of "little freedoms."

In particular, when the women put on stylish clothing to perform body service labor, they "reinforce a sense of dignity that is perpetually assaulted" by the conditions of their workplace, to quote Robin Kelley.[45] In the case of the nail salon workers, putting on style accomplishes this in surprising ways. It allows workers to stage an argument—internally, among the cohort of salon workers, and to a certain extent within the broader culture of clients and the owner in the salon. The argument: New York City might be the center of capital to which the nail salon workers are bound, but it is not the aesthetic center of the world. That privilege goes to Nepal. This "little freedom," then, provides a measure of dignity, and a different way, at least privately, and semi-privately, of reordering the hierarchies of the world.

It's worth establishing that the women claim a sense of themselves as fashionable. Here's Sita on the subject:

Everyone always says "Sita is so fashionable." Maybe because of the way I dress up . . . You ask me what I like about fashion? You ask if I like fashion? Yeah. I love it . . . *I* have a very good eye for fashion.

Like Sita, the other women are proud of their fashionability, and of each other's fashionability. "Everybody has their own quality," Renu put it, referring to her colleagues' individual style. The women are also *emphatic* that they did not acquire their fashionability when they migrated to the

United States: They brought it with them. As Sita explained, speaking of family members who are all in Nepal:

> My sister—she's also really fashionable. And my mom was really fashionable . . . Short skirts. Big goggle sunglasses. Block heels. At the time, *nobody* wear like that. She used to wear all this stuff . . . Maybe I was inspired by my mother. The way she always dressed us. Whatever she used to buy for me was perfect. She has a really good eye. I am so proud.

The conversation with Sita took place in the salon in front of clients. Sita was wearing an electric blue tiger-striped mini-dress from H&M. In the context of the salon, the aesthetic sensibility of beauty and fashion that Sita was attributing to her family in Nepal "should" be the privilege of the client. But when she made this speech, she was actively constructing and performing a genealogy of beauty and fashion that contravenes the one in which the clients who visit the salon are steeped. Because what she was saying is that her historied aesthetic sensibility of beauty and fashion is not rooted in the salon culture to which the clients are committed, or even more broadly in present-day US culture. She was declaring that she does not parrot contemporary American ideals of fashion and beauty when she puts on style to work at the salon. Rather, she is exercising an aesthetic sensibility that she constructs as a continuance of her family's traditions of fashion and beauty practices in Nepal. For Sita, putting on fashionable dress to work at the salon is also therefore not an emulation of the clients' class standing, as might be imagined—that's not what's in all those bags from H&M. Sita's attachment is to her own familial class/caste standing and cultural capital in Nepal.

Surely what Sita was saying was in no way strictly true. Like other immigrants, it's far more likely that some of the nail salon workers' fashionable aesthetics were carried with them from Nepal, some were made in the United States, and some were being newly improvised on the spot. For example, even as she denied it, there can be no doubt that Sita and her colleagues were borrowing from the immense cultural and social value placed on beauty and fashion in the salon in the heart of New York City to "dignify [her] own devalued labor," to quote Nan Enstad.[46] There were times when Sita and her colleagues told me specific aesthetic details they'd admired at the salon—the way one client layered her clothing, the way another combined colors. And those "short skirts," "big goggle sunglasses," and "block heels" have the distinct sound of Western fashions of the 1980s. But whether the nail salon workers' sense of fashion was one they brought with them, one they invented out of whole cloth, or one they found in the United States is largely beside the point. The point is what Sita and her colleagues forged from these carried, invented, and borrowed aesthetics: a potent, dignifying tale. This tale, told and enacted at the nail salon, suggested that the real world of fashion and beauty resides somewhere else entirely.

In Sita's construction, fashion belongs to her and her family. It doesn't belong to the salon's owner, who belongs to a different ethnic group, and it doesn't originate with the owner. Thus, Sita's alternative narrative of the history of fashion distances herself from the salon owner's attempt to harness her employees' fashionability as an economic benefit for the business, even as Sita fulfills the owner's injunction that she wear stylish dress to the letter.

The workers' alternative genealogy of fashion also resists a key logical and affective structure of the client/nail worker relationship. Part of the mechanics by which fashion works as a lubricant in the intimate public of the "high service" salon is by trafficking in a fantasy about women's universal commitment to beauty and fashion. As a magazine I found at the salon put it: "Women all over the world are interested in looking their best!" Clients and body service workers in this expensive salon are divided starkly by economic security and immigration standing, race, nationality, and culture; the fantasy of a feminine essentialist love of beauty and fashion unites them in a seemingly borderless world. By creating a story in which the origins of fashion and beauty are situated far outside of the salon, Sita refused or at least defused this fantasy. For her, fashionable dress was not a sign of a cozy feminine universalism, but part of her own highly particular, precisely located familial and Nepali history. Clients might compliment the way Sita put on style to lubricate their own experience of receiving body work, but chances are they could never really share in it.

Sita's sharp eye for fashion also has the sharp edge of social critique. It undermines a cherished—we might say foundational—narrative of the Western modernity and superiority. In the history of clothing, all dress could be seen "as ethnic, that is as geographically and culturally bounded," as the historian Kristin Hoganson points out.[47] But this of course is not how fashion has worked discursively. Instead, fashion has long served as an index of national and civilizational standing. To look to Paris, New York, Milan, and London has meant that dress from everywhere else signifies marginality. Indeed, as Hoganson puts it, beginning in the nineteenth century, "to buy into the fashion system . . . meant to distinguish oneself from penurious, colored, and colonized people."[48]

Sita's memory of her mother's and sister's style defies this powerful narrative, disrupting the historical racialization and spatialization of fashion as exclusively European, American, and white. According to Sita, Kathmandu, and not Paris or New York City, is the fashion and beauty capital of the world.

Perhaps the mere idea that fashion can perform this role in the workplace of the nail salon is inflaming. The women are not buying these clothes of their own choice. They endure hardships that cannot be ameliorated by fashion. Yet, nevertheless, when the workers put on style in the workplace, they were participating in another meaningful tradition: of subjects outside dominant structures of power and privilege connecting fashion to dignity and resistance. The garment workers at the turn of the twentieth century Nan Enstad writes about, who put on style not only for leisure, but to work, and to strike; and the workplace dress-code violations Robin Kelley discusses "as subtle and not-so-subtle but conscious acts of rebellion and resistance among a black working class," are but two examples. This chapter in turn draws on a long tradition of scholarship by scholars such as Kelley and Enstad that concentrates on subjects doing just this. To be sure, in the case of the nail salon workers, their subtle and not-so-subtle conscious acts of rebellion may add up to "a little freedom"—in part because they necessarily are working within a system of capitalism and hierarchies of distinction and not outside of them. Resources poured into dignity may be resources not placed somewhere else. This lands us in two places: The fundamental need people have for dignity, even if at the seeming expense of other seemingly more fundamental needs. And the long history of judging certain people's consumption as appropriate to their station and some as inappropriate.

In a purely economic calculus, the nail salon workers' expenditures on fast fashion don't make any sense. "Everything we ever earned in tips went into clothes," Samten told me only half-jokingly. But the cheap, chic clothes this group of body service workers wear to their jobs do at least two crucial things: They fulfill the owner's mandated dress code that the workers dress fashionably. And they re-emphasize the women's dignity and personhood in the context of labor that often erases it. For these workers, then, personhood, subjectivity, and dignity *can* be produced through fast-fashion fashion. And this is something that fast-fashion companies, advertisers, textile makers, and wearers all participate in. It's hard to imagine how the women could fulfill the owner's mandate or exercise their particular strategy of "little freedoms" without a plentiful supply of cheap, new, fashionable clothes.

Unimagined Subjects

The body service workers, who put on fast fashion to labor in the globalized, feminized service economy, remain unimagined subjects for the authors of *To Die For* and *Overdressed*. Cline writes that cheap fashion results in "the empty uniformity of cheapness." She announces the arrival of the "so-called fashion democracy where everyone can afford to be stylish and follow trends." And she decries it: "My wardrobe ultimately left me feeling slavish and passive." The result is a classist disregard for fast-fashion users and their use, and is blind to the strategies of people such as the workers at the salon.

It's not only Cline's and Siegle's imagined consumer that is classed in a highly particular way. The "ethical" solutions they propose are also class-based. Take for example a discussion I had with the nail salon workers about whether they'd ever thought about alternative ways to source the stylish clothes they were required to wear to work. In a group conversation, I floated Elizabeth Cline's idea that an alternative way to get cheap, chic clothes was to shop at secondhand stores. Jaya responded: "Very interesting. Vintage style. Secondhand? For us . . . [long pause] Not really." Sita added: "We don't like to wear these things." "We would rather go [to] H&M to buy new," concluded Jaya. For these body service workers, thrift stores aren't treasure troves of beautiful or interesting things from times gone by. They are other people's discards, and provoke not enchantment but disgust.

When the ethnographic data I've been collecting at the nail salon is set next to the data presented in books like *To Die For* and *Over-Dressed*, two very different kinds of consumers emerge. Where Cline's and Siegle's imagined fast-fashion consumer is overstocked, overstuffed, and blasé, the workers in the nail salon, by contrast, are interested, invested, and actively involved in the use of fast fashion as part of the construction of their own personhoods and the continuation of a lineage of aestheticization. At the same time the workers are required to wear fashionable clothes to their workplace. So part of my point is that when we think about fast-fashion companies' massive global retail presence and the ever-growing number of fast-fashion consumers, we can't use any singular form of consumption as the rubric to understand fast-fashion's users or the meanings users attach to their clothing.

Beyond this, when we complicate the paradigms we have of fast-fashion users, we are also going to have to complicate the paradigms of how to respond to fast fashion. Because my argument is not to re-vindicate fast fashion as a desirable value. The nail salon workers' use of fast fashion as a way to shore up their dignity and personhood doesn't justify the situation of textile workers in Bangladesh. And it doesn't mean that nail salon workers can't participate in change. To argue that the nail salon workers can't participate in change—or don't already— would reinscribe "the distribution of the sensible," to use Jacques Ranciere's phrase, that "renders some people visible as political actors while pushing others below the threshold of note."[49] In other words, we should not abandon a critique of fast fashion.

But the ethnographic evidence that not all fast fashion consumers are alike also indicates that consumers are not going to be—or maybe even that they should be—ethical in the same ways. My instinct is to say any movement that is going to rely on the ethics of consumers is going to have to be rewritten.

This presents the opportunity to better understand the uses of a massively circulating media—fast fashion—that has been barely explored. At the same time, the reminder that the nail salon workers may have different ethical and political positions because of who they are also presents an opportunity to take into account other, less visible ethical and political possibilities.

If "ethical" is taken in Foucault's sense of the "arts of existence"—i.e., "all those actions and rules of conduct through which we organize ourselves according to particular ethical and aesthetic criteria"—then the nail salon workers' practices, like Cline's and Siegle's, can be understood to "presuppose a set of specific learned ethical competencies."[50] For the nail salon workers, wearing cheap chic helps them feel a measure of dignity, and helps them fulfill what they understand as powerful ethical obligations to their families, who depend on the income they earn in the salon. It's worth pointing out that, in the case of the nail salon workers, it's not that they are uneducated about how fast fashion is made—that they lack potentially transformative *information*, as we might suppose. Rather, their location vis-à-vis global capitalism is different from subjects we may be more familiar with, and their uses of fast fashion are different.

"I Don't Think That I Ever Talked about the Workers of Textile Factories of Bangladesh, Ever."

When I asked the women at the salon in the days after Rana Plaza collapsed if they had been discussing the news, one person responded: "I don't think that I ever talked about the workers of textile factories of Bangladesh, ever." Maybe the nail salon workers, who feel so deeply their own disenfranchisement in their own workplace, were indifferent to the plight of the workers who made their clothes? If not, how do we account for the nail salon workers' brusque dismissal?

The sympathy Cline's and Siegle's imagined subject feels is generated by, if not predicated on, the vast socioeconomic, cultural, and geographical gap she feels between herself and the textile workers. In the Cline/Siegle framework, the textile worker is conceived as radically other. The worker's otherness is secured by the predictable, stable, unchanging racialization, class and economic differential, and spatialization of the fast-fashion consumption/production dyad. In this dyad, the imagined consumer is in a major Western fashion capital; the women "behind the label" are in faraway Asia in a sweatshop. The imagined consumer has not just a plentitude, but a surfeit of what she needs; the textile worker from the imagined consumer's point of view has next to nothing. These differentials produce in the imagined consumer feelings of shame and feelings of sympathy. Which in turn produce in her feelings of ethical incompleteness and personal dissatisfaction, igniting a desire for change. This set of affective responses is what Bruce Robbins calls "the sweatshop sublime."[51]

For the Cline/Siegle subject, the solution to the problem of what to do in the face of the iniquities of global capitalism is a fantasy of non-participation. The imagined consumer re-draws her relationship to the textile workers by withdrawing from the relationship to textile workers. She will no longer buy fast fashion. Instead, she'll shop differently, at venues she feels to be at a greater distance from the workings of global capitalism, and that are presumably more transparent and less iniquitous. One of her strategies of "being ethical" is understood in terms of avoiding or diminishing one's implication in the reproduction of harms "along broadly consequentialist lines that anchor 'responsibility' firmly around an analysis of the intended and unintended consequences of one's own actions."[52] For nail salon workers, this strategy is not an option or even a desire. They are banking on the fact that their families' livelihoods in Kathmandu—and their families' chances to participate in upward mobility—are derived from the women's service industry jobs in New York City.

For the women who labor in the nail salon, an ethics that depends on sympathy for textile workers based on their otherness is not going to work. Bangladeshi textile workers are not "the other" to Nepali body service workers. I don't want to overplay the parallels between these two groups of women. But arguably, there is a kind and degree of intimacy and familiarity that Nepali nail salon workers share with Bangladeshi textile laborers. Beyond the geographical proximity of Nepal and Bangladesh, the women are, in some cases and some ways, socially proximate. For a number of the nail salon workers, their own families are only one generation out of rural agriculture, as is the case with many Bangladeshi textile workers. Two women in the salon claimed higher caste status, but the rest did not. And as I've tried to underscore, the kind of work they do is not as dissimilar as might be imagined. Both jobs are overwhelmingly occupied by Asian women migrants working for scant pay, under obligations to remit income to their families, and in conditions dangerous to their basic health, well-being, and often also their dignity, for commodities/services bought and sold within the global fashion and beauty industry. (I found this argument much more readily apparent to people after the *New York Times* exposé on nail salon workers was published, and follow-up articles with titles such as "Three Ways to be a Socially Conscious Nail Salon Customer" took their place alongside pieces such as "Before You Buy That T-Shirt."[53])

Yet for the women I've been interviewing, migration to the United States and labor in the nail salon seems to intensify their need to distinguish themselves from other women who work in low-paying global service and manufacturing jobs, and perhaps in particular other South Asian women. Insofar as migration and body service work has narrowed or scrambled or merely rendered less legible the distinctions of caste, region, religion, culture, urbanity, education, and ethnicity that they hold dear, the women can seem to practice these distinctions even more brusquely.

Part of the labor for the Cline/Siegle subject is to keep the textile workers in mind so as to stick to the program of renouncing fast fashion. For nail salon workers, in contrast, it takes effort to keep up the socioeconomic, temporal, and spatial distance between themselves and textile laborers. Fierce distinctions—and new clothes—are part and parcel of a desire to keep the possibility of upward mobility on the horizon and downward mobility at bay. As one of my subjects put it, *Then why else would we have come here?*

This in turn sheds light on the dislike the women I met in the salon had for wearing the uniform typically found in nail salons. The hotel clerk's snappy suit, issued to Sita by the global hotel chain for which she'd worked in Kathmandu, felt to her like a badge of membership in a global business community about which she was deeply curious, and that she longed to join. She missed her work at the hotel, she said. At the nail salon it's all women, and they are all Nepali, she told me. This was not her dream of the United States, she said, finding herself in this narrow ethnic and gendered enclave. I like meeting people from all over the world, she said. (It's worth noting that clients don't count for Sita as people she meets.) In contrast to the hotel uniform, wearing black pants and a white shirt did not signal membership in the global community of international business. Rather, it signifies membership in a global community of low-paid, nearly invisible, seemingly indistinguishable, even extinguishable, immigrant service workers. At least wearing fast fashion to work in the salon could be styled to look and feel like upward mobility.

Finally, I don't think the women who work in the nail salon imagine themselves to be in a position to act in the way that the Cline/Siegle model of ethical consumption proposes. At the center of Cline/Siegle's vision is an exalted consumer, whose decisions about how to shop are of consequence, not only to herself but to the world. Her imagined future is one where shopping is both rich in meaning and without contradiction. Clothes that fit her beautifully will reflect an inner state of ethical soundness and well-being that will in turn connect to the well-being of her community. In other words, this is a fantasy that her consumer choices do not represent "little freedoms," but substantive ones. The women who labor in the nail salon don't see themselves as agential in a system of global capitalism in the way the subject imagined by Cline and Siegle seems to. Labor in the nail salon provides daily lessons to the body service workers in the specific ways they are constrained. If one reading of the nail salon workers' indifference is that it is bad faith—i.e., "the plight of Bangladeshi textile workers has nothing to do with me"—another interpretation of what appears to be indifference might be understood as: "the plight of Bangladeshi textile workers is so much bigger than me!"

Little Freedoms for All

I've argued so far for the necessity of acknowledging diversity among fast-fashion consumers. My bid is to better understand the massively circulating, largely untheorized form of global manufacture, exchange, sociality, and culture that is fast fashion. I've also suggested that strategies on the part of consumers to make these forms of exchange less extractive cannot be one-size-fits-all. In particular, I've suggested that the differences between nail salon workers and the imagined subject exemplified in Cline's and Siegle's books highlight the fact that fast-fashion consumption, use, and ethics demand an analysis of the specific contexts of class, race, gender, nation, and citizenship that shape particular subjects' acquisition and use of cheap chic. In this section, however, I want to try to think about some of the things the nail salon workers and the Cline/Siegle subject may share. I'm thinking of the larger structural ways all fast fashion consumers are being shaped by the quintessential form of global capitalism. And I'm thinking of the ways both the nail salon workers and the Cline/Siegle subject exemplify the delimited forms of freedom possible within it.

What if we understood "ethical fashion" programs like the one Cline and Siegle offer not as exalted cure-alls for the ills of the garment industry but instead as what they more closely resemble: "little freedoms"? "Little freedoms" that are designed to ameliorate and shift to a certain delimited degree, the affective experience of everyday life of these particularly located subjects, without in the end being able to change the larger structural systems in which they are located?

Trying this idea on for size calls for an additional interpretation of the classism in Cline's and Siegle's books. We can read the nail salon workers' dismissive attitude toward Bangladeshi textile workers as a class/caste-based form of disdain—because it well may be. But, as I've argued, the dismissiveness of a statement such as "I don't think that I ever talked about the workers of textile factories of Bangladesh, ever" also highlights the fragility of the nail salon workers' social position, immigration status, economic survival, basic health and safety, and simple recognition as human within the push and pull of global capitalism. Precarities that are continuously highlighted both by global garment production and their own work in New York City's body labor industry—a symmetry for the nail salon workers that is too close for comfort. Perhaps Cline's and Siegle's positions likewise are best understood not primarily, or at least not merely, as forms of class-based disdain. They too may be a sign of the precarity the Cline/Siegle subject also experiences within the same globalized system of accumulation and exchange. To be sure, there are cavernous differences between the degrees of instability experienced by journalists, and nail salon technicians and textile workers that I have no intention of collapsing. But perhaps it's worth asking the same questions of Cline's and Siegle's "little freedoms" as of the "little freedoms" nail salon workers: What is the idea of freedom animating "ethical fashion"? The horizon of freedom?

We might notice that both authors' books are framed through narratives of decline. To take Cline's book in particular, she recounts an America of the past in which clothes were made in the United States, in US-owned factories, and then sold in locally owned department stores that anchored the downtowns across the nation. The clothes made in those factories and purchased in those stores were, according to Cline, well fitting, well made, and long lasting. And when they began to fray, Americans themselves (or at least the white American middle- and upper-middle-class women who shopped in the stores in the first place) possessed the skills required to repair them. In contrast, as we already know, for Cline, today's clothes are "crudely slapped together" overseas; downtowns have been eroded by fast-fashion chains (in fact, her book opens with a scene in a Kmart that Cline mournfully recalls was formerly the venerable American department store, Wanamaker's). Clothes last but a moment. And almost no one knows, or cares to know, how to repair them.

When Cline speaks in these ways, she's not speaking merely of clothes. Her story of clothing is an allegory for a whole way of American life that no longer exists, or at least not as it once did for some people. Cline's "before"—of US factories, department stores, home sewers, and so on—is located at a historical moment in which there was something like a US middle class (perhaps more particularly a white US middle class). An era in which it still was possible "to maintain the structured totality of income, lifestyle, cultural capital, and occupational status that . . . defined and sutured together the category of the middle class," as Marianne Conroy puts it. Clothes are meaningful in this picture in this sense that Cline is mourning an era in which the commodities one purchased "operated in sync" with this "structured totality" and helped members of the middle class to experience a "unified, coherent social position."

In the world of *Overdressed*, this "structured totality" of middle-class life is no longer in place. Indeed, toward the end of the book, the reader learns that these constitutive elements of this life have been ruptured in Cline's own existence. "Like many Americans," she writes, "I have dealt with financial hardship since the recessions started."

> I lost my job at a magazine in 2008 and went on unemployment. Then the real estate market in my neighborhood plummeted, and the value of my home fell along with it. Eventually I was able to sell it at a loss.[54]

Seen through this lens, Cline's program of "ethical fashion"—a diet of "buying less but buying better," shopping for vintage clothes (Cline singles out the kind sold in the US department stores she's nostalgic for), shopping locally, and learning to sew is significant. The imagined subject in Cline's book rejects fast fashion and re-clothes herself in the garb of an era when white middle-class stability still seemed possible. When she drapes herself in this imaginative projection into the past, she wishfully rejects the very real instabilities of global capitalism. Cline never quite fully makes the connection, but the housing crisis, widespread layoffs in journalism, especially print journalism, and fast fashion's meteoric rise in this sense are all linked.

The nativist tendencies that crop up in Cline's book might also be understood through the lens of her longing for a more stable economic and social world. She dreams that Americans, and not Bangladeshi or Chinese workers, will again make her clothes. This is also part and parcel of a fantasy of a protectionist world that's not so much about protectionism qua protectionism, but rather a world imagined to be without the immense precariousness of global capitalism. "Like many Americans," as Cline points out, perhaps including Sita and her colleagues at the salon, the author is not getting the America she dreamed of. Little freedoms have replaced bigger ones.

Where Nepali salon workers use fast fashion in part to distinguish themselves (at least in their minds) both from the upper-class women they service and the Bangladeshi women who make the clothes they wear, the Clines and Siegles of the world draw on the "little freedom" of "ethical fashion" to practice their own class, racial, national, professional, and citizenship positionalities more brusquely. Clothes don't remain just clothes in these stories—they index and allegorize much more. Part of what little freedoms seem to provide are compensatory practices of distinction within a form of globalization that seems to collapse difference even as it everywhere re-inscribes it.

Conclusion

How does fast fashion emerge as a problem when studied in this light? What kinds of "solutions" to this problem seem imaginable? Do little freedoms have the capacity to become, or even to indicate, more substantive potentialities?

Part of where this leaves us is with the unhappy thought that in our era of global capitalism, little freedoms is what we get. The overlap between the theorization on the part of the nail salon workers of little freedoms with scholars of neoliberalism including Wendy Brown and Judith Butler is apparent.[55] Part of the problem with an ethical fashion program like the one Cline and Siegle suggest is the way it fits so neatly into a neoliberal worldview: Instabilities of capitalism are taken up as responsibilities of individual consumers. It's not just that Cline and Siegle imagine themselves as exaltedly agential, it's that they see no other option. Following the neoliberal imperative, the whole system is placed on the individual to fix. They become, indeed *must* become, the solution.

But if we look at the nail salon workers and the Cline/Siegle subject from a larger, structural economic picture, would corporations such as H&M or Inditex distinguish between them very much? Both groups spend similar amounts of time shopping, similar percentages of their money on clothes, and rely on a credit economy to do so. Credit, of course, with interest rates that could be high as 20 percent or more was the answer to the mystery of how you can make six dollars an hour plus tips and still shop so much. (Of course, there is a cavernous difference between the ability of a nail salon worker and a Cline/Siegle subject to get themselves out of debt.)

The fact that little freedoms smooth edges of a rough day cannot and should not be overlooked. But whether they take the form of heating up your lunch on top of the towel and hot rock heater; shopping during working hours for clothes you are required to wear to work; dressing in a way that reminds you of home; erecting a boundary between yourself and demanding, well-heeled clients, and the desperately poor people you are afraid you will become; or making you feel like you can stitch or shop or repair yourself back into middle-class stability by "buying better and less"; buying from small, local ecologically conscious fashion brands; shopping for secondhand garb; or learning to make or alter clothes—little freedoms are too small to encompass bigger dreams.

But what little freedoms can do is help us to see both their own small, meaningful uses, and delineate the big freedoms they can't address. Being able to make these kinds of distinctions—between freedoms small and large—*is* a tool of active existence.

NOTES

1 I have changed the names of the subjects in this piece to protect their anonymity.

2 Miliann Kang, *The Managed Hand: Race, Gender, and the Body in Beauty Service Work.* Berkeley: University of California Press, 2010, 133–134.

3 See "Health Hazards in Nail Salons," Occupational Safety and Health Administration, US Department of Labor, https://www.osha.gov/SLTC/nailsalons/.

4 See Kang, *The Managed Hand.*

5 "Update: Brands' Responses to Tazreen and Rana Plaza Compensation Demands," *Clean Clothes Campaign.* 2014. http://www.cleanclothes.org/.

6 Elizabeth L. Cline, *Overdressed: The Shockingly High Cost of Cheap Fashion.* New York: Portfolio/Penguin, 2012; Lucy Siegle, *To Die For: Is Fashion Wearing out the World?* London: Fourth Estate, 2011.

7 Vikas Bajaj, "Fatal Fire in Bangladesh Highlights the Dangers Facing Garment Workers," *New York Times,* November 25, 2012; Jim Yardley, "Horrific Fire Revealed a Gap in Safety for Global Brands," *New York Times,* December 6, 2012.

8 Julfikar Ali Manik and Jim Yardley, "Building Collapse in Bangladesh Leaves Scores Dead," *New York Times,* April 24, 2013; Dina M. Siddiqi, *To Act or Not to Act? Section 377 of the Bangladesh Penal Code: Summary Report.* Dhaka: James P. Grant School of Public Health, BRAC U, 2009; Shelley Feldman, "Historicizing Garment Manufacturing in Bangladesh: Gender, Generation, and New Regulatory Regimes," *Journal of International Women's Studies* 11, no. 1 (2009): 268–288.

9 See Shelley Feldman and Naila Kabeer, *The Power to Choose: Bangladeshi Women and Labour Market Decisions in London and Dhaka.* London: Verso, 2000.

10 Manik and Yardley, "Building Collapse in Bangladesh"; Siddiqi, *To Act or Not to Act?.*

11 Manik and Yardley, "Building Collapse in Bangladesh."

12 Julfikar Ali Manik and Vikas Bajaj, "Killing of Bangladeshi Labor Organizer Signals an Escalation in Violence," *New York Times,* April 10, 2012.

13 See Kabeer, *The Power to Choose.*

14 For a comprehensive list of the brands sourcing from the factories housed at Rana Plaza and Tazreen, see Clean Clothes Campaign, 2014, "Brands Responses to Tazreen and Rana Plaza Compensation Demands," http://www.cleanclothes.org/.

15 Pankaj Ghemawat and Jose Luis Nueno, "ZARA: Fast Fashion." Harvard Business School (9-703-497). Cambridge, MA: Harvard Business School, 2006.

16 James Suroweicki, "After Rana Plaza," *New Yorker,* May 20, 2013.

17 Gehmawat and Nueno, "ZARA: Fast Fashion," 13.

18 Juliet Schor, *Born to Buy.* New York: Scribner, 2005, 313.

19 Suzy Hansen, "How Zara Grew into the World's Largest Fashion Retailer." *New York Times,* November 10, 2012.

20 Ibid.

21 Vikas Bajaj, "Before You Buy That T-Shirt," *New York Times,* May 18, 2013; M. T. Anderson, "Clothed in Misery," *New York Times,* April 29, 2013; Lindsay Poulton, Francesca Panetta, Jason Burke, and David Levene, "The Shirt on Your Back: The Human Cost of the Bangladeshi Garment Industry," *Guardian,* April 16, 2014; Nathan Fitch, "'The Deadly Cost of Fashion,'" *New York Times,* April 14, 2014.

22 See for example Siddiqi, *To Act or Not to Act?*; Feldman, "Historicizing Garment Manufacturing in Bangladesh"; Kabeer, *The Power to Choose.*

23 Thuy Linh N. Tu, *The Beautiful Generation: Asian Americans and the Cultural Economy of Fashion.* Durham, NC: Duke University Press, 2011.

24 Vikas, "Before You Buy That T-Shirt."

25 A selection of Cline's television and radio appearances in the aftermath of Rana Plaza include: "The Real Cost of Cheap Clothes." NBC Nightly News, 2.22. May 14, 2013. http://www.nbcnews.com/; "Search Ends for Bodies after Bangladesh Garment Factory Collapse." MSBNC, Jansing & Co., 4: 18. May 13, 2013. http://video.msnbc.msn.com/; "The Price of Fashion." New York Times TimesCast, 2:19. May 8, 2013. http://www.nytimes.com/; "Ethical Fashion: Is the Tragedy in Bangladesh a Last Straw?" Fresh Air with Terry Gross, 38:54. May 2, 2013. http://www.npr.org/. Siegle wrote about Rana Plaza in its immediate aftermath for the *Guardian* on May 6, May 12, and May 26, 2012.

26 Siegle, *To Die For*, p. 39.

27 Ibid., xi; also see p. 3.

28 Ibid., pp. 2–3.

29 Ibid., p. xi.

30 Cline, *Overdressed*, p. 8.

31 Ibid., p. 7.

32 Ibid., p. 1.

33 Ibid., p. 4.

34 All interviews were conducted by the author, unless otherwise noted.

35 Cline, *Overdressed*, p. 4.

36 Mark Seltzer, *Bodies and Machines*. New York: Routledge, 1992, 84.

37 Kang, *The Managed Hand*, pp. 133–165.

38 Ibid., p. 147.

39 Ibid., p. 146.

40 Jonathan Glennie, "Remittances Are Not the Only Reason Young Nepalese Decide to Migrate," *The Guardian,* July 5, 2012. Despite the title of the article, Glennie offers powerful statistics about remittances by Nepali workers.

41 Sarah Maslin Nir, "The Price of Nice Nails," *New York Times*, May 9, 2015, and Nir, "Perfect Nails, Poisoned Workers," *New York Times*, May 10, 2015.

42 Nan Enstad, "Fashioning Political Identities: Cultural Studies and the Historical Construction of Political Subjects," *American Quarterly* 50.4 (1998): 751–752.

43 Kang, *The Managed Hand*, p. 202.

44 Personal communication, January 25, 2013.

45 Robin D. G. Kelley, *Race Rebels: Culture, Politics, and the Black Working Class*. New York: Free Press, 1994, 18–19.

46 Enstad, "Fashioning Political Identities," p. 751.

47 Kristin L. Hoganson, *Consumers' Imperium: The Global Production of American Domesticity, 1865–1920*. Chapel Hill: University of North Carolina Press, 2007, 80.

48 Ibid., p. 81.

49 Jacques Rancière, *The Politics of Aesthetics: The Distribution of the Sensible*. London: Continuum, 2004; see also Jane Bennett on Rancière, from whom the gloss on "the distribution of the sensible" comes: *Vibrant Matter: A Political Ecology of Things*. Durham, NC: Duke University Press, 2010, 105.

50 Michel Foucault, *The History of Sexuality, Volume One*. New York: Random House, 1978. The gloss is Gay Hawkins in *The Ethics of Waste: How We Relate to Rubbish*. Lanham, MD: Rowman & Littlefield, 2006, 24.
51 Bruce Robbins, "The Sweatshop Sublime," *Pmla* 117.1 (2002): 84–97.
52 Nick Clarke, Clive Barnett, Paul Cloke, and Alice Malpass, (2007). "Globalising the Consumer: Doing Politics in an Ethical Register." *Political Geography* 26, no. 3 (2007): 231–249.
53 Sarah Maslin Nir, "3 Ways to Be a Socially Conscious Nail Salon Customer," *New York Times*, May 7, 2015.
54 Cline, *Overdressed*, p. 190.
55 Wendy Brown, *Undoing the Demos: Neoliberalism's Stealth Revolution*. New York: Zone Books, 2015; Judith Butler and Athena Athanasiou, *Dispossession: The Performative in the Political: Conversations with Athena Athanasiou*. Cambridge, UK: Polity, 2013.

9

Cartographic Imaginaries of Fast Fashion in Guangzhou, China

NELLIE CHU

One afternoon, Mrs. Wu, the owner of a small clothing factory located in the heart of Guangzhou's garment district, was diligently working at her sewing station. As she carefully constructed a garment sample using jagged pieces of fabric, she cheerfully sang the praises of Xiao Yu, her favorite and most important client. She stated, "I really respect her. For a twenty-six-year-old woman, I'm impressed by how she has already succeeded in her business. She travels around the world, and she can speak many foreign languages. Xiao Yu has the courage to go out into the world. You have to have courage just like her!" In Mrs. Wu's view, Xiao Yu possessed the unique and enviable combination of cosmopolitanism and local Cantonese identity. As a native of Guangzhou, Xiao Yu left home to attend college in Australia. After only two years of study, her mother suddenly passed away. Shortly thereafter, Xiao Yu returned to Guangzhou to take over her mother's garment business. Since their initial encounter two years ago, Mrs. Wu and Xiao Yu's professional relationship blossomed into a fictive mother-daughter kinship. Xiao Yu's cultural fluidity, transnational experiences, and business acumen led Mrs. Wu to live vicariously through her client's transnational travels and entrepreneurial endeavors.

In many ways, Xiao Yu's stories of her worldly travels served as discursive projections of a woman Mrs. Wu could never become given her socioeconomic status. She proudly explained to me, "In the beginning, the dresses I produced for her (Xiao Yu) did not sell so well, but look at the number of international orders (*waidan*) she has now!" Indeed, Xiao Yu's experiences of traversing the global circuits of fast fashion contrasted with Mrs. Wu's migrant journeys out of Guangdong's countryside and into the mega-metropolis of Guangzhou as a factory worker before becoming a factory owner in her own right.[1] At the age of 18, Mrs. Wu left her native place to labor as a migrant wage worker in one of Shenzhen's massive garment factories while China's market reforms were gradually being implemented. For more than 20 years, Mrs. Wu's life revolved around the factory space. She met her husband in a garment factory and started a family before branching out into small-scale entrepreneurship a few years ago. Since then, Mrs. Wu's role as the factory boss fixed her firmly within the confined space of an industrial workshop that resembled a household garage. Day in and day out, she constructed each and every garment that passed through her hands before they were sent to different corners of the world, only to imagine what traveling to these places would be like. As a witness to the rise of Xiao Yu's fledging business venture into a thriving enterprise, Mrs. Wu imagined herself as a participant in her client's worldly exchanges.

To be sure, Mrs. Wu's friendship with me as a student researcher, which blossomed while I was conducting ethnographic fieldwork in Guangzhou from 2010 to 2012, also augmented her desire to explore a wider world. When I introduced myself as a Hong Kong–born, Chinese American student from California, who arrived in Guangzhou's garment district to study factory laborers in southern China, she seemed as interested in my experiences as an overseas Chinese as I was in her life as a rural migrant in the city. Oftentimes, Mrs. Wu asked me how flying in an airplane felt, or how long an airplane ride from China to the United States took, demonstrating her curiosity about seeing and experiencing a wider world.

Using these women's life histories as a point of departure, this chapter analyzes how Chinese rural migrants' participation in the global commodity chains for fast fashion in Guangzhou intersects with their geographic imaginaries of the "global." Specifically, it examines how migrants come to know the extent of their displacement as low-wage laborers in one of China's "workshops of the world." Their senses of dislocation are place-based and are evidenced by how they imagine the faraway people and places to which the fashion commodities they produce are distributed. Through ethnographic description, this chapter reveals how migrant laborers' geographic imaginaries inform the ways in which Chinese migrant laborers come to understand the conditions of their class-based labor and displacement vis-à-vis other market participants along the wider commodity chain, in which production processes are segmented and workplaces are geographically dispersed. Through their embodied labor in garment manufacturing and exchange, they create mental maps of the commodity chains in which they participate, while they situate their class-based roles along the production chains.[2]

In contrast to Fordist factories where assembly lines are centralized and workers can thus gauge their class-based positions as laborers vis-à-vis their managers across a hierarchical chain of command, low-waged producers in the global fast-fashion industry organize their labor and livelihood across segmented production sites where processes of outsourcing and mass assembly are often rendered invisible. Migrant laborers in southern China, including factory owners, temporary sewers, and sourcing agents, in turn, realize the class-based conditions of their exploitation and displacement through processes of envisioning the cross-regional markets that they serve. Without access to the pathways of transnational mobility that many of their clients possess, these rural migrants experience the paradoxical feelings of desire and confinement in the course of their business transactions with the customers and commodities they watch come and go. At the same time, their mapping practices offer migrants a means of negotiating and protecting themselves from demanding and unreliable clients who, in large part, determine the conditions of their low-wage labor. Cartographic imaginaries of the global thus enable rural migrants to orient their class-based positions along the transnational commodity chains that they serve, as they envision the faraway places that lay beyond the physical confines of their wage labor. Through these discursive practices, migrant laborers across the fast-fashion commodity chains in Guangzhou understand their relative positions along the chains of power and inequality.

Migrants' discursive categorizations of the global demonstrate what Frederic Jameson describes as cognitive mapping. In his book, *Postmodernism, or, the Cultural Logic of Late Capitalism*, Jameson describes cognitive mapping as an aesthetic, "a pedagogical political culture which seeks to endow the individual subject with some new heightened sense of its place in the global system" (1990: 92).[3] Cognitive mapping, as Jameson explains, underscores a person's sensibilities and imaginations of the world in connection with or in contrast to a socioeconomic world order brought about by the material conditions of late capitalism. Since

Jameson's introduction of the concept a few decades ago, other scholars have demonstrated how cognitive mapping practices serve as a form of critical engagement, an alternative perspective into the ways ordinary people orient their sense of personhood in relation to their imaginations of the world. As Robert Tally (1996) argues, "alternative ways of (worldly) imagining . . . is necessary for any pedagogical, not to say political, project that attempts to deal with the present condition (of late capitalism) (401).

In Guangzhou, migrants' experiences and cartographic narratives demonstrate the usefulness of cognitive mapping as an ethnographic method. Rather than taking global commodity chains as heuristic devices fixed concretely upon social formations as they emerge on the ground, this chapter seeks to explore the humanistic dimensions of transnational supply chains by taking cognitive mapping as a form of critical practice. Participants' cartographic imaginaries of the "global" unfold through their affective and embodied engagements with the manufacture and exchange of fast fashion. Aspirations, desires, and fears of exploitation emerge through these engagements, informing their sense of personhood as well as their "place" in an unequal world. Rural migrants' work in linking the transnational supply chains for fast fashion thus entails not only the embodied and affective dimensions of low-waged labor, but also their imagined sense of self in an increasingly globalized world.

Specifically, by appropriating the language of fashion and style, factory owners, wage workers, and sourcing agents in Guangzhou's fast-fashion sector sketch their mappings of the world, a type of embodied engagement that is tied intimately to their bodily experiences of garment exchange and manufacture. Such forms of embodiment include migrants' memories and experiences of the physical pain and sense of confinement they must endure when they work long and intensive hours in order to produce or source clothing for particular fashion markets. They also include female migrants trying on or wearing the stylish clothes that they labor to produce but could never afford to purchase.

Migrants' embodied engagements with the material objects and discursive qualities of fashion style also enable them to map the financial possibilities and risks involved in conducting business and wage employment in Guangzhou's factories and wholesale markets for low-cost

Figure 9.1. Photo of a typical *jiagongchang* informal workshop in the garment district of Guangzhou, China. Photo taken by author.

garments. The following ethnographic vignettes trace garment producers' various cognitive mapping practices along the supply chains for fast fashion. These producers, the majority of whom are rural migrants from China's countryside, include factory owners, wage workers, and intermediary agents, who manufacture and distribute low-cost garments to fashion wholesalers around the globe. Ethnographic descriptions show how garment producers and distributors in Guangzhou chart worldly aspirations, economic opportunities, and financial losses that emerge through their encounters with clients from abroad. Through their discursive cartographic practices, migrants situate their class-based labor across the transnational organization of supply chains for fast fashion. In short, they try to make sense of the transregional dynamics of power and inequality within which they find themselves.

Imagining the World's Supply Chains for Fast Fashion

As a case in point, Mrs. Wu would often try to locate her own position as a small-scale factory owner along the transnational supply chain for fast fashion by describing the distances to which Xiao Yu's merchandise traveled. Even though Mrs. Wu's role as a garment manufacturer physically confined her within the spatial limits of the small factory where she and her husband and older son lived and worked, she and her workers frequently charted conceptual maps of the global supply chains they served. The fabrics, magazine photos, clients, and garment samples that drifted in and out of the factory floor shaped the workers' understanding and imagination of the places to which the garments traveled.

For instance, Mrs. Wu once informed me that Xiao Yu's garments were distributed to various wholesale markets throughout Bangkok and Southeast Asia. She speculated that the dresses passed through the hands of many agents and wholesalers across city, township, and national boundaries. Mrs. Wu then proceeded to draw a map of Xiao Yu's traveling dresses. She explained, "In Thailand, the dresses travel (zou) from large markets to the smaller ones" (you da huo zou dao xiao de). In her view, smaller markets branched out from larger markets, with Guangzhou as a primary production hub in Asia. As Mrs. Wu stated, "This city (Guangzhou) is the center (zhong deem or zhong dian) of garment and fashion production."

Mrs. Wu further elaborated how the commodity chains that linked smaller to larger wholesale markets determined the scale of Xiao Yu's profits. She stated, "She (Xiao Yu) relies on production volume as well as geographic distance for the successes of her business." Mrs. Wu explained that as a direct wholesaler, Xiao Yu, relied on selling large volumes of clothing abroad, rather than solely on a diversity of styles in local markets in order to achieve business success. With each passing of hands, the prices of the garments would skyrocket, underscoring the speculative dynamics of the transnational exchange of fast fashion. To be sure, as Mrs. Wu explained, Xiao Yu's participation in the global exchange of fashions required her to travel to countries, such as Vietnam, Thailand, Indonesia, and New Zealand. Her overseas experiences afforded her the privileged position as a globe-trotting agent and fashion entrepreneur.

As Mrs. Wu described Xiao Yu's business to me, I was surprised to hear her description of Guangzhou as the hub of the world's garment and fashion production, while neglecting to mention other metropolises such as London, Milan, Tokyo, New York, Paris, or Shanghai as popular centers of the fashion world. I wondered whether she implicitly drew a distinction between garment manufacturing and creative design, so as to place Guangzhou as the hub of garment manufacturing while reserving more cosmopolitan cities as the global cores of fashion design. Over the course of my research with Mrs. Wu, however, I began to realize that through her everyday experiences in garment production, the conceptual distinctions she drew among apparel design, construction, and manufacture had always been blurred.

In fact, in the two years that I observed her work in the factory, she repeatedly emphasized the conceptual labor involved in running a full-scale garment factory. For example, she once complained to me about the growing numbers of clients who brought new, unfamiliar designs to copy. She and her husband faced the challenge of constantly imagining and sketching new patterns that corresponded to the latest designs. During the off-season (*dam gui*), I would often catch Mr. Wu, the husband of Mrs. Wu who labored as the in-house sample-maker, hover his entire upper body over his worktable, while busily constructing original garment patterns and experimenting with new T-shirt and dress designs which he would eventually bequeath to his wife to serve as his model and muse. I also observed the couple advising their clients, including Xiao Yu, on how to best reconstruct the garment samples they wished to replicate, as well as which fabric types would be appropriate for a specific pattern or design.

Based on his wide-ranging knowledge and expertise in garment construction and manufacture, Mr. Wu identified himself as a designer (*shejishi*), though far from the globe-trotting, internationally trained, and cosmopolitan fashion designers most people would commonly imagine. "I'm a designer," Mr. Wu declared with utmost certainty during our initial introductions. Indeed, the thought-labor entailed in their work as garment manufacturers compelled Mrs. Wu to describe her work as conceptual. As she once emphasized to a friend visiting the factory for the first time, "Our work requires much thinking and planning. You must first think about what you have to do, and how you're going to do it. Our work is conceptual."

The Wu's self-identifications as garment designers as well as manufacturers made them distinct from other factory owners that I encountered around the Zhongda garment district. Whereas most factories in the area oversaw merely one aspect of garment production, the Wus' factory served as a full-scale garment operation, which coordinated most production processes under one roof. These processes included sample-making, garment assembly, and packaging. Their work experiences and skills motivated them to brainstorm other entrepreneurial pursuits so as to occupy other market niches related to garment design and manufacture.

In fact, Mr. Wu once acknowledged that he was learning to become a fashion designer through experimentation and other methods of self-teaching. In another instance, I overheard Mr. Wu brainstorm with a client from the Shi San Hang wholesale market in Guangzhou about the pros and cons of creating a line of counterfeit goods. Since competition among stall owners in the market had become increasingly fierce, the client was struggling to sustain his fledging business. With an air of resignation, he sought Mr. Wu's advice regarding the potential risks and rewards in pursuing a counterfeit fashion line. Upon overhearing the men's conversation, Mrs. Wu openly rejected their ideas by declaring, "Of course, that's a bad idea! By the time you copy someone else, that trend has already passed. Everyone knows that you have to sell original designs to make yours stand out!"

Indeed, the passing of globe-trotting clients across the shop floor, along with the transnational circulations of fabrics and garments in and out of the factory space, shaped how the couple imagined and positioned their roles as manufacturers within the transnational circuits of fashion production and exchange. By discursively claiming Guangzhou as the world center of garment manufacturing, the Wus paradoxically acknowledged their displaced positions as migrant laborers along the fashion and garment production hierarchy, while using their skilled labor, hard work, and client networks to connect themselves with these transnational circuits of garments and fashion.

These connections enabled the Wus to extend their social worlds beyond the physical confines of their factory. For example, during the two years that I worked with the couple, they bequeathed countless samples of their work for me to bring back to America and show to my peers. Besides their immeasurable generosity, they prided themselves on the fact that the products of their unwavering dedication and hard work were gifted to faraway worlds beyond the spatial limits of the factory and beyond their emplaced roles as garment manufacturers. Through their everyday encounters with traveling clients, garments, and designs that floated in and out of their factory space, they adopted the discourse and practices of garment production and fashion-making in order to imagine and construct themselves as part of a wider world.

Imagining Spaces: Global Encounters on the Factory Floor

By appropriating the discourse of fashion style, factory wage workers also imagine the countries to which the garments are sent.[4] These discourses serve as the cultural signifiers through which they situate their wage labor and their migratory displacements across the global circuits of commodity exchange. Workers' practices of cognitive mapping via the discursive and material language of fashion shed light on the ways in which the spatial fragmentation of commodity production and exchange via supply chains shapes migrants' embodied encounters with the material objects linked to garment manufacture and exchange. In turn, these encounters augment rural migrants' spatial and subjective senses of displacement as factory workers in Guangzhou.

For instance, one afternoon, Mrs. Wu was working among the sewers at one of the workstations along the back wall of her factory. She was carefully attaching ruffled sleeves to a stack of girls' multicolored dresses. While she was working, I asked Mrs. Wu to which country the girls' dresses were being shipped. Mrs. Wu replied that the dresses would be sent to Xiao Yu's clients in Thailand and Singapore. She then added that these dresses were better suited for markets in Indonesia, Thailand, and Singapore, because women in those places preferred bright colors, such as red, pink, blue, and yellow. In contrast, as Mrs.

Wu explained, Chinese consumers would deem these patterns and colors too bright and eye-catching and would prefer colors that were a bit darker and more subtle. Besides, as Mrs. Wu continued, consumers in the Southeast Asian markets preferred the so-called *mo nu zhuang,* or the matching mother and little girl outfits, a look that Chinese consumers would view as odd and even comical. Mrs. Wu implied that Chinese consumers tended not to prefer these styles. To be sure, Mrs. Wu and her workers were well versed in the consumption preferences of women across Southeast Asia, since they saw themselves as consumers of the very same clothes that they produced. Some workers would even wear some of the clothes that they manufactured.

Later that day, Mrs. Wu continued to explain that these flashy and eye-catching trends and styles offered Xiao Yu the opportunity to extend into the realm of women's fashions through her experience of designing children's clothing. She speculated that although Xiao Yu's client base remained in Southeast Asia, her clients' growing business and knowledge of the markets might enable her to expand farther across the geographic reaches of the world. Through Mrs. Wu's experience in garment manufacture, she developed her personal knowledge base about the distant countries, markets, and peoples to which these garments traveled. Her impressions of Thailand were further concretized by her statement, "People say that it doesn't cost much to fly to Thailand from here, but I have never had the chance to go. I only know the place based on the colors of these dresses." Mrs. Wu's revelation attested to the fact that she situated her displacement as a migrant laborer through her imagined experience of airplane travel, an opportunity she might never realize.

In another instance, I was sitting along the left-hand side of the front work table, slowly snipping loose threads off of stacks of finished girls' dresses. An older female worker from Guangxi province was sitting closely behind me at the end station, lightly elbowing me every now and then as her hands swayed monotonously front and back, while guiding the fabric underneath the rapid movements of the needle on the sewing machine. Yang Yang, the teenage worker from Hunan, sat down at a surge machine beside the woman to sew lace borders onto a batch of light blue denim skirts that had dark blue flower trimmings embroidered along the hem. Suddenly, she gushed with excitement, "These dresses must be for Africa! I know Africans like loose-fitting styles (*pang*

Figure 9.2. Scene of street life in the urban villages that comprise the garment district of Guangzhou. Photo taken by author.

pang de)." She then pressed the garment against her body in order to imagine how she would look if she had it on. I then asked how she knew this, and she responded that she had seen African styles before (possibly because she had previously encountered similar pieces in other garment factories).

Yang Yang's passing comments left an impression on me, because her statement revealed how she situated the various fashion markets and places across the globe through the language and materiality of clothing styles. They also showed how the structural dynamics of displacement among low-wage migrant laborers served to create Yang

Yang's discursive categorization of what she imagines "African" styles to be through the language of fashion and materiality. Her comments impressed me in particular, because Mrs. Wu informed me that these denim dresses were meant for markets in Southeast Asia, not Africa. Yang Yang's comment signified the disjunctures or gaps in the workers' conceptual understanding of the supply chains they critically served. Garment workers imagined but perhaps would never discover for whom the clothes were meant and where the garments were going. Yang Yang's comment made clear to me how influential the spatial segmentation of mass manufacture across transnational supply chains operated in shaping workers' impressions and categorical ordering of the world within the physical confines of the factory workshop.

Mapping Limits: Charting Guangzhou's Wholesale Markets

Factory workers' imaginative descriptions of faraway places also reveal the risks they encounter as they intensify their participation in the broader circuits of fast-fashion production and exchange, particularly when they face instances of labor exploitation. More specifically, their struggles in mass producing garments for the global supply chains for fast fashion inform the workers of the hypercompetitive and money-oriented environments of some of the world's wholesale markets without even having to step foot inside these market spaces. Such struggles are frequently marked by bodily pain, which include exhaustion, headaches, and other physical ailments, which migrant workers must endure when they labor to keep up with the timely demands of garment mass manufacture. Their everyday experiences in low-cost garment manufacture lead them to constantly negotiate their sense of immobility as low-wage workers and their desires for physical and social mobility as small-scale factory owners.

In her study of Fuzhounese transnational migrants to the United States, Julie Chu (2010) uses the notion of emplacement to highlight Chinese rural villagers' feelings of being out of place as a result of being immobile or "stuck in place," while other villagers in their native places move abroad. She challenges theories of displacement that focus on the departure of a people from a literal or an imagined "home." Such conceptual focus, she argues, overemphasizes migrants' condition of nostalgia for a lost "home" and their realization of their impossible return. Similarly, garment workers in Guangzhou experience the conditions of emplacement as they remain confined within the factories, only to watch clients and commodities come and go. More importantly, workers gradually begin to realize that their socioeconomic conditions of immobility leave them vulnerable to undue exploitation by transnational and domestic clients who regularly come and go on the factory floor. Their sense of emplacement underscores the relationality between the subjective conditions of mobility and immobility.

In their efforts to minimize their exposure to market risks and exert control over the production process, they assess market risks based on the geographic extensions of various commodity chains. More specifically, they evaluate the risks of disappearing clients, unpaid orders, and exploitative working conditions based on the geographic markets they serve. As manufacturers and sourcing agents in one of China's hubs for the world's fast fashion, they must frequently calculate the limits and possibilities of their specific roles as producers of fast fashion based on the specific supply chain they operate. More specifically, they must negotiate the risks and exploitative effects of low-wage labor. Discourses of unpaid orders or "*zou dan*" (literally meaning fleeing orders), along with the languages of quality and style, reveal the uneven terrains that constitute the world markets for fast fashion through the eyes of those who make and manufacture the very goods upon which the supply chains depend.

For instance, the Wus must frequently assess the risks of entering a business relationship with an unfamiliar client, particularly those who operated their businesses within Guangzhou's hypercompetitive wholesale markets such as Sha He or Shi San Hang.[5] These long-standing markets sold clothes that were often exported to markets across East Asia and Southeast Asia. Because of the extremely high rents that were demanded within the buildings, the markets often featured high turnovers of small-scale shopkeepers, transnational clients, and low-cost commodities that were exemplary of fast fashion's so-called race to the bottom. In light of Sha He and Shi San Hang's notoriously competitive atmospheres, the Wus frequently refused clients whose garments were sold directly to these wholesale markets in their efforts to minimalize their exposure to labor exploitation. For the Wus, the practice of mapping Guangzhou's wholesale markets based on indexes of price, quality, and monetary return became matters of market survival.

The couple's reluctance stemmed from their experiences of being mistreated by demanding clients who once worked out of the Shi San Hang market. One husband and wife duo once commissioned the Wus to produce batches of women's trendy skirts to sell at the Shi San Hang market. They submitted daily orders for women's skirts, each with different styles and at small volumes of two to three hundred pieces at a time. Because new styles required the labor-intensive work of drawing patterns and sample-making, the clients' flood of orders demanded disproportionate time and effort of more than 16 hours a day of labor, even though the return for the workers' hard work was exploitatively minimal. (The owners received about 5 RMB per garment while workers were paid only 2–3 RMB per piece). In addition to these oppressive conditions, the clients rotated around the factory space in order to monitor the workers' movements day in and day out. In one instance, the clients penalized the Wus by deducting their pay without negotiation after flaws were discovered in one of their batches. After about three months of toil, Mrs. Wu admitted to the heart-breaking struggles of their back-breaking labor. She stated, "We can't endure this any longer. We can't eat. We can't sleep."

After this bitter experience, the Wus learned to filter their prospective clients' requests by mapping the wholesale markets to which their garments were sent. Their strategy became apparent to me one afternoon when a male prospective client approached the factory doors to inquire about a garment sample. He carried a bag containing a hot pink dress with bright golden buttons attached symmetrically as decorations on its front centerpiece. The man asked whether Mrs. Wu could create a sample based on the dimensions of this garment along with specific modifications. As he tried to describe the modifications he pictured in his mind, Mrs. Wu interrupted him and suggested that he instead bring in a sample that displayed his specifications, so that she could visualize his requirements and contribute her input on the design. She then proceeded to ask him where he intended to sell his merchandise, adding that they refused any orders to the Sha He and Shi San Hang wholesale markets.

In reply, the man asked why Mrs. Wu would care whether he sold his goods in the Sha He or Shi San Hang markets. Mrs. Wu stated, "Because the clothes that are sold there are too cheap! We can't make any money with each garment priced at 3 RMB. That price doesn't even cover the cost of hiring workers here. We pay them (the workers) at least 5 RMB. What can we make with that low price?!" The man then asked what kind of orders the Wus' factory handled. Mrs. Wu immediately answered, "Exports (*waidan*)." Afterward, he left without a word, though Mrs. Wu continued a barrage of complaints about producing garments for the Shi San Hang and Sha He markets. She repeatedly grumbled, "Right, that's why we don't do business with any clients dealing with Sha He and Shi San Hang. We can't make a living with those prices."

Shortly afterward, another potential client, a younger, more petite-sized man with glasses, arrived with a cream and burgundy long-sleeved, lace woman's dress. Before the man had a chance to explain his specifications, Mrs. Wu immediately jumped in by asking, "Where do you intend to sell your goods (*shemme huo*)?" The man replied that he intended to sell his goods overseas to Thailand. Immediately upon hearing the word Thailand, Mrs. Wu softened her tone of voice and cheerfully replied, "Well, the dresses that we're making here are going to Thailand." She then went on to explain that the dresses they produced were for children, though they manufactured women's clothes as well. As this prospective client elaborated his specifications, Mrs. Wu beckoned him to wait upstairs in the second floor living space until Mr. Wu returned from his grocery trip. Mrs. Wu's welcoming tone contrasted sharply from her diffident stance toward the previous client.

When a third prospective client came in that day with a long, floral-patterned summer dress, Mrs. Wu approached him with the same biting question about where he intended to sell his clothes (*shemme huo*). When the stranger replied that he worked in the Sha He market, Mrs. Wu immediately declined his offer, saying that they refused any business that dealt with Sha He. Baffled, he stumbled out of the factory floor, confused and dumbfounded by Mrs. Wu's abrupt refusal in handling his requests. As Mrs. Wu turned away from him, her gaze met mine. She immediately flashed a smile, comically acknowledging her hasty rejection of the perplexed man.

After this series of encounters, I reflected upon Mrs. Wu's links between her work in the factory and the geographical locations of the various wholesale markets around Guangzhou. Since the prices of the garments ultimately determined the cost and labor of manufacturing them and vice versa, her conceptualization of these market places was mapped along overlapping indexes of price, quality, rent, and geographic locations. As a former wholesaler from Shi San Hang had previously explained, insiders within the local garment industry knew that the Sha He market featured garments with the lowest quality at the lowest price. Moreover, insiders of Guangzhou's garment industry often complained that the exorbitant rents at the Sha He and Shi San Hang markets contributed to the hypercompetitive business practices in these markets, including the extreme practice of undercutting garment prices among the stall owners. Thus, the low prices of Sha He and Shi San Hang clothing in turn determined the garment processes by squeezing the profit margins of the workers and manufacturers' labor.

The quick turnover of the styles in these markets added pressure to the Wus' already tedious manufacturing process to the point that Mrs. Wu claimed that they could not eat or sleep if they continued to manage their orders for Sha He and Shi San Hang. The Wus' experiences of physical stress and mental exhaustion on the shop floor led them to associate particular styles of clothing with the geographical supply chains that they served. As the Wus experienced firsthand, wholesalers who operated out of the Shi San Hang market frequently attempted to limit their overhead costs by maintaining strict oversight over the Wu's production processes. Clients often stayed with the Wus into the late hours of the evening, overseeing how each garment was assembled and packaged so that every fraction of their cost was tightly controlled. As a result, Mrs. Wu believed that Shi San Hang orders were simply too difficult to handle, a common struggle for low-waged producers of Guangzhou's fast fashions.

Mrs. Wu's preference for producing exports (*wai dan*) over garments for the local wholesale markets revealed the couple's strategic orientation toward specific market niches that enabled them to manage their work lives in the face of harsh exploitative practices. Producing exports not only connected them to wide-ranging networks of diverse markets, but geographic distance also demanded larger production volumes and slower turnaround time for different styles. As they once explained to me, the Wus preferred a steady flow of export orders which for the previous year had supported their business. Mrs. Wu also attested that Xiao Yu's orders for girl's dresses had been the most manageable to produce, since many of her orders were familiar styles or copies from previous orders, to which industry participants often referred colloquially as *fan ban* (or turnover of samples). As she explained, *fan ban* or in this case repeated orders were the most manageable types of orders for them since they would not have to spend time and effort in familiarizing themselves with new or different garment styles. As garment manufacturers, the Wus also received higher returns from exports, since these goods often demanded relatively higher prices.

The Wus' categorizations of markets based on prices, styles, and geographic locations demonstrate how their mapping of the global market places for fast fashions determines their strategies for minimizing the painful effects of labor exploitation while sustaining their dreams of entrepreneurship. As migrants originating from China's countryside, their connections to the wider world are enabled by their participation in the diversity of fast-fashion markets as low-end and small-scale garment designers and manufacturers. However, their precise role as manufacturers along the hierarchical garment production chain emplaces them within the confines of the factory, while exposing them to the vulnerabilities associated with market fluctuations and various forms of labor exploitation. Their strategies for market survival in the face of these market inequalities reveal how manufacturers negotiate the tensions produced by their desires for mobility and by the emplacements they confront as low-wage factory laborers. Consequently, they conceptualize the world markets for fast fashions and position their roles within them by situating garment styles, clients, and market places within the cultural geographies of commodity chains.

Charting Losses: The Discourse of "Zou Dan" and Conflicts over Quality

In other instances, Chinese sourcing agents, or distributors, who are positioned further up the supply chains for fast fashion, similarly draw mental maps of the customers and geographic markets that they serve. These distributors often operate as intermediaries between Chinese manufacturers and transnational consumers along the fashion supply chains. As agents who are positioned along the intermediary segments of the supply chains, distributors must often balance their relationships between their foreign clients and their Chinese manufacturer-employees. This work involves coordinating the delivery of production orders with their clients' expectations and demands for timely output and quality control. Consequently, distributors must formulate certain categorizations of the various markets they serve through the discursive ordering of place, quality, and style in order to assess the financial risks and gains of a business relationship with a transnational wholesaler. Through their discursive categorizations of place, quality, and styles, distributors strategically position themselves based on careful approximations of temporal cycles of trends, price, and client credibility. As in the case of factory owners and wage workers, mapping practices similarly reveal the uneven terms of exchange upon which the global markets for fast fashions are situated.

Fanny, an experienced sales representative for a long-standing Chinese trading company, sources women's contemporary shoes to consumers in markets all over the world. As a wholesale agent, she negotiates with countless overseas and domestic clients who travel to Guangzhou in order to browse through the expansive showrooms displaying the latest designs in women's low-cost shoes. At my initial meeting with her, she immediately lays out a mapping of the world markets for women's shoes, primarily determined by geographic regions. As she explains, there are four main consumer markets for the world's shoes for women. They are: (1) Africa, (2) North America, (3) Middle East, and (4) Europe. These regional distinctions index the discursive categorizations of styles, clients, and business practices that comprise these distinctive markets.

For example, Fanny explains that her company prefers working with clients who serve the European markets. In contrast to the United States, the markets for women's shoes in Europe seem comparatively stable and profitable for her company's business interests. In particular, she describes her company's involvement with the annual trade shows in Dusseldorf and in Milan. As she elaborates, participation in the trade shows enables her company to achieve greater exposure in the global markets for fashion. Her company uses these trade shows as a form of marketing and advertising in order to attract new clients. Later in the conversation, she elaborates that since the company relies heavily on its long-term clients with whom it already has familiar relationships ranging from four, six, to ten years, the company has recently deliberated whether participation in these trade shows is a worthwhile investment.

She further elaborates that styles for the European market are simpler and more sophisticated, so they require lower production costs, thereby allowing higher profit margins. Interestingly, her designation of Europe refers exclusively to Western Europe, particularly Spain, Italy, Germany, and France. She contrasts these countries with those that comprised the former Soviet bloc. According to her, these markets remain unstable primarily due to government corruption and the black market. Interestingly, she cited the case of the Ukraine, whereby businesses often have to deal with sudden changes in government policies that pertain to the taxation of imports, including women's fashions and gold. At any time, corrupt governments may disallow the importation of certain commodities such as gold or raise exorbitant taxes to the point of rendering the importation of such goods unprofitable.

Fanny stresses that her company avoids cooperating with American clients, because of the high risks involved in entering into business deals with them. She describes a recent case in which the company has lost a male American client, with whom they had positive relations for nearly three years. During the course of those three years, he has successfully placed three orders of three to five containers of shoes, with nearly 40,000 pairs of shoes in each container. As a general policy, this company does not usually assist clients in shipping the containers once the goods are lifted onto boats and once they depart from ports in China. Goods are then declared Free On Board, designating the client's financial responsibility of the products.[6]

As Fanny explained, the American client dutifully submitted all his payments for his first two orders. However, during the course of his last order, the client suddenly disappeared (a practice colloquially referred to as *zou dan*), neglecting to submit nearly 60 percent of his bill for the last five containers of shoes (nearly 200,000 pairs). As she described, "We simply could not understand what happened. He paid us properly during his first two orders, but after his last order he just disappeared (*zou dan*). I just don't know why." His disappearance coincided with the US credit crisis that began in 2008, so she speculated

that the downward fluctuations of the global market must have nega-
tively affected the client's shoe business. As a result of this troubling
incident, Fanny's company lost nearly 60 percent of profits from the
client's order. As a precaution, the company now refuses to accept credit
and maintains a cash-only policy toward overseas clients, particularly
those from the United States.

Though fragmented and incomplete (she remained reticent about
the African and Middle Eastern markets), Fanny's discussion on the
regional specificities of the fast-fashion markets underscores the difficult business strategies and market environments that contextualize
the particular imaginaries of place. Her company's position as a wholesaler for shoes in the global market requires Fanny to occupy the critical vantage point of assessing market risks by conceptually situating the
regional markets for shoes based on geography, client groups, and business practices. In a way, these variations in turn make up her company's
conceptual mapping of market uncertainty along spectrums of market
volatility.[7]

Fanny and her company's direct encounters with clients' demonstrations of unaccountability, disappearance, and sudden financial losses
shape their own business practices in navigating the uneven conditions
and practices of trust-building and exchange. These events also inform
Fanny and her company of the world's changing market landscape, inducing them to strategically calculate the constraints and possibilities of
their participation with these regional markets from the position of intermediary distributors along the fashion supply chain. For example, the
company attempts to hedge unpredictable clients and unstable market
conditions by requiring 40 percent deposits and by mandating a cash-
only policy. In addition, they handle fewer quantities of shoe orders for
new clients and bill the clients for the production costs at the end of
each stage of the production process rather than bundling the costs into
a single lump sum. Furthermore, Fanny stresses her company's long-
standing relationships with clients based on face-to-face interactions.

My conversations with other suppliers and distributors for garments
and shoes echoed similar sentiments regarding the risky business of
dealing with overseas clients, particularly those from Europe, the United
States, and Hong Kong. One manufacturer who operated a denim factory in Xintang, China's so-called jeans city, once explained to me the

challenges he faced when foreign clients used the quality of their merchandise as justification to reduce payments or to abscond from paying altogether. He observed that since the global economic slowdown in 2008, overseas clients frequently disappeared without submitting full payments or canceled orders on short notice. He explained, "If clients say that the quality is bad, then they just simply won't pay."

He recalled one specific client from France who requested a voluminous order of women's jeans online via the website Alibaba. While in the process of preparing his order, the European consumer market slowed down, inducing the client to realize that he could not sell his merchandise in time to catch up with the fashion seasons. Fearful that he could not cover his financial obligations, the client returned all the goods to the manufacturer, citing poor quality in the dyes or wash of the jeans. The client subsequently refused to pay the remaining 60 percent of the 500,000 RMB deposit, even though production of the remaining jeans had already begun in full swing. The client eventually disappeared, leaving only a fictitious company name and a non-existent P.O. box number. Left in mounds of debt from the costs of producing those jeans, the manufacturer remained near bankruptcy for the next four to five years.

After narrating his story to me, he retorted, "I wish we (as manufacturers) would someday be in the position to flee from an order!" His comment reflected the vulnerabilities he faced as a garment manufacturer along the hierarchical supply chain for fast fashions. Despite the signing of contracts, he acknowledged the harsh reality that there was no guarantee that clients, particularly those from overseas, would pay as promised. In order to minimize the risk of fleeing orders, the manufacturer subsequently required overseas clients to pay in increments every three months before production in the factory commenced.

During the course of my research, similar cases of disappearances, unaccountability, and fleeing orders from overseas clients occurred, highlighting the ways in which the discourse of quality became pretexts for renegotiating the terms of exchange and financial obligations, often through unfair and sometimes coercive means. One friend who worked for an American wholesale company based in Guangzhou, which designed and sourced shoes for well-known retail chains in the United States, described a case in which a high-end department store chain deliberately canceled an order on short notice after it failed to meet a retail deadline.

Figure 9.3. Fashion commodities on display in a wholesale market for fast fashion in Guangzhou, China. Photo taken by author.

After deliberating on a collection of women's shoes for some time, the department store chain missed the trend cycles for particular styles. With full knowledge of its miscalculations, the department store chain canceled its production orders for a large volume of shoes, leaving the wholesale company responsible for paying the entire costs of production to the local manufacturers. In an effort to protect its own financial liabilities, the wholesale company simply canceled all the orders it placed with the local manufacturer on short notice while complaining about the poor quality of its shoes. Enraged by these displays of unaccountability along with the accumulation of outstanding balances, owners of the local factory later sent a number of hired security guards and workers to the offices of the American shoe company in order to protest, using picket signs and rally slogans. At one point during the demonstrations, some of the hired guards barged through the office doors of the American company, threatening to inflict acts of violence upon targeted bosses and employees.

Conclusion

In conclusion, industry participants' cartographic imaginaries of the world's supply chains for fast fashion in Guangzhou lead many to realize their physical and subjective displacement as migrant laborers. By appropriating the language of fashion, migrants map indexes of place, price, quality, and style in order to situate their class-based positions along the supply chains as well as to imagine the destinations to which fashion commodities are sent. These transregional connections highlight the relational conditions of fixity and mobility, as well as displacement and emplacement, in which migrant laborers in Guangzhou find themselves as they observe and speculate on the clients, objects, and stories that move around them.

Migrants' cartographic narratives also demonstrate the significance of cognitive mapping as an ethnographic method. This chapter challenges the conceptualization of global commodity chains merely as heuristic devices by seeking to explore the humanistic dimensions of transnational supply chains. Specifically, it takes cognitive mapping as a form of critical practice, whereby low-wage producers and migrant laborers understand their labor as well as their relative positions across the fast-fashion commodity chain. Participants' cartographic imaginaries of the "global" emerge through their affective and embodied engagements with the manufacture and exchange of fast fashion. Their experiences of bodily pain, immobility, and financial loss inform their sense of personhood as well as their "place" in an unequal world. Migrant laborers' struggles in linking the transnational supply chains for fast fashion entail not only the embodied and affective dimensions of low-waged labor, but also their imagined sense of self as producers and consumers of fashion in an increasingly globalized and unequal world.

NOTES

1 I use "fast fashion" as a descriptive term to denote a historically specific form of production that lends insights into the subjective dimensions of human labor characteristic of supply chain capitalism (Tsing 2009). For more conceptual analyses of fast fashion, see Sprigman and Raustiala (2006), Horning (2011), and Moon (2014).

2 To be sure, Chinese migrants' mapping practices may be roughly interpreted as a form of creative agency in relation to the global capitalist economy. My reading of the migrant laborers' cartographic mapping activities attempts to extend this practice beyond the notion of agency by presenting a more nuanced picture of the everyday struggles that these workers confront. Cartographic practices do not assume that migrants, as individual actors, take on full agency in resistance to a world capitalist system. (The term, agency, tends to suggest this.) Rather, I underscore the moments of ambivalence and negotiation among migrant laborers who must balance their desires in going out into the world with the social constraints that keep them emplaced upon the factory floor. These moments emerge most clearly, as I demonstrate, when migrants participate in the transnational circuits of clients and commodities.

3 Since the introduction of this concept several decades ago, literary critics and other scholars of cultural studies have disagreed on Jameson's precise definition of the term. They have debated the extent to which Jameson's use of the term adequately describes an individual's sensibilities and imaginations of the world in connection with or in contrast to a socioeconomic world order brought about by the material conditions of late capitalism. Moreover, scholars have expressed critiques that question the extent to which cognitive mapping can potentially be counter-hegemonic by tapping into what Jameson calls a group's political unconscious (Tally 1996).

To be sure, these critiques have underscored the dilemmas of representation characteristic of the postmodern condition, which pertain to the questions of who is doing the representing and who is represented. Collectively, they challenge Jameson's conceptualization of cognitive mapping as a form of critical practice that is linked to a world-scale capitalist order (Tally 1996). Beverly (1996), for example, argues that cognitive mapping remains bound up with historical relations of domination such that the analytic takes away any form of self-representational authority from the figure of the subaltern (ibid.). In a similar vein, Bartolovich (1996) criticizes Jameson's notion of cognitive mapping based on his contention that a totalizing vision of utopia that undermines the global system of late capitalism excludes marginalized groups from adequate representation. Those from the global South, as Bartolovich points out, may not find a utopic totality as liberating as those from the developed world. He thereby highlights the unevenness of late capitalism as a world order, thereby demonstrating the impossibility of Jameson's totalizing vision of resistance or utopia. In an attempt to extend Jameson's cognitive mapping beyond the urban landscapes of the developed world, Bartolovich suggests the notion of the itinerary in lieu of mapping to emphasize people's conditions of uncertainty and displacement over even lines and stable relations (Tally 1996; Bartolovich 1996). Though these debates have elucidated the political and theoretical stakes involved in Jameson's critiques of late capitalism, I approach the study of transnational capitalism not as a totalizing entity per se, but rather as webs of social relations that have historically been organized as global supply chains. Furthermore, I echo Robert T. Tally's (1996) call to link literary theory with historical formations in order to cast a humanistic perspective onto what Anna Tsing (2009) calls supply chain capitalism. To this end, I attempt to employ Jameson's notion of cognitive mapping as an ethnographic method within the context of transnational subcontracting in southern China. By using Tally's (1996) conceptualization of cognitive mapping as a critical practice, I demonstrate the ways in which migrant workers' imaginations of faraway places across the world are linked through their participation in the mass manufacture of low-cost garment exports across global supply chains.

4   In recent years, anthropologists have increasingly theorized fashion and adornment as social practices that critically intersect with notions of the self and of the body (Entwistle 2000). Primarily focused on marginalized groups that are conventionally excluded from Euro-American standards of fashion, their works have conceptualized the body as a site of contestation and cultural difference. Wilson, for example, celebrates the dreams and fantasies that fashion elicits among its participants. She writes, "(Capitalism) manufactures dreams and images as well as things, and fashion is as much a part of the dream world of capitalism as of its economy" (Wilson 2003: 14). Meanwhile, Jones (2007) demonstrates that certain veiling practices within Indonesia's Islamic fashion culture enable women to feel more pious and modern at the same time. While Wilson and Jones emphasize the fantasies and religiosities that certain adornment practices generate, other scholars underscore the anxieties, alienation, and violence often associated with clothing. Macaraeg (2007), for example, links clothing practices to the ornamentation and display of weaponry across various historical contexts. While Stoler (2002), Niesson, Leshkowich, and Jones (2003), and Tarlo (2007) note that particular clothing and adornment practices have enabled violence and alienation through the exercise of colonial power, Woodward (2005, 2007) explores how some women's desire to "look good" and "feel right" through clothing paradoxically produces anxiety about what they should wear for certain occasions. Although these studies illuminate the significance of fashion and adornment as practices of embodiment, their works tend to focus on the consumers of fashion rather than on the producers, particularly low-waged factory workers across the Global South. In southern China, garment laborers construct notions of the self through their bodily engagement with the mass manufacture of fashion garments and accessories. They situate their roles as migrant laborers along the supply chains for

low-cost fashion vis-à-vis their globe-trotting clients through the materiality of the styles and clothing that they mass manufacture along the assembly line.

Furthermore, Barthes's (1983) seminal book *The Fashion System* introduced a semiotic reading of fashion by deconstructing the networks of relationships and symbols that constitute the fashion industry. Drawing from Ferdinand de Saussure, Barthes conceptualized clothing as a system of signs that communicate meanings. By following Saussure's approaches in distinguishing the signifier from the signified, Barthes demonstrates that meanings attached to garments depend upon specific historical contexts. He thus argues that communication through clothing is a matter of individual expression, and not a systemic object of study (Carter 2003).

5 Sha He and Shi San Hang are two of Guangzhou's largest wholesale markets. Thousands of small-scale, informal workshops like the Wu's factory across the Pearl River Delta (PRD) region in southern China manufacture clothing that is sold in these markets. Domestic and transnational wholesalers and retailers arrive here to source the trendiest low-cost fashion of the season. Garments are sold in bulk and resold to other retail and wholesale markets across China, South Korea, Japan, and countries in Southeast Asia. Many of the clothes are eventually passed onto markets across Europe and North America.

6 As a side note, I have learned that the company usually charges clients a 40 percent deposit before the goods are shipped and then charges the remaining 60 percent sum once the client receives his or her shipment in his or her home country.

7 At the time of this conversation, the political and economic instabilities in the Ukraine during 2014 had not yet become prominent in the international media. Therefore, at that time, Fanny assumed that the socioeconomic environment in the Ukraine was more stable than that of the United States.

BIBLIOGRAPHY

Barthes, Roland. 1983. *The Fashion System*. New York: Hill and Wang.
Bartolovich, Crystal. 1996. In Rolland G. Paulston, ed., *Social Cartography: Mapping Ways of Seeing Educational and Social Change*. New York: Garland, 375–397.
Bear, Laura, Karen Ho, Anna Tsing, and Sylvia Yanagisako. 2015. "Gens: A Feminist Manifesto for the Study of Capitalism." Fieldsights—Theorizing the Contemporary, *Cultural Anthropology Online*, March 30, http://www.culanth.org/.
Beverly, John. 1996. In Rolland G. Paulston, ed., *Social Cartography: Mapping Ways of Seeing Educational and Social Change*. New York: Garland, 347–356.
Carter, Michael, ed. 2003. *Fashion Classics from Carlyle to Barthes*. New York: Berg.
Chu, Julie. 2010. *Cosmologies of Credit: Transnational Mobility and the Politics of Destination in China*. Durham, NC: Duke University Press.
Entwistle, Joanne. 2000. *The Fashioned Body: Fashion, Dress, and Modern Social Theory*. Cambridge: Polity.

Horning, Rob. 2011. "The Accidental Bricoleurs." *n+1*. June 3, https://nplusonemag.com/.

Jameson, Frederic. 1981. *The Political Unconscious: Narrative as a Socially Symbolic Act.* Ithaca, NY: Cornell University Press.

Jameson, Frederic. 1990. *Postmodernism, or, the Cultural Logic of Late Capitalism.* Durham, NC: Duke University Press.

Jones, Carla. 2007. "Fashion and Faith in Urban Indonesia." *Fashion Theor.* 11 (2/3): 211–232.

Macaraeg, Ruel. 2007. "Dressed to Kill: Toward a Theory of Fashion in Arms and Armor." *Fashion Theory* 11(1): 41–64.

Moon, Christina. 2014. "The Secret World of Fast Fashion." *Pacific Standard*, March 17, https://psmag.com/.

Niessen, Sandra, Ann Marie Leshkowich, and Carla Jones, eds. 2003. *Re-orienting Fashion: The Globalization of Asian Dress.* New York: Berg.

Sprigman, Christopher Jon and Kal Raustiala. 2006. "The Piracy Paradox: Innovation and Intellectual Property in Fashion Design." *Virginia Law Review* (92): 1687.

Stoler, Ann. 2002. *Carnal Knowledge and Imperial Power: Race and the Intimate in Colonial Rule.* Berkeley: University of California Press.

Tally, Robert. 1996. "Jameson's Project of Cognitive Mapping." In Rolland G. Paulston, ed., *Social Cartography: Mapping Ways of Seeing Educational and Social Change.* New York: Garland, 399–416.

Tarlo, Emma. 2007. "Islamic Cosmopolitanism: The Sartorial Biographies of Three Muslim Women in London." *Fashion Theory* 11(2/3): 143–172.

Tsing, Anna. 2009. "Supply Chains and the Human Condition." *Rethinking Marxism* 21(2): 148–176.

West, Cornel. 1982. "Frederic Jameson's Marxist Hermeneutics." *boundary 2* 11(1): 177–200.

Wilson, Elizabeth. 2003. *Adorned in Dreams.* New Brunswick, NJ: Rutgers University Press.

Woodward, Sophie. 2005. "Looking Good: Feeling Right—Aesthetics of the Self." In Susanne Küchler and Daniel Miller, eds., *Clothing as Material Culture.* London, UK: Berg.

Woodward, Sophie. 2007. *Why Women Wear What They Wear.* London, UK: Berg.

10

Times, Tempos, and the Rhythm of Fast Fashion in Los Angeles and Seoul

CHRISTINA H. MOON

Daniela tells me that lately work has been especially stressful. Whatever free time she has left, after work and her kids, she devotes to
keeping motivated by exercising and reading self-help books. She tells
me about her Chinese astrological signs, what her personality tends
to lean toward and work against, and worries that this might influence the kind of decisions, good or bad, she might make in her next
business move. She's tired of having to come up with so many new
ideas, new designs, and new ways to make fashion. She's tired of all
the different ways to get the attention of buyers and of dealing with the
fast-changing, finicky tastes of the people who may wear her clothes.
The trends come quickly and to keep up, she has to be out there in the
world, constantly reading magazines, watching celebrity news, checking online and scrolling through Instagram, poring over all kinds
of printed and online trend reports. Daniela tells me that what she
needs to know in fashion is now wide—from what's on the runway
to what's worn down on the Venice Beach boardwalk, to what's even
sold or worn in the Jobber Market in downtown Los Angeles, the largest clothing wholesale market in the United States and dominated by
Koreans, where she sells her clothes. She and her husband, Sung Joo,
dream of the day they will break out on their own and create their own
clothing label—helping to run her family's wholesale clothing business
with her parents is just so much work. It can get too exhausting with
all the differences in opinion among the four of them (her husband
and her parents) from what factories to use in China, to design ideas,
even down to the size of a button. She and Sung Joo haven't had the
courage to start their own business yet, since they fear that without
her parents' knowledge or help, things will fall apart quickly. Who can

survive this fast-fashion business at this fast pace, when one minuscule mistake can cost their family all that they have built?

On this particular evening, Daniela wants to tell me about the latest thing to catch on in the market, which she goes on to describe with both marvel and disgust. Most of the downtown Los Angeles jobber market's Korean wholesalers and manufacturers have joined "online showrooms" or "malls" to feature their small clothing labels and lines. This has been popular for some time since it is cheaper to purchase a monthly "showroom space" online than lease a brick and mortar showroom in the downtown market, which can cost nearly $25,000 a month. In fact, nearly every one of the Korean fast-fashion families wholesaling in the market is a member of one of these online showrooms to advertise their clothes, since increasingly buyers' budgets have been shrinking. Rather than spend on travel, it's now easier for a buyer from an American retailer to just log into an online showroom—L.A. Showroom, Fashion Go, or Orange Shine—and look at all the different new styles that the Korean wholesalers have to offer, and make their purchases for their stores. The problem was that were too many wholesale vendors trying to get the attention of buyers. A local wholesaler who owns one of the most popular online showrooms had come up with a great idea—after setting his own showroom website and populating it with jobbers who were willing to pay a high fee to have their clothes listed on its side bar, he also created an advertising banner that would run along the top bar of the website, featuring images of one's clothing looks or line. Daniela's Korean uncle, who also has a business in the neighborhood, encouraged Daniela to shell out the money to advertise her clothing label on the showroom site's banner. He told her that both advertising and selling larger sizes in clothing attracted more buyers placing orders in his store.

Daniela learned that this was, in actuality, a daily auction where the top five bidders paid to have their clothing featured on the site for one 24-hour day. The top bidder, who pays more than others, gets the first featured banner that appears on the webpage. Daniela tells me it doesn't last all that long—just a quick 5 seconds before switching out to feature the clothing of the next wholesaler who has won the bid. She won the fifth spot in the auction, which meant that in 24 hours her banner would come up fifth in line—a flash of clothes—for just five seconds. In the end, she bid $5,000 in cash for her clothes to be featured on just this one day of advertising. Though she's not all that sure it worked, she didn't re-gret the money spent. In this game of fast fashion, from manufacturing it in Asia to selling it in the United States, these are the kinds of things you have to do to keep ahead: act quickly, make quickly informed deci-sions, and take high risks on your designs. Daniela marvels at the good idea this guy had—this is something that she loves about fashion—there is always an ingenious idea right around the corner and you can make money from it. But she's also so tired of it. After working in the industry for more than a decade, this fast pace of designing, producing, think-ing, being, and reacting has changed her. Each year she works harder, deals with even quicker tempos in production, trends, and styles, and yet makes less money. There are days when she tells me she just wants to quit.

Fast fashion is clothing that is often defined by its accelerated rate of consumption and disposability—clothing that is trendy, produced cheaply, and sold for rock bottom prices at stores like Forever 21. Schol-ars often analyze it from the perspective of the material object itself, in its quick consumption and disposability among shoppers in the age of Instagram, Snapchat, and Amazon Prime, in a culture that demands immediacy and the constant desire for the new. Though the industry continues to attribute fast fashion's "fast" nature as the result of top-down corporate innovations and productivity, my research attributes fast to a small immigrant community of Korean fast-fashion vendors in downtown LA, whose daily work practices connect retail, design, and production Asia in the making of fast fashion. What are the rhythms of the workday among fast-fashion clothing vendors in the Los Ange-les jobber market? What does their daily work say about the complex multi-rhythm tempos that have emerged in fast-fashion global supply chains between the United States and Asia? In downtown LA, Korean jobbers, producers, and manufacturers of fast-fashion clothing diaspori-cally connect design in LA with production across Asia for American corporate retail. I argue that their multilayered and complex relation-ship with time in fast fashion is informed by their daily work practices, generational knowledge and relationships, and a history of industrial capitalism in Asia, all of which plays a role in newly emergent global commodity chains of fast fashion. In other words, the majority of fast fashions that most Americans wear are structured by the work practices and management of multiple timings in design, production, and retail encountered across fast fashion's global commodity chains, and the ability of an immigrant Korean fast-fashion community to quickly match the complex industrial timings between formal capitalist structures of American retail with informal production economies in Asia alongside the quickly shifting and finicky tastes of American consumers in what are uneven global markets.

Time is on everyone's mind in the LA Jobber Market, a wholesale clothing market in a neighborhood of just a couple of miles that includes more than 3,000 clothing labels and jobbers. Time can be felt everywhere, especially in the quick and rushed walking of the buyers and sales agents, and especially among the local vendors and jobbers, since no one wants to be accused of staring too long at some neighbor's clothing displayed on a mannequin or in a showroom—in a highly competitive market of slim profit margins, copying—of the runways or your neighbor's styles—is rampant—one can simply memorize the designs and make a phone call to sample-makers in China for reproduction. Time is also visible in the quickly changing geographic contours of the neighborhood, which is constantly expanding and shrinking, and follows the foot traffic of retail buyers who represent companies both big and small across different regions of the United States, and Central and South America. Showroom-store leases in the neighborhood are incredibly expensive, as much as $100,000 in cash key money deposit for just a 500-square-foot space, and up to $12,000 a month in cash to the Korean and Persian landlords who have dominated the ownership of the district since the 1970s. It's also the reason why so many small-time vendors are beginning to abandon these brick and mortar shops for "online showrooms," where one may lease virtual online space that can feature their clothes to the department store and chain store buyers who frequent them. This also reflects the enormous and rapid growth of online retailers who increasingly rely on "social media influencers" to spread the word on fashions and trends. Shoppers now look more at their Instagram and Snapchat feed for fashion inspiration rather than the runways.

The names of the clothing labels, showroom spaces, and the mom and pop companies themselves—teeny bop–sounding labels such as Blushing Hearts, Bella Chic, Dancing Queen—line the streets of the market and constantly change like the styles of clothing themselves. In these "private label" practices, the labels will frequently change since they are irrelevant anyway, eventually switched out and replaced by the name of retail stores—Macy's, Kohl's, Urban Outfitters. When the market opens at 8 am, the mannequins hung up on showroom walls are outfitted with clothes with new trends and styles day-by-day and week-by-week. Jobbers must keep track of how long the designs have been hanging on the wall on display, or how long they have been featured on the online showroom. They tell me that buyers always want to see something new. Most vendors stagger the 12 or 20 designs and styles that show up in their warehouses each day, so that it always seems as if there is something new tomorrow and more designs and styles arriving the next day. In back inventory rooms, Latino workers pack and unpack boxes of the plastic-sleeved merchandise, individually wrapped pieces of clothing from size 0 to size 18 in every color imaginable, to be trucked out to varying regions of the country during the day. On weekends in the Jobber Market, these workers run sample sales, often keeping track of what's selling for their own entrepreneurial enterprises, selling trendy fast-fashion clothing to Mexico City, Central and South America and beyond.

Trends are everything in fast fashion, and one must keep up with its study and analysis constantly, from what celebrities are wearing to where it is worn in various locations around the world. Though one takes note of what is worn down the runways of New York, Paris, Milan, and London fashion week, vendors now consider what's seen on the "street" and what shows up in their social media feeds—what clothing labels are worn by young celebrities or "social media influencers," what materials are popular and available, what styles are worn frequently and in a variety of body sizes. Vendors often highly specialize in what to make, considering what their wholesale neighbors are selling (plus sizes or pleather jackets?), distinguishing themselves in types and varieties. Vendors not only study what styles do well in different parts of the country (the jobber market is considered a test market for varying demographics differentiated by tastes and price points) but also keep note of what boxes are coming in and out of the neighboring showrooms—boxes Made in China, Made in Vietnam—using which particular factories for production. Vendors also constantly worry about timing—will the trend hit the stores before one has to receive their own shipment of the goods? If one is not careful and sells the trend a little too early, she will be out of luck—no one will even think to buy the clothes. If one sells the trend a little too late, then likely there will be trend saturation with others who have beaten you to the punch, selling the clothes for even less.

Daniela worries about how much the work of fast fashion has aged her—her own youth and beauty are important for the business. She keeps up with popular culture and knows what celebrities are wearing in major global cities. She's always carrying magazines, and shopping for "samples" in Santa Monica, Venice, Robertson Blvd, the Grove, and Rodeo Drive, checking out new designs and trying them on for fit. Daniela quietly worries that things might really change for her as she nears her late 30s. Since the business is based on ideas of youth and beauty—and though she is still young and beautiful, looking at least a decade younger than most her age—she worries about keeping up with styles and trends to convince buyers that someone young will want them. As a mother of two in her thirties, will she look youthful enough for her buyers to trust that she knows what will sell to those who are young? Daniela herself wears the clothes she creates and styles her own hair. She tells me that when buyers walk into the store, her older parents will scurry back to the inventory room, since buyers only want to see young salespeople in the store, wearing youthful, and hip clothes. This is why she and her mother hire young interns and sales girls—for help with the store, gaining knowledge on trends, but also convincing buyers in the store. In fact, Daniela has an eye for hiring young, fashionable Latina shop girls who also model the clothes in her lookbooks, which she creates herself and sends out to buyers constantly. Daniela and her mother mention how they love to be around young people, how much energy and inspiration they get from them, and how it is important to surround oneself with youth in this fast-fashion business. It seems that the whole neighborhood consists of these mother and daughter teams like Daniela and Magdalena, who have come together intergenerationally to make, design, and sell the clothes.

Daniela is nostalgic for the way things used to be—gone are the days of that single, big order from a major American retailer who will put in an order four times a year, order 30,000 pieces of clothing, and pay in advance. Now, with fast fashion, money can only be made by selling a small incremental continuation of orders—50 items of one style of clothing ordered one day, 1,000 by the end of the week, 2,000 at the end of the following week. As if riding a small wave that grows in size, fast fashion's orders and numbers increase as the demand for the trend continues to grow. Keeping track of multiple trends, all the time, Daniela tells me there is an art to pulling the plug and stopping production before the trend peters out, with the risk of being stuck with boxes of stuff that won't move off your shelves. The waves come small and quickly, and once the cash is made, several stops are made at the bank where times on the wall read for Los Angeles, Guangzhou, and Seoul. By late afternoon, phone calls are made to China to check in with factories on the multiple production lines and schedules. And in the back of everyone's mind is the timing of factory production in Asia (along with its holidays when workers take off), the arrival of the goods at the Port of LA, and—with the changing of the week and season—the movement of merchandise off the store floor. New designs and ideas are Skyped in at the end of the day in Los Angeles just as morning begins in Guangzhou. This collaborative work, in design and production, in this global supply chain of fashion, is a continual 24-hour workday.

Within the United States, large branded and logoed clothing companies such as Abercrombie and Fitch and GAP, which sold solid colors and "basics," once dominated the US retail scene. Quietly within the last decade, however, no-brand, non-logoed fast-fashion stores such as Forever 21 have come to dominate the American retail scene. These stores offered cheap, specialized, and trendy fashions that could be worn by women and men of all sizes, in multiple styles, colors, and varieties, capturing a wider audience and markets interested in trendy fashions for bargain prices. They were also successful in their different approach to selling clothing, offering a limited number of pieces produced per style, but ordering a great many different kinds, styles, and varieties to replenish store shelves every single day. The fashions could be consumed rapidly and continuously, and once out of stock, replenished with new varieties and styles.[1] Astonishingly, what was once the traditional three-month season—the time it took to draw up a design, prototype the samples, factory produce in Asia, then distribute from Los Angeles to retailers across the United States—had collapsed in timing from four times a year to every two weeks. Though most had attributed the fast nature of fast fashion to the development of data-collecting marketing technologies, much of my research shows that, within the context of the United States, it was only made possible by a community of small-time immigrant Korean fast-fashion families, who design, produce, and manufacture clothing from downtown Los Angeles and Asia, and often under the most precarious, risk-taking conditions. Instead of initially taking orders from retailers for production, vendors must study and predict the trends in advance, and put designs into production without knowing whether it will ever be sold or ordered by retailers. Though fashion is often studied by its quickly changing forms, aesthetics, styles, and trends, I'm interested in how work practices among this immigrant community make fast fashion possible, structure its sense of timing, and how memory, history, and geography might inform its "fast'" nature.

Timing in the LA fast-fashion market wasn't just about the quick clothes and quickly changing trends; it is also reflected in the coming together of two generations in Korean American families whose divisions of labor could make fast fashion "fast" and design and produce fast fashion efficiently. Though Koreans in the Los Angeles are known to have been in the rag trade as early as the 1970s, it was their children, many who had "come of age" throughout the 2000s, who had come back to Los Angeles to help join their parents' ailing businesses. Having gone off to receive training or American college degrees in marketing, merchandising, international relations, and business, design, and retail, this 1.5 and second generation returned to the district to help revamp their parents' ailing garment businesses after dramatic changes to the industry— the liberalization of trade laws in the late 1990s, the offshore of garment manufacturing in the United States to Asia, China's entrance into the WTO in 2001, and the expiration of the Multi Fibre Trade Agreement in 2005. These families and their work in fast fashion represented both the precarity and risks of global production—much of the business is still done in cash, clothing markets are often volatile with consumers' finicky tastes, and much can go wrong while over seeing a complicated global process of production—but also an opportunity to transform their businesses into formalized, small, and branded labels. To do so, families intensely relied on one another to carry out all parts of the design and production process from design, pattern-making, fabric sourcing, and management of factory production. As a result, large department stores—what were once the traditional places in which shoppers bought their fashions—and their bureaucratic structure of management and approvals, could not keep up with the quickly changing trends and the efficient ways in which these families could quickly design and produce the latest trends from not just the runway but also social media.

In order to survive the challenge of time in fast fashion, you need to have each other, Daniela tells me. For each family in the LA jobber market, each member provides different skills, with connections to the diaspora working in the rag trade abroad in Asia, and rapid communication that makes the process more efficient. Daniela explains how her family is typical in their work practice in the LA Jobber Market, where husband and wife teams work alongside their adult-aged children who often bring into the business spouses, partners, cousins, etc. Daniela's mother, Magdalena the expert pattern-maker, handles garment construction, pattern-making and fit, understanding the curves of the many shaped bodies, from a size 2 to size 18 of what is now the average size of the "American female body." Magdalena was born in Korea in the early 1960s and her family migrated to Brazil after the Korean War. She grew up in a large Korean Brazilian community that now controls much of the wholesale clothing and textile markets in Brazil. Daniela's father, Fernando, is Korean but born in Brazil and though he studied to become an engineer, chose to work in the rag trade in his twenties since everyone he knew—his Korean relatives and friends—all worked it. As newlyweds, Daniela's mother operated a small fashion retail store in Sao Paulo while her father ran his own fabric cutting factory. Soon after the peso crisis of the 1990s, and with the motivation to educate their children within the United States, the Kim family immigrated to Los Angeles, where a large Korean community had already been working in clothing and textiles since the 1970s. Daniela, by then in middle school, grew up in Los Angeles and after moving to Korea after college, met her Korean husband Sung Joo in 2001. After completing his military service in Korea, Sung Joo went on to pursue an undergraduate degree in graphic design from Parsons School of Design. Joining their parents' business in the mid-2000s, Daniela deals with sales and design, Magdalena her mother is in charge of pattern and sample-making, her father handles fabric and factory production, while her husband Sung Joo lends an eye in design but also keeps track of the complicated quotas, customs, and trade laws that are crucial knowledge in order to avoid receiving large fines by retailers. Sung Joo also travels regularly to China to meet with their factory manager and intermediary broker, an old friend from his Korean military days, who oversees the timing and quality control of garment production in China. Among generations with knowledge on production and design, alongside the transnational connections among a diaspora that works in garments in Asia, Los Angeles's Korean fast-fashion families successfully and efficiently create fast fashion, by intensely relying on one another.

If generational time informs the quick, efficient nature of design and production coming together in fast fashion, nostalgia and one's relationship for another time, another place, and another country inform and structure its *bbali bbali* or "'fast" nature. Daniela's family, along with the many vendors I interviewed, often cite Dongdaemun, the historic garment district and largest wholesale fast-fashion market in Seoul, South Korea. Strangely, there is an uncanny sense of familiarity while walking the small alleyways and streets of the jobber market. One experiences the same *bbali bbali* work culture, fast pace, and flexibility that is found in Dongdaemun. Throughout the neighborhood, jobbers talk about, remember, remark, or mention Dongdaemun constantly, some who have worked that market at another time or have family members or friends working there. Though an older generation might reminisce about shopping there in the 1980s, today's young Korean American designers in the LA jobber market often talk about all the new trends and fashions that emerge from Dongdaemun, often visiting to get new ideas. Dongdaemun, in fact, is where Daniela and I first truly connected after meeting, both of us having first heard about it from our Korean mothers and aunts.

Originating as far back as the Chosun era, Dongdaemun market snakes alongside the Cheongyecheon River in central Seoul and was, during the 1960s and 1980s, the central site for Korea's manufacturing factories and manual labor in garment production. Today, its urban structure still evidences those yesteryear factories, where upper floors of its mile-long buildings were (some still are) filled with garment factories. Its ground level and first floors often contain wholesale shops. This market was the site of large numbers of rural to urban migrants who had come into the city to work throughout the 1960s through the 1980s, driven by the calls of an autocratic military government to develop the country and rebuild post-Korean War, by making export-oriented goods toward industrialization. By the 1980s, it also became the key site to Korea's trade unions and democratic movement, its most famous activist Chun Tae Il leading a protest against garment factory working conditions by self-immolation. As this garment district began to deindustrialize throughout the 1980s, with garment production offshored to China, the 1997 IMF crisis spurred the neighborhood's transformation from manufacturing into retail, department stores, and tourism.

Diasporic cultural ties, including those between Korea and China, were driven and developed by American, European, and Asia firms, and informed the opening up of new territory for foreign capital in South China. In the next two decades, industrialization throughout Asia in garments created new cultures of fast and just-in-time operational systems of garment production, and Hong Kong, Singapore, South Korea, Taiwan, and South China would come to dominate the world's collective share in clothing and textile production throughout the 1970s and 1980s. It must be said that the development of southern, coastal regions of China in garments, what is known as the world's factory especially in fast fashion, occurred in direct geographic, spatial, diasporic, and entrepreneurial relation to Korea, Hong Kong, and Taiwan, which had become their own hubs in fast-fashion flexible production and wholesale fast fashions. These "modernization successes," however, were also the direct result of suppressed labor as well as the establishment of state-privately owned special economic zones and export processing zones. These special economic zones were first developed and experimented with in Korea and Taiwan (with US and Japanese capital), then spread throughout China to provide tax deductions as well as foreign investment, evolving along the eastern seaboard of China.[2] Between 1980 and 1994, China's exports of clothing and textiles increased eightfold.[3]

Throughout the 2000s, Dongdaemun market transformed into a transnational space of wholesale and retail shopping, attracting first Japanese shoppers but with time, Chinese shoppers of a growing middle class. Korean wholesalers and sewing operators alike formed and developed their own wholesale communities in Guangzhou and Shanghai, transnationally linking markets and connections between Los Angeles,

Seoul, Guangzhou, and Shanghai. In recent years, the Korean government established a Special Act on Support Small Urban Manufacturers
in Dongdaemun to protect the further deindustrialization of this manufacturing ecology and network. If fast fashion can be produced in just
two weeks' time from factory production in Asia to the LA jobber market,
time is even further condensed in Dongdaemun market. It takes just
one 24-hour day to design, produce, and distribute fast fashion across
South Korea and other parts of Asia from this market. Today there exist
over 10,000 sewing factories, 39,000 fashion distributors, and 120,000
workers within Dongdaemun, as well as a cluster of some 80,000 fashion businesses that attract 600,000 people a day to the market. While
the workday begins at 8 am in Los Angeles, peaking in the afternoon,
in Dongdaemun, the market opens at 7 pm, peaking at around 2 am.
Korean fast-fashion families in Los Angeles tell me that Dongdaemun
has been recreated and reimagined in other cities where a diaspora of
Korean immigrants live and work in fashion, including Los Angeles, Sao
Paulo, Shanghai, and Guangzhou. It is no coincidence that the jobber
market in LA, the central hub for fast fashions within the United States,
invokes Dongdaemun market in Seoul, whose 24-hour wholesale and
retail markets have become the central hub for design and coordination
of fast-fashion clothing production across East and Southeast Asia. A
transnational, diasporic community of Korean jobbers, wholesalers, and
fast-fashion families are now the intermediaries and cultural interpret-
ers of a transnational, trans-Pacific, and inter-Asia global commodity
chain in fast fashion, supplying fast fashion to markets across the United
States and Asia. They produce clothing across spatial divides while managing the multiple velocities and timings of design and production and
retail. These migrating immigrant entrepreneurs have acquired the ability to quickly match complex industrial processes of timing between
formal capitalist structures of American retail with informal production
economies in Asia for the quick making of an ephemeral material object.

Fashion is often thought of as the experience of the new, of modernity and time-space compression, of the kinds of consumer cultures
Zygmunt Bauman describes as a twenty-first century characterized by
instantaneity, what Kate Fletcher states satiates desires. This is all true,
but here fast fashion in Los Angeles occurs among immigrant entrepreneurs and their families, in their daily rhythms and work practices,

as generational timing and the coming together of certain divisions of labor through the family, out of the memory and nostalgia of another time and place, when tiger economies and an authoritarian state put out calls to an entire nation to "bbali bbali," quickly modernize and industrialize. These fast-fashion intermediaries are informed by deeper histories that link industrial capitalism with the emergence of multiple, complex, industrial tempos that have emerged from the export-oriented production and development of "just in time" production throughout Asia. The emergence of wholesale fast-fashion markets in Seoul and Guangzhou as outcomes of modernization drives in Korea and China from the 1970s and 1980s points to fast fashion's multiple tempos and its relationship to new forms of making and spatial imaginations.[4] In this way, the clothes reflect this history, migration, the neighborhood in which they work, their work practices and divisions of labor in the design and production process. It reflects a history, knowledge, and migration that is transnational, trans-Pacific, and inter-Asian. The quick, ephemeral nature of clothing reflects the timings of the LA Jobber Market, the work practices and labor of fast-fashion families that have emerged in these new and precarious global productions of fast fashion's commodity chains.

Daniela likes to play around with the idea of perfect time for the design, making, and selling of her clothes. For her, this means that a retailer with many different stores—a franchise all across the United States, perhaps at every single major US airport—that reorders a popular style—the very same thing, over and over again as the years go by. It is just the opposite of planned obsolescence. Perfect time, Daniela explains, is when luck and opportunity meet and one is prepared for it. It's when the color predicted two or three months ahead of time—today she tells me its mauve, a dusty pink, or a muddy rose—has hit the downtown market just on time, which means not too early or not too late. Perfect time means finding your ideal match in a customer and buyer, among those who love your product, who want to order and order it, without you ever having to change it. Perfect timing is like dating, she explains to me, like meeting that right person at the right time under the right circumstances—the buyer who is going to sell out of the style you created and come back for more. But today, Daniela is dealing with her fear that it's not going to be a cold enough winter on the east coast, and that the pleather jackets she's already designed and made won't be ordered so far ahead of time. She complains that her retail buyers just want to order just enough for what will sell by the weekend. In other words, the buyers no longer want to take the chances of thinking too far ahead of time and won't run the risk, so who will? What's the weather going to be like this weekend? Daniela asks me again. Daniela is waiting for it to get cold. She's waiting and waiting for that perfect time. She's got jackets on the shelf that can't sit there for too long.

NOTES

1 Rob Horning, "The Accidental Bricoleurs," n+1 online, June 3, 2011.
2 Ching Kwan Lee, *Gender and the South China Miracle: Two Worlds of Factory Women* (Berkeley: University of California Press, 1998); Pun Ngai, *Made in China: Women Factory Workers in a Global Workplace* (Durham, NC: Duke University Press, 2005); Pun Ngai, "Becoming Dagongmei (Working Girls): The Politics of Identity and Difference in Reform China," *China Journal* 42 (1999): 1–18. See also Keller Easterling, *Extrastatecraft: The Power of Infrastructure Space* (New York: Verso, 2014) for information on SEZs and EPZs; Leslie Chang, *Factory Girls: From Village to City in a Changing China* (New York: Spiegal and Grau, 2009). Andrew Brooks, *Clothing Poverty: The Hidden World of Fast Fashion and Second-Hand Clothes* (London: Zed Books, 2015).
3 Andrew Brooks, *Clothing Poverty: The Hidden World of Fast Fashion and Second-Hand Clothes* (London: Zed Books, 2015).
4 Nellie Chu, "Uncertain Encounters: African Migrant Entrepreneurs and Chinese Manufacturers," *China Policy Institute Blog*, October 7, 2015; Soon Ok Chun, *Small Urban Manufacturers: Artisans of Our Times* (Seoul, South Korea: Puriwa Ipari Press, 2016); So Young Park, "Stitching the Fabric of Family: Time, Work, and Intimacy in Seoul's Tongdaemun Market," *Journal of Korean Studies* 17, no. 2 (Fall 2012).

ACKNOWLEDGMENTS

This book was inspired by the "Global Circuits of Fashion and Beauty" Symposium that the three of us co-organized in 2015 and was jointly hosted by New York University and The New School Parsons MA Fashion Studies Program. The symposium brought together interdisciplinary scholars to consider new geographies of fashion and beauty. Specifically, we wanted to examine how the production, consumption, and transit of beauty and fashion are connected to contemporary, post-American networks that, rather than routing through the global North, instead map other forms of exchange in Asia and Africa. The conversations and collaborations generated from the day's workshops and roundtables were not only inspiring but a refreshing change of pace from most academic disciplines and spaces that rarely center fashion and beauty as central to regional histories, economics, and politics. We would like to thank the participants of that symposium, many of whom are also contributors to this collection: Hazel Clark (The New School), Denise Cruz (Columbia), Tanisha Ford (University of Delaware), Jessamyn Hatcher (NYU), Kimberly Hoang (University of Chicago), Ann Marie Leshkowich (Holy Cross), Laura Liu (The New School), Minh-Ha Pham (Pratt), Seo Young Park (Scripps), and Priti Ramamurthy (University of Washington, Seattle).

Through this collection, we hoped to make these interventions more widely available and to catalyze many more such fruitful discussions in the emerging field of Critical Fashion and Beauty Studies. We would like to thank Eric Zinner, Alicia Nadkarni, and Dolma Ombadykow, our editors at New York University Press, along with our peer reviewers for guiding this project to publication.

Finally, the three of us would like to offer some individual acknowledgments:

Heijin: This volume is a material tribute to the intellectual community that we have been able to cultivate over the years that first began with the "Global Circuits" world tour of conferences that spanned the

American Studies Association, Asian Studies Association, and Association for Asian American Studies from 2013 to 2014. I'd like to thank the women I met through those series of roundtables that sparked the idea for the "Global Circuits of Fashion and Beauty" Symposium who have now become friends as well as intellectual and political allies: Denise Cruz, Tanisha Ford, Christina Moon, Minh-Ha Pham, Priti Ramamurthy, and Thuy Tu. In particular, Christina and Thuy, thank you for being invaluable co-conspirators in bringing both the symposium and the volume to life. Working with you has been a pleasure in every sense. All my love to Dean Saranillio, our Hyun and Yuna, and my Abba, Myung Ho Lee, for supporting me and loving me so unconditionally. Finally, I dedicate this book to my Umma, Song Za Lee, with whom I have not only learned but lived fashion and beauty and its connections to Korea and being Korean. For all her love, pushing, protecting, and preening, I dedicate this book to her.

Christina: My deep gratitude to Heijin and Thuy, my co-hosts and co-editors, for all the inspired ideas and conversations that went into the making of this book—it is so meaningful to me. I thank all those who participated in the symposium and contributed to this volume, along with all the panels, roundtables, and talks that were a part of the conversation. Thank you, Denise Cruz, Heijin Lee, Minh-Ha Pham, and Thuy Tu, for giving me the opportunity to share my work at your universities. I am also honored to be among a community of scholars that includes Hazel Clark, Ann Marie Leshkowich, and Priti Ramamurthy. Among my colleagues, many thanks to the Fashion Praxis Working Group and MA Fashion Studies faculty at Parsons School of Design, the India China Institute and Spatial Politics of Work Working Group, the Graduate Institute of Design, Ethnography, and Social Thought, and the Zolberg Center on Migration and Mobility at The New School— all have played such a significant and supportive role in my thinking, research, and writing. For my chapter contribution, I thank all those I interviewed in the L.A. Jobber Market for their time and generosity. Special thanks to the Moon Caccamise families, most especially Chris, Ada, and Roman, for all the love and ongoing encouragement. Finally, my love to Kim Young Ja and Ham Pok Soon, who have always been the most fashionable, the most beautiful among them all.

Thuy: I'd like to echo the thanks already being offered by Christina and Heijin to the symposium participants and book contributors, who have been so patient with us during this publication process. I took on this project for no other reason than to think alongside and work with this fantastic group of women, all trusted teachers and dear friends. Thanks especially to Christina and Heijin (co-writing is not always easy, but it's always fun with you guys); to Denise for launching us on this journey and for hanging in there with us; and to Ann Marie, for teaching me so much about Vietnam and warmly welcoming me into the field. Thank you to all the friends, family, and kind folks in Saigon who took time to talk to me, and thanks finally to my little crew on Bleecker Street, beautiful in every sense.

ABOUT THE CONTRIBUTORS

Nellie Chu is Assistant Professor at Duke Kunshan University. Her most recent publication is "The Paradoxes of Creativity in Guangzhou, China's Wholesale Market for Fast Fashion" in *Culture, Theory and Critique Volume* 59 (2018).

Denise Cruz is Associate Professor of English at Columbia University. She is the author of *Transpacific Femininities: The Making of the Modern Filipina* (2012) and is working on a cultural study of the development of high fashion in Manila from the 1940s to the present.

Jessamyn Hatcher is Clinical Professor of the Humanities in the Global Liberal Studies program at New York University. Her work has appeared in the *New Yorker* and *Women's Studies Quarterly*.

Miliann Kang is Associate Professor in Women, Gender, Sexuality Studies at the University of Massachusetts, Amherst, where she is also affiliated faculty in Sociology and Asian/Asian American Studies. She is author of *The Managed Hand: Race, Gender and the Body in Beauty Service Work* (2010).

S. Heijin Lee is Assistant Professor of Social and Cultural Analysis at New York University. Lee is co-editor of *Pop Empires: Transnational and Diasporic Flows of India and Korea* (2019) and the forthcoming *The Geopolitics of Beauty: Transnational Circulations of Plastic Surgery, Pop and Pleasure*.

Ann Marie Leshkowich is Professor of Anthropology at College of the Holy Cross. She is author of *Essential Trade: Vietnamese Women in a Changing Marketplace* (2014), for which she was awarded the 2016 Harry J. Benda Prize from the Association for Asian Studies.

Christina H. Moon is Assistant Professor of Fashion Studies at Parsons School of Design, The New School. Her most recent article, "Fashion City: Diasporic Connections and Garment Industrial Histories Between the US and Asia," appears in *Critical Sociology* 44, no. 3 (May 2018).

Minh-Ha T. Pham (@minh81) is Associate Professor in the Graduate Program in Media Studies at Pratt Institute. She is the author of *Asians Wear Clothes on the Internet: Race, Gender, and the Work of Personal Style Blogging* (2015).

Emily Raymundo is a Provost's Postdoctoral Fellow in Asian American Studies at Dartmouth College. Her article, "The End of Whiteness and the Rise of Multicultural Asian America," appeared in the October 2017 issue of *Journal of Asian American Studies*.

Thuy Linh Nguyen Tu is Associate Professor of Social and Cultural Analysis at New York University. She is the author of *The Beautiful Generation; Asian Americans and the Cultural Economy of Fashion* (2011) and of the forthcoming *Experiments in Skin: Making Race and Beauty Across the Pacific*.

INDEX

Afghanistan, 98n39; burqa in, 79, 82; humanitarianism in, 79

Alibaba, 44, 262

ASEAN: formation of, 9; Vietnam and, 130

Asian beauty, 8

Asian Debt Crisis, 85–86, 91

Asian taste, 7, 13–14

aspirations, 7, 17; in Vietnam, 23–24, 26, 29, 34; VINTA and, 166

Bangladesh: Nepalese nail salon workers and textile workers in, 231, 232, 234, 235; Rana Plaza in, 212, 214, 215–16, 219, 231; unions in, 214

Bauman, Zygmunt, 280

bbali bbali (fast fast) culture: fast fashion and, 278, 281; global economy and, 10; industrialization and, 8

beauty industry: aged bodies and, 17; Asian beauty and, 8; Chinese consumerism and, 110; civilizational thinking and, 79–80; Euro-American, 10; gender and, 6–7; Japanese, 2; luxury market for, 22; for mother and daughter, 16–17; regime and regimen of, 103–4, 105, 107, 116, 122; soft power and, 110. *See also* cosmetics; plastic surgery, in South Korea; YouTube beauty

beauty industry, in South Korea, 2, 3–4; class and, 36; consumerism and, 7, 35, 110; development and, 36; nation and, 35–36; skin care and, 35–36; suitability of, 32–33; Vietnam purchasing from,

31–33. *See also* plastic surgery, in South Korea

beauty industry, in Vietnam, 38n7; cosmetics and, 22–23, 26–27; Korean cosmetics in, 31–33; suppliers by country of, 32

beauty standards and aesthetics: Hollywood and *Hallyu* and, 117; Korean, 116–17, 119–21; Suh in "Korean *vs.* American Makeup" video of, 116–17, 119–20; Western, 24, 116–17, 119–22, 125n30

Bell, Derrick, 46

Bolton, Andrew, 41–42

Bourdieu, Pierre, 128, 129, 147

Brave New World (Huxley), 77, 80

bright (sáng), 27

brightness, 29, 37; compared to whiteness, 27, 31

burqa, 79; Afghan women and, 79, 82; as oppression symbol, 72, 78; pity and, 24

Butler, Judith, 109, 237

Canada: Filipino formal wear in, 154–55; Filipino migrant population in, 160. *See also* VINTA

capitalism: cognitive mapping and, 244; cosmetics and, 106–7; digital, 78; fast fashion and global, 231, 234; global neoliberalism and, 104; *Overdressed* and global, 236–37; plastic surgery in Korea and, 85, 100n54; Rofel on, 103; Womenlink and, 85

and, 77; Korean War and, 79, 98n38; K-pop and, 117–18, 119; lookism and, 81–82, 83–84, 85, 87–88, 95, 99n48, 99n50; medical tourism and, 89, 90, 91, 92; Middle Eastern women compared to, 78–79, 81, 82; Miss Korea gif and, 69–70, 73; new media and, 74; racialized uniformity and, 69–70, 72; self-esteem movement and, 93–94; self-love and, 95; as self-management, 76, 85–86, 87, 88, 90, 95; social media and, 94; in South Korea, 3–4, 16, 69; techno-orientalism and, 80, 82; US obsessions with, 72; Vietnamese sex workers and, 89; visual economies and, 71. See also *Jezebel*; Korean Womenlink

Pony. *See* Hye-min, Park

Postmodernism, or, the Cultural Logic of Late Capitalism (Jameson), 244

power, 10; globalization and, 5; lightness and, 24, 30; soft, 110, 116, 117, 119; whiteness in Vietnam as, 24, 26; YouTube beauty and cultural, 116

property and whiteness, 46, 57

PSY, 69, 70, 71

quick response (QR), 214–15

Rabinow, Paul, 129

race: cosmetics and, 107, 110–11; creativity and, 13; neoliberalism and, 110–11; YouTube beauty and, 104, 105, 111–15

Ramamurthy, Priti, 158

Rana Plaza: aftermath of, 215–16; building capacity of, 215; collapse of, 212, 214, 219, 231

Ranciere, Jacques, 230

Ray, Krishnendu, 224–25

Rofel, Lisa, 103

romantic Orientalism, 41–42, 55–56; cultural appropriation and, 58; as emotional strategy, 46; historical inequali-

ties and, 58–59; public feeling and, 58; role of, 45; Said and, 53; white feelings and, 47, 49

Rose, Nikolas, 106

Safire, William, 84, 99n48

Said, Edward, 53, 58

sales associate: cash policy of, 261; conceptual mapping of, 259–61; long-term clients and, 260

sáng (bright), 27

self-esteem movement, 93–94

self-management: femininity and, 6; neoliberalism and, 106; plastic surgery as, 76, 85–86, 87, 88, 90, 95

Seltzer, Mark, 221

shanzhai cultures (imitation cultures), 12

Shaw, Linda M., 161–62

Siegle, Lucy, 219; on news, 216–17; *To Die For* by, 14, 212, 213, 216–18, 229–35, 236, 237–38

Sita (nail salon worker), 209; dress of, 210–11, 219, 221, 225–26, 227–28; family of, 226, 227, 228; fast fashion and, 211; infertility of, 222; on little freedoms, 224; uniform for, 224, 233

skin color: brightness and, 27, 29, 31, 37; geography and, 23; lightness of, 22, 23, 24–27, 30, 31, 37. *See also* whiteness; whiteness, in Vietnam

Skov, Lise, 144

slow fashion, 160–61

Smith, Randall, 192–93

"The Social Skin" (Turner), 16

soft power: beauty markets and, 110; culture as, 116, 117; *Hallyu* and, 119

South Africa, 26

Southeast Asia. *See specific topics*

South Korea (Korea), 5; Asian Debt Crisis and, 85–86, 91; *bbali bbali* culture of, 8, 10, 278, 281; brightness in, 27, 29, 31, 37; child rearing in, 16–17; Cultural Content Office in, 91;